Children's rights, Eastern enlargement and the EU human rights regime

Manchester University Press

European Policy Research Unit Series

Series Editors: *Simon Bulmer, Peter Humphreys* and *Mick Moran*

The European Policy Research Unit Series aims to provide advanced textbooks and thematic studies of key public policy issues in Europe. They concentrate, in particular, on comparing patterns of national policy content, but pay due attention to the European Union dimension. The thematic studies are guided by the character of the policy issue under examination.

The European Policy Research Unit (EPRU) was set up in 1989 within the University of Manchester's Department of Government to promote research on European politics and public policy. The series is part of EPRU's effort to facilitate intellectual exchange and substantive debate on the key policy issues confronting the European states and the European Union.

Titles in the series also include:

Children's rights, Eastern enlargement and the EU human rights regime

Ingi Iusmen

Manchester University Press
Manchester and New York

distributed in the United States exclusively by Palgrave Macmillan

Published by Manchester University Press
Oxford Road, Manchester M13 9NR, UK
and Room 400, 175 Fifth Avenue, New York, NY 10010, USA
www.manchesteruniversitypress.co.uk

Distributed exclusively in the USA by
Palgrave Macmillan, 175 Fifth Avenue, New York,
NY 10010, USA

Distributed exclusively in Canada by
UBC Press, University of British Columbia, 2029 West Mall,
Vancouver, BC, Canada V6T 1Z2

British Library Cataloguing-in-Publication Data
A catalogue record for this book is available from the British Library

Library of Congress Cataloging-in-Publication Data applied for

ISBN   978 0 7190 8822 3 hardback

First published 2014

The publisher has no responsibility for the persistence or accuracy of URLs for any external or third-party internet websites referred to in this book, and does not guarantee that any content on such websites is, or will remain, accurate or appropriate.

Typeset
by 4word Ltd, Bristol
Printed in Great Britain
by CPI Antony Rowe Ltd, Chippenham, Wiltshire

Contents

List of tables

Acknowledgements

I have benefited from much support and guidance in writing this book. The main argument and accompanying empirical findings took shape as part of my doctoral research, at the University of Strathclyde (Glasgow), under the supervision of Laura Cram. I am deeply grateful to Laura for her constant academic and moral support during my doctoral studies and for instilling in me the passion for researching EU politics and European integration. The Economic and Social Research Council (ESRC) postdoctoral fellowship, held at the University of Sheffield, enabled me to further develop and broaden the arguments of my doctoral research and, particularly, to carry out empirical research, which underpins the findings of the book. Therefore, I am very grateful for the funding I benefited from the University of Strathclyde (university studentship for my PhD, 2006–2009) and from the ESRC (postdoctoral fellowship grant PTA-026-27-2846 'The EU Human Rights Regime: Policy Feedback and Children's Rights', 2011–2012) in order to conduct the research for the book. I am immensely grateful to and appreciative of the substantial support and guidance of Simon Bulmer and Jean Grugel at Sheffield University. I am particularly indebted to them for providing me with the much-needed encouragement and motivation to write the book. Thanks must also go to Helen Stalford (Liverpool University) whose passion and dedication for researching European children's rights has proved so influential in the latter stages of writing this book. I am thankful to all those at Manchester University Press for their patience, professionalism and efficiency in preparing this book for publication.

I am deeply grateful for the support, loyalty and friendship over the years of all my friends in Glasgow and Sheffield. The ceaseless support and help of my dear friends Ruxandra Arsene, Dawn Morrow, Fernanda Jäkel, Alessandra Negreiros and Dine (Christine) Haider, as well as Vicky Ward and Caz Rouse, have been vital over the last 2 years.

A special acknowledgement must go to my family in Romania: I will be eternally grateful to my parents, Saime and Ilhan, whose love truly knows no boundaries. They have been such an enormous support over the years by offering uplifting advice and encouragement and, particularly, by simply believing in me. I am grateful, as ever, for the love and good humour of my sister, Meral.

The final word of thanks must go to Alan D. Donaldson, who, unfortunately, is no longer with us. Alan's unstinting love, patience, sense of humour, bright mind and gentle spirit have guided my doctoral research in Glasgow and, at a deeper level, have rendered the completion of this book possible. This book is dedicated to Alan and his memory.

Ingi Iusmen
February 2013

List of abbreviations

AFSJ	Area of Freedom, Security and Justice
ANPCA	National Authority for Child Protection and Adoption in Romania (in Romanian: Autoritatea Nationala pentru Protectia Copilului si Adoptii)
CARDS	Community Assistance for Reconstruction, Development and Stability in the Balkans
CEECS	Central and Eastern European Countries
CFI	Court of First Instance
CFSP	Common Foreign and Security Policy
CRC	UN Convention on the Rights of the Child
CRC Committee	UN Committee on the Rights of the Child
DC	Democratic Convention
DCP	Department for Child Protection
DG	Directorate General
DG EAC	Directorate General Education & Culture
DG ELARG	Directorate General Enlargement
DG EMPL	Directorate General Employment, Social Affairs and Inclusion
DG JLS	Directorate General Justice, Freedom and Security
DG RELEX	Directorate General External Relations
DG SANCO	Directorate General Health & Consumers
EC	European Commission
ECHR	European Convention on Human Rights
ECJ	European Court of Justice
ECtHR	European Court of Human Rights
EIDHR	European Instrument for Democracy and Human Rights
EP	European Parliament
EU	European Union
FoR	Focus on Romania
FRA	EU Agency for Fundamental Rights
FYROM	Former Yugoslav Republic of Macedonia
ICA	inter-country adoption

IGIAA	Independent Group for Inter-country Adoption Analysis
IiP	Investing in People
ILO	International Labour Organization
IMAS	Institute for Marketing and Polls
IPA	Instrument for Pre-Accession Assistance
ISG	Inter-Service Group
ISPA	Instrument for Structural Policies for Pre-Accession
JHA	Justice and Home Affairs
LIBE	European Parliament Committee on Civil Liberties, Justice and Home Affairs
MEP	member of the European Parliament
NATO	North Atlantic Treaty Organization
NGO	non-governmental organization
ODIHR	Office for Democratic Institutions and Human Rights
OECD	Organization for Economic Cooperation and Development
OSCE	Organization for Security and Cooperation in Europe
PHARE	Poland and Hungary: Assistance for Reconstructing their Economies
PKK	Kurdish Workers' Party
SAA	Stabilization and Association Agreement
SAPARD	Special Accession Programme for Agriculture and Rural Development
SERA	Solidarité Enfants Roumains Abandonnes
TEC	Treaty establishing the European Community
TEU	Treaty establishing the European Union
UN	United Nations
UNICEF	United Nations Children's Fund
USA	United States of America

Introduction

Human rights and minority protection have been at the core of the Eastern enlargement process of the European Union (EU). Human rights norms also underpin the European project and are constitutionally enshrined at treaty level. The EU accession conditionality, in particular, has provided EU institutions with the necessary 'stick and carrot' clout to trigger structural reforms regarding the human rights provision and minority protection in the Eastern candidate countries. Indeed, Eastern enlargement saw the EU-driven overhaul of the human rights provision in Eastern candidates on an unprecedented scale in the history of the EU (Sedelmeier, 2003; Smith, 2003). The EU's human rights mandate, however, is far more limited in relation to EU Member States than candidate states and, subsequently, this has raised harsh criticisms regarding the EU's use of double standards in its approach to human rights (Alston and Weiler, 1999; Williams, 2000, 2004; De Witte and Toggenburg, 2004). This critique is even more pertinent given the violation of human rights in the Member States, a fact regularly denunciated by various international non-governmental organizations (NGOs) (Pop, 2009; Human Rights Watch, 2012a; Amnesty International, 2013), and human rights bodies, such as the Council of Europe (Council of Europe, 2008). Furthermore, the profile and political salience of human rights protection at the EU level has been recently augmented due to the constitutional and legal changes introduced by the Lisbon Treaty (2007) and the binding nature of the EU Charter of Fundamental Rights (2000). Additionally, the EU's recent policy initiatives aimed at establishing an area of freedom, security and justice (AFSJ) in Europe, along with the EU's external role in international politics, have all boosted the profile of human rights principles at the EU level. However, the underlying dynamics between EU external policy, such as Eastern enlargement, and EU internal processes regarding human rights protection has not been thoroughly scrutinized so far. Indeed, there is no analytically rigorous and empirically robust research exploring how, why and the extent to which the human rights conditionality applied to Eastern candidates, as part of the accession negotiations process, has had feedback effects and far-reaching consequences for the EU's human rights provision, and for the broader European integration.

This book offers a timely exploration of the nature and scale of this emergent EU human rights regime as a consequence of Eastern enlargement. The human rights conditionality applied to Eastern candidates went well beyond the EU's internal role and mandate in human rights in relation to the Member States and led to the radical transformation of the human rights provision of the former communist states. Nevertheless, the implications and far-reaching consequences of this interventionist policy on the EU's own approach to human rights matters have not been scrutinized. By drawing on the human rights conditionality (particularly in relation to children's rights) as applied to Romania, the book interrogates *whether*, *how* and *why* the extension of EU human rights remit externally has resulted in extensive institutional and policy feedback on the EU human rights policy in general.

A set of crucial analytical, conceptual and empirical questions are raised in this book. Empirically, what shape did the feedback effects and processes take? What factors and actors triggered these feedback effects and why? Or what was the impact of EU accession conditionality on human rights provision in Romania? What were the consequences of Eastern enlargement on EU human rights provision? To what extent can the empirical findings scrutinized here be generalized? Analytically, how are these empirical processes explained most cogently? What kind of insights does the empirical evidence provide into Europeanization, EU enlargement and EU human rights scholarship? What analytical and conceptual frameworks capture best the emergence and impact of feedback effects? Ultimately, how do the empirical findings and the accompanying analytical debate inform our understanding of European integration and the role of human rights within it?

The feedback effects regarding the protection of children's rights have transformed the EU institutions' role and scope in this policy area both in EU internal and external human rights dimensions. The key findings of this book also provide a process-tracing approach to the EU's recent developments in the field of children's rights and the broader human rights areas – for instance with respect to Roma protection, mental health or international adoptions – by unearthing why the EU has intervened in these areas in the first place. The process-tracing dimension demonstrates why policy issues emerge on EU agenda and why other policy structures and issues persist over time, hence becoming entrenched. At the same time, the analytical and empirical foci of the book move from the specific case of human rights in Eastern candidates (the case of Romania) and their feedback effects to the broader EU human rights provision by showing how certain feedback effects are interlinked with the broader EU human rights actions, particularly after the entry into force of the Lisbon Treaty in December 2009, which underlines the emergence of a well-defined and robust EU human rights regime.

The key arguments of the book

The feedback effects of Eastern enlargement on the EU itself have shaped and continue to influence the EU's institutional and policy structures. The empirical findings of the book provide evidence in relation to the depth and scale of the impact and feedback effects triggered by the EU's advance of human rights measures – via the EU accession conditionality – on the EU itself. At the same time, by drawing on the human rights conditionality as applied to Romania, the empirical findings of the book provide substantial insights into the effectiveness of EU accession conditionality to radically transform the human rights provision in the former communist states. One of the main empirical findings of this book centres on the conditions and factors generating policy development, and hence agenda-setting processes, at the EU level due to Eastern enlargement. It is argued, therefore, that provided the availability of certain factors – such as propitious institutional and political conditions and policy entrepreneurs at the EU level – then EU actions in human rights outside the Union (e.g. as part of Eastern enlargement) will prompt feedback effects *qua* policy development at the EU level by shaping EU policy agenda. The policy feedback effects are shown to be most evident in relation to the protection of children's rights, where policy entrepreneurs at the Commission level seized the window of opportunity (Kingdon, 1984; Baumgartner and Jones, 1993; Mintrom, 1997, 2000) to import an EU external policy issue into the EU internal dimension.

Furthermore, the feedback effects constitute a function of the intrusive human rights policy applied by the Commission as part of the political accession criteria. The EU's intervention in human rights provision in Romania, with a key focus on child protection, demonstrates how the Commission crafted and applied a wide range of conditions and mechanisms to transform human rights sectors – where the Commission had no expertise and internal mandate – and particularly the sensitive and highly controversial issue of children's rights. In the Romanian case, policy entrepreneurs at the European Parliament and Commission level are shown to be the main driving forces behind the radical reforms in and the political salience attached to areas such as children's rights and the issue of international adoption. In other words, given the scale and high profile of the EU's intervention in areas such as child protection, it was deemed that Romania's case would have repercussions on the EU's approach to human rights in general. In the same vein, EU intervention in child protection in Romania also produced feedback effects on the current EU enlargement policy, as children's rights have now become an entrenched and standardized EU accession condition, which signals the continuation of the policy framework developed initially in relation to Romania. Meanwhile, other Eastern candidates did not experience the same level and depth of EU scrutiny in children's rights as Romania had and, consequently, they could not shape the EU's internal approach to child rights.

A range of post-accession impacts are examined in relation to high-profile areas such as the Roma minority, protection of disabled people and mental health. The process-tracing approach demonstrates how and why certain human rights matters have landed on the EU policy agenda after Romania's accession to the EU in 2007 and because of Eastern enlargement in general. The accession to the EU of new members from Eastern Europe, therefore, meant that new human rights violations or deficits of rights protection had to be addressed as part of the EU's internal policy framework. Indeed, Eastern enlargement galvanized the need for EU institutions to devise policy tools and mechanisms to address new human rights issues, which had been 'imported' with the accession of Eastern candidates.

Last but not least, one of the key empirical findings of this book is that the feedback effects generated by Eastern enlargement in general and the Romanian case in particular have shaped the scope and function of the emergent EU human rights regime after the entry into force of the Lisbon Treaty (2007). The consequences of Eastern enlargement for EU human rights policy, along with the constitutional and legal provisions brought about by the Lisbon Treaty and the binding aspect of the EU Charter of Fundamental Rights (2000), have further augmented the profile of certain human rights areas, such as child rights and Roma protection, at the EU level. Therefore, this book offers a timely empirical scrutiny of the EU human rights policy after Eastern enlargement and post-Lisbon.

The empirical findings examined in this book make analytical contributions to agenda-setting theories, the Europeanization analytical framework and historical institutionalism. The existing analytical frameworks, along with a set of new conceptual heuristic devices, are employed and adjusted to capture the dynamics and diversity of the feedback effects under scrutiny. The feedback effects of the EU's intervention in child protection in Romania on the EU's internal policy dimension are explained via the agenda-setting analytical framework, whilst the specific effects are envisaged as policy development processes. The driving force behind agenda-setting processes in the area of children's rights is policy entrepreneurship. To this end, Kingdon's (1984) model of agenda-setting via the role played by policy entrepreneurs in coupling the separate streams of politics, problems and policies is adjusted and applied to capture the emergence of child rights as an EU policy area. Kingdon's model of agenda-setting provides insights into the complexity and dynamics of EU policy process regarding human rights by accommodating both contextual factors and agency-based changes to explain *how*, *why* and *when* new issues emerge on EU political agenda.

The EU's interventionist policy in child protection in Romania, whereby the Commission applied human rights standards and principles for which it lacks an internal mandate, is described as an indication of promoting an EU-topia[1] in the field of human rights. The advancement of a human rights EU-topia in candidate countries sheds new light on the enlargement-led Europeanization, by unpacking how and the extent to which the EU intervened and sought changes in areas where it had no expertise or experience of involvement. To this end, the feedback effects triggered by the EU's enlargement policy on the EU's internal dimension are coined as the 'import of the EU's human rights EU-topia', initially intended for external consumption. Therefore, the findings of this book make two significant analytical contributions to the Europeanization East scholarship: first, they distinguish the human rights conditionality applied to candidates as a form of EU-topia in human rights; while, second they unveil the consequences of the external EU-topia on the EU internal structures. In brief, the EU's import of its own EU-topia into the EU internal dimension amounts to processes of agenda-setting and policy development.

The impact of the EU's intervention in human rights provision in Romania on the current enlargement process is analytically explained via historical institutionalist accounts. The continuation and entrenchment of policy structures and mechanisms developed initially during the accession process with Romania in the current enlargement process reflect aspects of *path dependency*, *lock-in effects* and *institutional self-reinforcement*, in this case observed in relation to the European Commission (EC). Therefore, historical institutionalist insights are shown to shed light on the key reasons and processes for which aspects related to child rights policy as part of EU enlargement have become entrenched and hard to roll back.

The key empirical findings and analytical accounts of this book reveal why and the extent to which EU intervention in human rights provision of the Eastern candidate Romania had feedback effects on EU internal and external human rights policies. At the same time, the processes under scrutiny provide a glimpse into the EU's role as a human rights actor, both inside and outside the Union, and the broader processes of European integration and EU enlargement after the entry into force of the Lisbon Treaty.

Eastern enlargement, policy feedback and EU children's rights

This book makes a vital contribution to the existing scholarship on Eastern enlargement, post-communist transition, Europeanization and EU human and children's rights protection. More specifically, the book advances the field of EU governance and human rights promotion, with a particular emphasis on Eastern enlargement and the emergent EU human rights regime, by providing new insights into: (a) EU policy feedback and the resulting EU human rights regime, (b) the key factors that explain the feedback effects of EU external action on the EU internal dimension, (c) historical institutionalism and policy entrepreneurship providing an analytical account of feedback effects in relation to EU human rights policy, (d) the bridging of the gap between EU internal and external human rights dimensions, and (e) the nature and scope of the developing EU human rights regime. The analysis of the causal factors that triggered feedback effects due to EU intervention in child protection in Romania in particular set a parameter for the analysis of other policy areas where the EU enjoys limited internal remit but a broad external role.

Methodologically, the empirical findings of this book are based on an in-depth case study analysis, i.e. the feedback effects generated by the EU human rights conditionality as applied to Romania (with a key focus on EU intervention in child protection), before 2007. The book draws on an extensive set of qualitative interviews (sixty) conducted between 2008–2009 and in 2011 with key EU officials (in the European Commission and European Parliament), children's NGOs, child rights experts and national actors (NGOs, government officials, civil servants) in Romania. Also, extensive documentary analysis of key EU and Romanian official policy documents, legislation and letters was conducted.

Chapter 1 provides an overview of the historical background to the EU's involvement with human rights and, at the same time, fleshes out the main analytical frameworks employed in the book to explain the feedback processes. The enlargement-led Europeanization analytical perspective describes how the EU, mostly the Commission, transformed candidate states' institutions and policies during the EU accession negotiations. It is argued that the EU 'Europeanized' candidate countries with respect to those conditions which involved the transposition of the already existing EU set of laws and rules – the *acquis communautaire* – at the national level. Yet, given that there is no EU *acquis* with respect to most human rights matters, the EU exported a human rights 'EU-topia' (Nicolaidis and Howse, 2002) to non-EU countries with regard to those human rights issues where the EU has limited internal mandate and has no EU *acquis communautaire*. The feedback effects triggered by this intervention are conceptualized as conducive to policy development (via policy entrepreneurship and agenda-setting) in EU internal policy sphere and to policy continuation (in line with historical institutionalism) in EU enlargement policy.

The breadth and depth of the EU intervention in human rights and minority protection provision in Romania during the Eastern enlargement process is scrutinized in Chapter 2. The human rights conditionality applied in Romania went beyond the existing EU *acquis* and internal mandate in human rights, particularly in relation to those politically sensitive sectors such as Roma minority, mental health and prison conditions. By deploying a wide range of financial, technical and international instruments, the EU sought to transform the provision of a wide spectrum of social, civil and political rights, including minority protection. This chapter shows that EU intervention in these sectors led to substantial institutional, legislative and policy changes. Additionally, this external involvement with human rights matters provided the European Commission with invaluable experience and expertise regarding the reform of the human rights systems of former communist countries.

Chapter 3 examines in great depth the transformation of the child protection sector in Romania due to EU accession requirements. EU intervention in children's rights in Romania was the most visible and highly politicized EU human rights accession condition both among Eastern candidates and in relation to Romania's accession agenda. All former communist countries had child protection systems that violated children's rights. However, due to the role of EU policy entrepreneurs, such as the European Parliament's rapporteur for Romania and the Commissioner for Enlargement, the child protection in Romania saw the most substantial EU intervention – in terms of the EU pressure and instruments to forge change – compared with other former communist states. The children's rights provision was radically over-hauled only in Romania before 2007; a similar transformation did not occur in other former communist states. The EU's interventionist policy in the protection of children's rights in Romania – an area where the EU lacked any expertise and experience – led to the 'root-and-branch' reform of the legislative and institutional framework underpinning this sector. Due to the EU's transformative role, today Romania boasts one of the most advanced child rights systems among the former communist states.

The feedback effects of EU intervention in children's rights in Romania on the EU itself are scrutinized in Chapter 4. Two distinctive sets of feedback effects are examined: one set focusing on the EU internal sphere, and the other on EU external policy dimension. The internal feedback effects, due to the entrepreneurship of EU actors such as Franco Frattini, the former Commissioner for Freedom, Justice and Security, led to the introduction of children's rights as self-standing issue on EU policy agenda via the adoption of the Commission Communication *Towards an EU Strategy on the Rights of the Child* in 2006. It is argued that the ensuing institutional and policy developments led to the emergence of children's rights as an overarching policy issue, addressed cross-sectorally and via targeted actions by the EU institutions. The feedback effects on the current enlargement policy amount to the entrenchment and formalization of child rights as an EU accession condition. Children's rights have become a more standardized and embedded EU accession conditionality as the European Commission employs benchmarks to assess the child rights provision in the current candidates. It is contended that the children's rights policy template – particularly focusing on 'children in crisis' – employed in the current accession process has been developed due to the Romanian children's case.

Chapter 5 provides insights into the analytical frameworks explaining the feedback effects triggered by the EU's intervention in child rights in

Romania, and the institutionalization of this policy area at the EU level. Kingdon's (1984) model of multiple streams coupling accounts for agenda-setting processes, via policy entrepreneurship, which led to the emergence of an EU child rights policy as part of EU internal policy. It is argued, therefore, that policy feedback occurred due to the opening of a window of opportunity which allowed EU entrepreneurs to push certain human rights issues, such as children's rights, high up on the EU's policy agenda. In line with the Europeanization scholarship, it is claimed that the EU has started to import its own EU-topia, which was initially intended only for external consumption. Historical institutionalist elements, such as path-dependency, lock-ins, institutional development and self-reinforcing institutions, are employed to explain the feedback effects on the EU enlargement policy. Path-dependency and lock-ins illustrate how and why the protection of the rights of the child is now an entrenched EU accession condition, which was initially developed in relation to Romania's accession agenda.

Chapter 6 explores the key features and functions of the emergent EU human rights regime in light of Eastern enlargement effects and the Lisbon Treaty provisions. It is shown that human rights areas, such as the Roma, mental health, disability and international adoptions, have acquired a high profile at the EU level due to Eastern enlargement and post-accession developments. Additionally, the legal and constitutional provisions in the Lisbon Treaty have further enhanced the political clout and visibility attached to human rights at the EU level. It is contended that, in light of the developments and changes explored in this chapter, the EU's human rights provision, or regime, has become more robust and more firmly entrenched in terms of its constitutional, legal and institutional clout. The Conclusion briefly outlines some of the key and more general conclusions that can be drawn from the analysis presented throughout the book. It is contended that feedback effects constitute contingent processes, but, once they have occurred, they have far-reaching implications for the EU's human rights remit and the broader European integration process.

Notes

1   The term was first employed by Nicolaidis and Howse (2002) in relation to EU norm-promotion via EU external policy.

1

The European Union and human rights: historical outlook and analytical frameworks

> We are not a human rights organization: our bread and butter business is the acquis communautaire; and the bread and butter of the accession negotiations are 'adopt the acquis communautaire'.
>
> (Commission official)

Introduction

The last rounds of enlargement saw the European Union's (EU's) intervention in a wide range of human rights matters in the Eastern candidates. The European Commission's pro-active role in applying the accession conditionality had a transformative impact on the candidates' institutions and policy structures upholding human rights. It is not surprising, therefore, that due to its strict application of human rights standards, the European Commission has been described as a 'human rights' actor (Sedelmeier, 2006) using a human rights discourse (De Burca, 2003). The human rights catalogue monitored and scrutinized in the Eastern candidates constituted the apex of the EU's engagement with human rights matters in non-EU countries. This chapter provides a brief historical overview of the EU's human rights policy and EU efforts to Europeanize the Central and Eastern European countries (CEECs) during accession negotiations. The feedback effects of EU human rights conditionality – as applied to CEECs – on the EU itself are conceptualized as amounting to policy development via entrepreneurial actions and policy continuation. This chapter, therefore, sketches the analytical frameworks employed in the book to explain how and why Eastern enlargement can trigger far-reaching effects on the EU's institutional structures and policies.

The EU and human rights: a contested relationship?

The EU's involvement with human rights matters has been contested throughout the history of European integration for a number of reasons, such as the EU's limited competence and *acquis* in relation to human rights. From the outset, the European integration was conceived essentially as an economic project, while the Council of Europe was regarded as the legitimate European organization in charge of upholding human rights protection in Europe. Indeed, after the Second World War, the Council of Europe was responsible for establishing a European human rights regime, while the European Community/EU was entrusted with the task of generating peace, stability and prosperity in Europe via economic integration. In other words, there was to be no overlap with respect to the EU and Council of Europe's missions in Europe after the end of the Second World War. Therefore, EU Member States retained the primary responsibility and mandate for safeguarding the protection of human rights at the domestic level, although processes of economic integration, as forged by the EU, would indirectly impact on the provision of fundamental rights across Europe. However, norms such as human rights, peace and democracy have always been at the heart of the European integration process and have shaped particularly the EU's external role as a 'civilizing power' (Duchene, 1972; Sjursen, 2006a, b), 'ethical power' (Aggestam, 2008), 'vanishing mediator' (Nicolaidis, 2004), 'normative power' (Manners, 2002) or 'gentle power' (Merlini, 2001; Padoa-Schioppa, 2001). The steady political and constitutional emergence of human rights matters at the European Community level starting with the late 1960s (Cassese *et al.*, 1991) came to fruition with the adoption of the EU Charter of Fundamental Rights in 2000, which places the protection of human rights, at least in terms of political visibility and constitutional salience, at the core of the EU processes (Von Bogdandy, 2000). Moreover, it has been claimed that the post-Lisbon reinforcement of human rights as general principles of law along with the EU's prospective accession to the European Convention on Human Rights (ECHR) 'together will change the face of the Union fundamentally' (Pernice, 2008).

The European Community – and later the EU – gradually engaged with human rights primarily in its external relations, although it lacked a solid and formal treaty provision for its involvement with human rights until the late 1990s. The European project was initially conceived as a model of economic integration, whereby economic cooperation was fundamentally aimed at securing peace and prosperity in Europe. The EU's core objectives, such as economic growth, peace and stability, were to be achieved via the creation of a common market, where the EU would play the role of a regulatory agency (Majone, 1998), and, therefore, politically sensitive issues like human rights and minority protection were to be part of the national competence; while human rights policing inside Europe was the remit of the Council of Europe. Indeed, all EU Member States are requested to be parties to the ECHR, although the Council of Europe system is deemed to be the lowest common denominator in terms of human rights protection within the EU (Alston and

Weiler, 1999), a fact which is also reflected by the gaps in the ratification of the ECHR protocols by the EU Member States.

Over the last 50 years, however, there has been a progressive advance-ment of an EU human rights provision.[1] The EU's engagement with human rights entailed two separate pathways: internally, the lack of explicit treaty references to human rights restricted the EU's scope in this area, whilst externally, human rights clauses and provisions became an integral part of the agreements concluded with third[2] countries (Fierro, 2003; Bartels, 2005). The founding treaties were silent with respect to human rights, although a vague reference was made in the Preamble of the Treaty of Rome (1957) to the constant improvement of the living and working conditions of the peoples of the Member States.[3] Yet, in the absence of clear and explicit arrangement in the founding treaties and in response to challenges of the supremacy of Community law over national constitutional law by the constitutional courts of Germany and Italy, the European Court of Justice (ECJ) took the lead in integrating human rights within the Community legal order. For instance, in 1969 the ECJ established for the first time that respect for human rights was part of the 'general principles of Community law' which have to be protected by the Court. The danger initially highlighted by the German Constitutional Court was that by giving away power to an organization outside the German constitutional structure, such as the European Community, it would actually empower a supranational executive which was not bound by the fundamental guarantees of the German Basic Law (Craig and De Burca, 2003: 269). To this end, the initial ruling of the German Constitutional Court was that the protection of fundamental rights in the German Basic Law would have to prevail over the Community law. The Court took the lead in developing a doctrine on the protection of fundamental rights (Craig and De Burca, 2003: 271) which eventually convinced the German Constitutional Court to accept the supremacy of the Community law at the national level. Furthermore, the ECJ played a key role in establishing the principles governing Community law, such as supremacy and direct effect, and the protection of human rights as a restraint upon the powers of the Community institutions rather than as a restraint upon Member States. The respect for human rights, therefore, was gradually introduced and embraced by EU institutions as a constraint on the discretion of the supranational institutions (Von Bogdandy, 2000:1308). The Court's actions have been compared to a 'quiet revolution' (Weiler, 1994) whereby the ECJ promoted 'integration through law' (Weiler, 1991), with the Court's remit providing an instrument to facilitate and advance European unification by means of judicial interpretation (Grimmel, 2011). It has been claimed, therefore, that the Court's judicial activism and case-law in the field of human rights led to the discovery of an unwritten Bill of Rights against which to check the legality of Community measures (Weiler, 1999: 108).

The explicit inclusion of fundamental rights and later, respect for human rights, at the treaty level, emerged in the early 1990s. Initially, the Preamble of the Single European Act (1986) made reference to fundamental rights;[4] however, it was Article F[5] in the Treaty of Maastricht (1992) that enshrined for the first time the 'respect for fundamental rights' in line with the ECHR provisions. Later on, Article 6(1) TEU as modified by the Amsterdam Treaty (1997) – which entered into force in 1999 – further reinforced this provision by stipulating that respect for human rights constitute the foundational principles of the Union.[6] The wording of human rights articles at the treaty level led to the contention that the EU attaches divergent functions to human rights in its internal and external policy spheres. For instance, it has been claimed that the wording of Article 6 (2) TEU (Treaty of Amsterdam) guarantees that EU institutions will respect fundamental rights, but it does not establish an EU 'objective' to respect these rights (Bartels, 2005: 204) and, therefore, the legal effect of Article 6(1) TEU is that it sets out certain assumptions on which the Treaty is predicated, without establishing clear-cut objectives. On the other hand, Article 11 TEU, as modified by the Treaty of Amsterdam, provides that one of the objectives of the Common Foreign and Security Policy (CFSP) is to 'develop and consolidate democracy and the rule of law, and respect for human rights and fundamental freedoms'. Thus, while Article 11 TEU makes the promotion of human rights an external objective of the Union, the EU does not have a corresponding objective – according to Article 6 TEU – of promoting human rights and democratic principles inside the EU (Bartels, 2005: 204). Therefore, the Treaty of Amsterdam signalled a clear disjuncture between the EU's internal and external objectives in relation to human rights, which was in place at the time of the accession negotiations with the CEECs. Put bluntly, when accession negotiations commenced with the CEECs, at the Treaty level there was a striking dissonance between the EU's role in human rights inside and outside the Union.

The entry into force of the Lisbon Treaty and the binding nature of the EU Charter of Fundamental Rights led to the constitutionalization of human rights at the EU level (Groussot and Pech, 2010). In legal terms, the inclusion of human rights in the Treaties, which have the force of EU primary law, has attached a constitutional role to the protection of human rights within the EU project, particularly due to the binding aspect of the EU Charter of Fundamental Rights. The Lisbon Treaty lists the protection of human rights among the values of the Union[7] and, subsequently, the EU aims to promote its values in its actions (Article 3 TEU). The reinforcement of human rights protection at the Treaty level has to be corroborated with the provisions in and binding nature of the EU Charter of Fundamental Rights. The Charter – stemming from the Treaties, ECJ case-law, the European Union Member States' constitutional traditions and the ECHR – brings together into a single text all the civic, political, economic and social rights enjoyed by the citizens and residents of the European Union. All EU institutions have to ensure that EU legislation and policies do not violate the principles and provisions in the Charter. Yet, the Charter applies to EU Member States only when they are implementing EU law and, above all, the Charter does not extend the EU's competences in the field of human rights as it acts rather like a brake on the powers of the EU institutions (Piris, 2010). A future accession to the ECHR, as provided by the Lisbon Treaty, will further boost the EU's human rights credentials, although this accession shall not affect the EU's legal competence in human rights.

A prolific involvement in the promotion of human rights has emerged as part of EU external policy dimension. Human rights, democracy and rule of law constitute values embraced by all EU Member States, although these norms mostly became the currency of EU external relations. The EU advances human rights norms through various agreements implemented with non-EU countries and through the political dialogues that it conducts with them as part of its foreign policy. In doing so, it uses a specific legal basis – a human rights clause – which is incorporated in nearly all EU agreements with non-EU countries. Since 1995 all association, partnership and cooperation agreements with third countries contain a human rights clause stipulating that human rights are an essential element in the relations between the parties (Muller-Graff, 1997). The use of human rights clause is intended to guarantee the protection of human rights in non-EU countries and it includes a suspension clause in case of serious violations of human rights provision. The human rights clause makes 'respect for the democratic principles and human rights as defined in the Helsinki Final Act and Charter of Paris for a New Europe' an essential element of the agreement, thereby enabling the EU to suspend or terminate such an agreement in connection with a failure of the non-EU country to comply with those standards (Pentassuglia, 2001). Therefore, the protection of human rights has become an integral part of the EU's external and development policy and the EU insists that all trade, cooperation, dialogue, partnership and association agreements with third countries include a human rights clause (Miller, 2004: 9). The employment of a human rights clause ascribes a normative and ethical dimension to EU external relations in general.

The protection of human rights also constitutes a key condition for EU membership. For instance, in 1977 a joint declaration – *Joint Declaration by the European Parliament, the Council and the Commission on Human Rights* – was issued by the three institutions and stressed the fundamental importance attached to the protection of fundamental rights and the commitment of these institutions – the Parliament, the Commission and the Council – to respect them both in the exercise of their powers and in the pursuance of the aims of the European Economic Community (Williams, 2004: 55). Furthermore, the European Council meeting in Copenhagen in 1978 re-stated the same principles according to which the 'respect for and maintenance of representative democracy and human rights in each member state are essential elements of membership in the European Communities' (quote in Smith, 2003: 110). However, it was the end of the Cold War and the EU's decision to enlarge to the East that signalled a new era for the EU's promotion of human rights norms. Indeed, Eastern enlargement entailed a qualitatively and quantitatively distinctive phase in the EU's external human rights policy, in terms of both the Commission's involvement with the CEECs and the high-profile attached to human rights during EU accession negotiations in general. For instance, on 16 December 1991, the EC Foreign Ministers issued a declaration – *Declaration on the Guidelines on the Recognition of New States in Eastern Europe and in the Soviet Union* – stating that formal recognition would be granted to the new states from Central and Eastern Europe provided that they respected the provisions of the UN Charter, Helsinki Final Act and the Charter of Paris 'especially with regard to the rule of law, democracy and human rights and guarantees for the rights of minorities' (quote in Bartels, 2005: 51). The boost to democracy and human rights was further reinforced by the requirement for EU applicants to join the Council of Europe and ratify the ECHR and all its protocols. The statute of the Council of Europe also requires the applicants to respect democratic principles, human rights and fundamental freedoms.[8] Compliance with the Copenhagen political accession criteria (June 1993)[9] was a prerequisite for the opening of the accession negotiations, as the European Council meeting in Luxembourg (1997)[10] made clear. Given the ambiguity and the broad spectrum of what the fulfilment of the Copenhagen political criteria may amount to, it has been argued that this vagueness was deliberate and the large room for manoeuvre implied that any judgment on the part of the Union would, to a certain extent, be subjective (Smith, 2004: 140). Unlike previous enlargements, the Eastern enlargement foregrounded human rights and minority protection as paramount to EU membership application and, implicitly, to what the EU stands for.

Before acquiring the status of a candidate country, all CEECs concluded the so-called Europe Agreements with the EU. The main aims of the Europe Agreements revolved around supporting the post-communist countries to manage more effectively the transition period by creating a climate of stability and confidence which would, in turn, favour reform and allow the development of close political relations, by strengthening the foundations of the new European architecture or by improving the climate for trade and investment (Smith, 2004: 92). Human rights clauses constituted the key requirements of the Europe Agreements (mixed agreements negotiated by the Commission and concluded unanimously by the Council) signed with Romania (1 February 1993) and Bulgaria (8 March 1993), although there were no human rights clauses in the agreements signed with Poland, Hungary and Czechoslovakia in 1991, i.e. the first generation of Europe Agreements.

In other words, it was contended that in countries such as Romania and Bulgaria the violation of human rights[11] is far worse than in other CEECs. Additionally, Member States decided to include a suspension clause, a measure that had not been included in the earlier Europe Agreements, which could be enacted if Romania and Bulgaria failed to meet their human rights obligations. Therefore, the key difference between the agreements signed with Hungary, Poland, the Czech and Slovak Federal Republic in 1991 and the second round of agreements signed in 1993 with Romania and Bulgaria is the human rights and suspension clause, which the first round of Europe Agreements lacked. Hence, it can be claimed that the second round of Europe Agreements are qualitatively different and stricter regarding human rights than other association agreements.

The Copenhagen political criteria and enlargement policy constituted significant milestones that shaped the EU's external engagement with human rights. The reasons for the political salience acquired by human rights during the Eastern enlargement are linked to the distinctiveness of the enlargement process *per se*. First of all, that which differentiates the post-1989 enlargement from the previous ones is the transformation of the EU itself (Hillion, 2004: v). What the new Member States joined in 2004 and 2007 was substantially different from what it was at the time of previous enlargements. The Union was different from the earlier European Communities in fundamental ways, such as the common currency, common market, common foreign and security policy and the EU Charter of Fundamental Rights. Second, Eastern enlargement had a symbolic meaning in the sense that the accession of CEECs amounted to a 'return to Europe' process (Cirtautas and Schimmelfennig, 2010), namely the reunification of Europe after half a century of communist rule in Eastern Europe. The Commission played a pivotal role in the assessment of the human rights performance of the candidates: for instance, the Commission's strict monitoring of the candidates' progress suggests a more systematic and allegedly 'depoliticized' process relying on more objective criteria (Hillion, 2004: 14). Meanwhile, the state of economic and political development of the CEECs required a much more elaborate pre-accession strategy than in previous enlargements, which meant that the European Commission was the main actor that devised and managed the pre-accession policies and formal negotiations (Grabbe, 2006: 26). Moreover, the Commission's role as a 'screening actor' was even more challenging due to the fact that the human rights conditionality, and more generally political conditionality, does not correspond to a Union's particular policy or even competence (Hillion, 2004: 11). Finally, unlike the previous accession procedures in which few Commission Opinions were given, the 2004/2007 enlargements led to a substantive number of assessments, leading to Commission's Progress Reports being delivered on an annual basis. This strict and systematic evaluation made the conditions for enlarging the Union more entrenched, which in practice amounted to the employment of more 'objective' standards for assessing progress (Hillion, 2004: 15). Hence, the Copenhagen criteria established in relation to the CEECs have become standard accession criteria to the extent that one can speak of a progressive 'constitutionalization' of these criteria (Hillion, 2004: 22). In a nutshell, EU external human rights policy, as exemplified by Eastern enlargement, extended the EU's role and scope in addressing a wide array of human rights matters, for which EU institutions lack a similar mandate in relation to the Member States.

Europeanization of the CEECs and human rights

The Eastern enlargement process consisted of the EU's application of a wide range of accession conditions in order to prepare CEECs to become EU members. At the same time, Eastern enlargement led to the EU's development and implementation of a sophisticated and complex version of human rights conditionality to non-EU countries. Both rationalist-intergovernmentalist as well as sociological-normative explanations have been put forward to describe the reasons behind the Union's Eastern enlargement. The EU's initial decision to accept the former communist states has been attributed to economic interests, as well as to power relations between EU members and candidates (Moravcsik and Vachudova, 2003; Plumper and Schneider, 2007). Others have proposed geopolitical explanations (Skalnes, 2005) by emphasizing the hard security dimension (Sperling, 1999; Smith and Timmins, 2000; Smith, 2005), rather than economic and commercial factors, as the key driving force behind the EU's decision to enlarge. However, security and economic considerations alone cannot explain why the EU had previously decided to open accession negotiations with countries such as Romania, arguably the most 'difficult' of the former communist states (Papadimitriou and Phinnemore, 2008: 14). Indeed, countries such as Bulgaria and Romania have been labelled as the laggards of post-communist transition due to their sluggish economic and political reforms (Gallagher, 2005; Ciută, 2005). To this end, norm-inspired accounts, involving the spread of liberal and democratic values to the former communist states, have emerged to complement rationalist and security-based explanations. Norms are integral to the very fabric and scope of the European project and, therefore, norms such as democratic rule, human and minority rights and the rule of law inspired Eastern enlargement (Friis, 1998) and became associated with the EU's post-Cold War reason for being (Fierke and Wiener, 1999). The EU's commitment to norm promotion via enlargement indicates the EU's moral obligation to accept the ex-communist states by re-uniting them with the family of Western democracies. No wonder, therefore, that the EU's decision to enlarge has been underpinned by its 'special responsibility' (Sedelmeier, 2005) and the 'sense of kinship-based duty' (Sjursen, 2002:508) towards the CEECs, as well as by the EU's identity as a pan-European liberal-democratic community (Schimmelfennig, 2001). In brief, both economic-instrumentalist reasons and normative-moral factors drove the EU's decision to expand to the East.

The EU's transformative impact on the CEECs during accession negations has been described as a process of Europeanization. Eastern enlargement was conceptualized as a form of Europeanization *qua* 'export', whereby the impact of the EU occurs beyond its own geographical confines (e.g. Lippert *et al.*, 2001; Goetz, 2001; Grabbe, 2003; Papadimitriou and Phinnemore, 2004, 2008). The EU's impact on CEECs was explained as an external incentives model of rule adoption according to which Europeanization is 'a process in which states adopt EU rules' (Schimmelfennig and Sedelmeier, 2005a: 7). According to a rationalist model of change, the CEECs transformed their institutional structures and policies provided that the EU incentives, including the membership reward, outweighed the costs incurred by these domestic changes. Therefore, the institutionalization of EU rules at the domestic level involved 'the transposition of EU law into domestic law, the restructuring of domestic institutions according to EU rules, or the change of political practices according to EU standards' (Schimmelfennig and Sedelmeier, 2005a: 7). The enlargement-led Europeanization, also defined as 'the impact of the EU accession process on national patterns of governance' (Grabbe, 2001:1014), generated two kinds of effects at the national level: on the one hand, it altered the domestic opportunity structures by empowering certain actors at the expense of others; on the other, it engendered changes in the actors' cognition and preference formation (Knill and Lehmkuhl, 1999:1–2). In brief, both rational institutionalist and sociological perspectives have been developed to provide explanatory frameworks for enlargement-led Europeanization.

The application of the accession conditionality and the high level of misfit between Eastern candidates' political and economic structures and those of the Member States point to a substantial transformative impact of the EU on the candidates' institutions and policies. The relationship between the EU and the CEECs was deeply asymmetrical (Hughes *et al.*, 2004) given that candidate countries, compared with the Member States, were in a weaker position vis-a-vis the EU, and subsequently these countries lacked a bargaining and negotiating clout (Grabbe, 2006). Second, the former communist states aspiring to EU membership were particularly eager to comply with EU rules, as the so-called 'return to Europe' had been their most important post-communist policy orientation. Furthermore, the breadth of the EU conditionality agenda involved no possibility of opt-outs from parts of this agenda. For instance, the Copenhagen accession criteria (1993) covered a wide spectrum of demands, ranging from economic to political and legal demands. The creation of formal accession conditions has given the EU much wider leverage to get the Eastern applicants to comply with its requests – compared with the former candidates (Grabbe, 2003) – and thus these applicant countries were committed to converge with a maximalist version of the EU rules and policies (Grabbe, 2006) as the EU was trying to export the *acquis communautaire* lock, stock and barrel (Bulmer and Radaelli, 2004: 2). Yet, it has been claimed that this asymmetry of power was described by uncertainty (Grabbe, 2003: 318–323) about the content of the EU accession agenda, its standards and thresholds and, ultimately, about whom to satisfy, namely the Commission, the Council or particular Member States. Despite this uncertainty, the asymmetrical relationship shaped both the extent and depth of the EU's impact on the former communist states.

The EU-driven changes in Central and East European countries were underpinned by a so-called policy of conditionality (Schimmelfennig and Sedelmeier, 2005a), based on the Copenhagen accession criteria which had to be met before CEECs could become EU Member States. The policy of conditionality, employed by the EU in its external relations context (Pridham, 2002; Smith, 1998), consists of a 'bargaining strategy of reinforcement by reward, under which the EU provides external incentives for a target government to comply with its conditions' (Schimmelfennig and Sedelmeier, 2004:662). The EU's ability to 'export' strong Europeanization pressures (Papadimitriou and Phinnemore, 2008:11) to the CEECs relied heavily on a strict policy of conditionality, an instrument the EU does not possess in relation to its members (Schimmelfennig and Sedelmeier, 2007: 97) and which gives the EU significant leverage to forge changes at the domestic level in the candidates. The EU's conditionality for the accession of CEECs is viewed as a powerful incentive and disciplinary structure including both the formal requirements on candidates but also the informal pressures arising from the 'behaviour and perceptions of actors engaged in the political process' (Hughes *et al.*, 2004: 2). The EU's application of the conditionality instrument took two guises: formal conditionality, based on the Copenhagen criteria and the EU's *acquis*, and informal, i.e. softer mechanisms of applying pressure or conditionality. To this end, it has been argued that the transformative effects of the accession conditionality depended upon three factors, namely the nature of the EU *acquis*, the policy area concerned and the political context in which conditionality was applied (Hughes *et al.*, 2004). The policy of conditionality was implemented via a set of EU instruments, such as benchmarking and monitoring, provision of legislative and institutional templates, advice and twinning, financial assistance or gate-keeping, namely access to negotiations and further stages in the accession process (Grabbe, 2001: 1020). In addition, given the breadth of the accession agenda and the EU's policy of conditionality, it has been claimed that insofar as Europeanization has the EU as its source, the 'Europeanization effect' of enlargement was very strong externally (Bulmer and Radaelli, 2004: 2).

The application of EU accession conditionality was also conceptualized as a process of gradual and formal horizontal institutionalization of organizational rules and norms (Schimmelfennig and Sedelmeier, 2005b). This horizontal institutionalization signals that the gap in rules and institutional arrangements between the insiders of a Union and the outsiders progressively becomes narrower, which is the outcome of successive rounds of reforms and institutional adjustments to EU norms and practices undertaken by outsiders (Mattli and Plumper, 2005: 59–60). Furthermore, international socialization in Eastern Europe, according to which Eastern candidates were induced to adopt the constitutive rules of the EU, was described as strategic action in an international community (Schimmelfennig *et al.*, 2006). According to this approach, the socialization of the CEECs occurred gradually via the adoption of EU rules and the main socialization mechanism was reinforcement by reward via political conditionality (Schimmelfennig *et al.*, 2006: 6–7). The socialization of the candidates was effective provided that two factors were at work: first, if the EU membership incentives were credible; and second, if the domestic political adaptation costs were low (Schimmelfennig *et al.*, 2006: 10). Institutionalist accounts, therefore, provide sociological and rationalist explanations for the array of changes triggered by EU accession in the CEECs.

The impact of the EU on CEECs, defined as 'EU rule adoption' (Schimmelfennig and Sedelmeier, 2005a), however, refers only to the adoption of the EU *acquis communautaire,* hence the body of the already existing EU rules and regulations at the EU level as adopted at the national level. This EU rule adoption is part of the Copenhagen accession criteria and it involves the applicants' transformation by the already existing EU legislation and rules which are at work at the EU level and in the Member States. However, the Copenhagen political criteria, particularly with regard to human rights matters, amount to transformative processes triggered by the EU in areas for which it lacks standards, templates or rules. Indeed, the Commission crafted a highly intrusive policy in the human rights systems of the candidates. According to Williams (2004: 77), all three levels of the internal–external human rights incoherence – in terms of human rights definitions, methods of scrutiny and measures of enforcement – were salient in the Commission's assessment of the CEECs' human rights performance. It has been argued that in the accession agenda presented to the CEECs the distinctions between the EU and national competences are not acknowledged (Grabbe, 2006:23), which means that through the accession policy the Member States gave the Commission competences in CEECs that they had never accepted for themselves (Grabbe, 2006:36). The EU's interventionist policy in the human rights provision of non-EU members resulted in a stark contrast between what the Commission does internally and externally in relation to human rights. Given that the former communist countries were to become future EU members, the stakes were high for the Commission to foster the compliance in CEECs with a wide spectrum of human rights standards and principles, for most of which the Commission lacked legal mandate in relation to EU Member States. Due to the lack of EU templates and standards on various aspects of human rights and minority protection, the policy of conditionality amounted to the Commission's creative role in spelling out what the standards ought to be, rather than forging a policy of rule of adoption of already existing EU rules and norms, as is generally the case with respect to EU *acquis*. Furthermore, the salience of human rights issues in the Eastern enlargement policy contributed to the creation of a new role for the EU as a human rights promoter, which was an unintended consequence of the EU's extensive involvement with human rights protection in candidates (Sedelmeier, 2006: 118–135).

The significant prominence of human rights in the 2004 and 2007 enlargements or in EU external relations in general is not matched by a similar approach internally. This 'policy of bifurcation' or internal–external incoherence (Williams, 2000, 2004) leads to the emergence of what might, drawing on Nicolaidis and Howse's (2002) depiction of EU external trade, be described as an EU-topia in the field of human rights. A clear disjuncture exists between the ideal promoted through the EU's external human rights dimension and the internal coherence of the EU's human rights role in relation to its Member States. The main reasoning behind the 'EU-topia' contention is that EU internal and external human rights dimensions are not coherent and the EU promotes externally norms and values that it fails to pursue to the same extent internally. Moreover, the EU pursues externally high standards of human rights protection, while inside the Union, EU Member States are often criticized by international institutions for human rights violations. In brief, 'what is being projected [externally] is not the EU *as is* but an EU-topia' (Nicolaidis and Howse, 2002: 769, emphasis in original). The EU-topia projected externally was clearly illustrated via Eastern enlargement when 'the Copenhagen criteria spelled out what the EU is (or is supposed to be) and therefore what candidate countries should become' (Nicolaidis and Howse, 2002: 774). It has been argued that the disjuncture between EU internal and external human rights dimensions has not been addressed by the Lisbon Treaty provisions and therefore 'the absence of a serious EU human rights mechanism, the double-standard as between internal and external policies, and the continuing emphasis on the autonomy of the EU's human rights regime' (De Burca, 2011:4) still cast doubt on the EU's efforts to promote human rights. In short, the Europeanization of the CEECs' human rights provision amounted to the export of an EU-topia in human rights, a process largely undertaken and steered by the European Commission.

Analytical framework(s): policy feedback effects

The breadth and depth of EU intervention in the human rights provision of the CEECs was unprecedented. By acting as a human rights actor (Sedelmeier, 2006), the EU has overhauled the institutional structures and policy mechanisms upholding human rights in the former communist states. However, the EU's intervention in a wide array of human rights matters has had far-reaching consequences and, hence, feedback effects on the EU itself. The feedback effects and unintended consequences of the EU's enlargement policy on the EU's institutional and normative frameworks have been little researched. It is generally contended that enlargement decisions and processes have a certain 'history-making' character since they significantly affect the future functioning of the EU (Baun, 2000). Broadly conceived, policy feedback occurs when policies – which are the effects of politics – in turn become causes and thus have effects on actors' behaviour, institutions and on broader political processes (Pierson, 1993:624). Yet, the conceptualization of and evidence for policy feedback with respect to Eastern enlargement and human rights has to be adapted to the dimensions of EU human rights policy. Therefore, by taking into account the EU's 'policy of bifurcation' (Williams, 2000, 2004) with respect to human rights and the enlargement context, the policy feedback involves two distinctive aspects: the internal policy dimension, where policy feedback affects the agenda-setting process via *policy development*; and the external policy dimension, where policy feedback entails *policy continuation* in line with a historical institutionalist framework. Whilst the internal policy feedback includes policy entrepreneurship, i.e. the emergence of policy entrepreneurs capable of shaping the EU's internal policy agenda, and therefore has a strong agency-related focus, the external policy dimension outlines the role of structures, i.e. institutions and policies, in becoming entrenched and hard to roll back over the longer term. Hence, policy feedback is conceived as policy development via entrepreneurial actions to set the EU policy agenda (EU internal policy sphere), and as policy continuation, which amounts to policy stability and entrenchment in time (EU external policy sphere). The main analytical focus here is on unveiling the extent to which the enlargement-led Europeanization of CEECs has had unintended consequences on and has prompted far-ranging changes of EU institutions and policies.

Policy entrepreneurship and agenda-setting processes

Policy entrepreneurship in relation to human rights at the EU level provides insights into the factors and conditions which lead to agenda-setting processes via entrepreneurial actions, given the EU's limited mandate in human rights in relation to the Member States. Policy feedback in EU internal policy dimension is conceptualized as agency-driven actions, i.e. entrepreneurship, aimed at influencing the policy agenda of the EU. Therefore, this study informs about the role of policy entrepreneurs with regard to agenda-setting and policy development processes (Peters, 2001; Pollack, 1997; Princen, 2007, 2009) triggered by the Commission's intervention in the human rights provision of CEECs. Agenda-setting theory is concerned with the factors that shape political agendas (Baumgartner and Jones, 1993; Cobb and Elder, 1972; Kingdon, 1984). In the context of the EU agenda-setting studies (Peters, 2001; Pollack, 1997; Princen, 2007) the central focus has been on investigating why certain issues get onto the EU political agenda and how the agenda-setting processes can bring new insights into the European integration (Harcourt, 1998; Peters, 2001; Pollack, 2003). Indeed, there is a strong connection between the breadth of the EU's political agenda and European integration as by taking up new issues the EU expands in scope and policy remit (Princen, 2007:22). In brief, the actions undertaken by policy entrepreneurs can shape the EU agenda and policy processes.

The literature focusing on entrepreneurship in politics uses the same concepts to explain a wide variety of policy processes, making it rather difficult to clearly define and conceptualize policy entrepreneurs (Barzelay and Gallego, 2006, 2010; Dyson, 2008; MacKenzie, 2004; Mintrom, 2000; Mintrom and Vergari, 1996; Oliver and Paul-Shaheen, 1997; Reinstaller, 2005). However, policy entrepreneurs, generally defined as 'advocates for proposals or for prominence of ideas' (Kingdon, 1984: 122) or as 'people who seek to initiate dynamic policy change' (Mintrom, 1997: 739, see also Baumgartner and Jones, 1993; Kingdon, 1984; Polsby, 1984) are generally deemed to play a pivotal role in the policy-making process, particularly in relation to policy innovation or policy development (for example Roberts, 1991; Mintrom, 1997, 2000; Schneider *et al.*, 1995; Schiller, 1995). Kingdon's (1984) conceptualization of policy entrepreneurs pays heed to the conditions and factors that can facilitate or hamper entrepreneurial actions. By contextualising the entrepreneur and his/her actions, Kingdon's analysis illustrates that entrepreneurs always operate in a setting, which in social terms means that it is imperative to consider both *agency* – the entrepreneur – and *structure* when seeking to explain policy innovation. It should be noted that, here, entrepreneurship is conceptualized as individuals acting in certain institutional settings, and therefore the focus is on the dynamics between individuals (entrepreneurs) and the institutional contexts where they act.

Kingdon's (1984: 191) multiple streams model analyses policy initiation as a function of three streams providing contextual factors, namely problems, policies and politics, which are joined together by agents or policy entrepreneurs. The *problems* stream denotes the issue of concern itself or those issues which require political action. Citizens, media and civil-society stakeholders often define problems and raise awareness of underlying societal problems.

The *policies* (or solutions) stream consists of policy alternatives which float around in a 'primeval soup' (Kingdon, 1984:122), with some ideas floating to the top of the agenda whilst others fall to the bottom. The *politics* stream consists of political events and conditions that may or may not be favourable to the policy. The multiple streams model is not linear as the three streams flow relatively independently from each other; yet, it is only when a 'policy window' or a 'window of opportunity' opens in any of the three streams that all streams are coupled by a policy entrepreneur. Concepts such as policy window (Kingdon, 1984) shed light on the reasons why certain policy issues become high on the agenda and action is taken in relation to them. The policy window is 'an opportunity for advocates of proposals to push their pet solutions or to push attention to their special problems' (Kingdon, 1984: 173). A policy window opens particularly because a new problem captures the attention of policy-makers and, while the problem becomes pressing, it creates an opportunity for advocates of proposals to attach their solutions to it (Kingdon, 1984: 176–7). Whether they open in the problems or politics streams, windows of opportunity do not stay open long (Kingdon, 1984:213) and, hence, the convergence of the three streams to advance a new policy issue is largely dependent on 'the appearance of the right entrepreneur at the right time' (Kingdon, 1984:214). Therefore, according to Kingdon's multiple streams model (1984:191), entrepreneurs link the independently floating streams – problems, policies (solutions) and politics (political events and conditions) – together via *coupling*, by taking advantage of the opened policy windows.

Policy entrepreneurship can also be brought about by a 'focusing event', which can provide the political visibility and necessary impetus to take action in initially excluded policy areas at the EU level. To this end, not only do timing and sequence influence the impact of events, but also they shape the strategic opportunities available to actors (Pralle, 2006:990). A focusing event generates a sudden rise of attention at top institutional levels by drawing attention to a problem that hitherto received less attention. Indeed, an external focusing event can provide policy entrepreneurs with a 'window of opportunity' (Kingdon, 1984) to take action in areas initially excluded from decision-making. Therefore, policy entrepreneurship in relation to human rights at the EU level entails favourable contextual conditions facilitating entrepreneurial actions, given the EU's limited mandate in human rights in relation to the Member States. By drawing on Kingdon's model of policy entrepreneurship, here the emphasis is placed on contextual factors (problems, policies and politics), the favourable timing (window of opportunity, focusing event) and the emergence of the right entrepreneurs to take advantage of all these opportunities in order to forge policy change at the EU level. Although Kingdon's model emerged as an influential framework explaining the public policy process in the US, it has been little applied across countries (Baumgartner *et al.*, 2006), particularly in relation to EU policy process.

According to EU agenda-setting literature (Princen and Rhinard, 2006), issues can enter EU policy agenda via two routes: 'from above' (the high politics route) or 'from below' (the low politics route). Issues arrive on the EU policy agenda from above when there is agreement between EU political leaders or high-level officials that EU-level action should be taken in relation to a policy matter; while issues emerging from below involve policy experts formulating new policy directions in low-level groups in the EU institutions. Usually, a focusing event can trigger the policy development from above, when the window of opportunity underpinning the attention span of an issue can initiate top-down policy change, while the low politics route takes longer to come to fruition. Hence, issues can emerge on the EU agenda from above due to actions taken by EU policy entrepreneurs by seizing the opportunity provided by a policy window. Concepts related to policy entrepreneurship, such as *policy venue* and *policy image* (Baumgartner and Jones, 1993), can also explain the feedback of EU external policy on the EU internal human rights agenda. The policy venue, which refers to the institutions that have the authority to make decisions concerning an issue, and the policy image, namely 'how a policy is understood and discussed' (Baumgartner and Jones, 1993:11), do influence policy entrepreneurship. Indeed, certain issues or policy matters are more appealing than others to policy-makers, and, subsequently, it is easier to place them on the EU agenda. In brief, agenda-setting processes, described as the interplay between venues and framing (Princen, 2009:36), can generate policy development due to the entrepreneurship of EU actors.

EU external feedback effects

Feedback effects in EU external policy dimension – due to Eastern enlargement – are envisaged as policy continuation and path-dependent processes. Historical institutionalist elements (Pollack, 2008; Pierson, 1993, 2004; Armstrong and Bulmer, 1998), such as path dependency and lock-ins, self-reinforcing institutions and institutional learning, explain how non-EU policy areas such as human rights can become embedded as part of the EU external policy, such as enlargement policy. *Policy feedback* and *self-reinforcing* institutions are some of the key concepts employed to explain the effects of policies and institutions over time. Self-reinforcing institutions and positive feedback explain how certain institutional choices and policy lines are hard to reverse due to their stickiness. In the same vein, institutions are self-reinforcing if the effects generated by these institutions in turn reinforce them (Pollack, 2008), causing actors to stick with the existing institutional arrangements. This is tantamount to the *positive feedback* generated by institutions.

In essence, institutions or policies generate positive feedback effects if they provide incentives for actors to stick with existing institutions and policy lines, which leads to path dependence and lock-ins (Pollack, 2008). The concept of path dependency has been adopted increasingly in studies of EU integration (for example, Holzinger and Knill, 2002; Dimitrakopoulos, 2001). Path-dependency effects amount to the fact that 'the entrenchments of certain institutional arrangements obstruct an easy reversal of the initial choice' (Levi, 1997: 28) and, thus, institutions and policies are hard to roll back due to their becoming embedded over time.

The feedback effects of Eastern enlargement on the current EU enlargement process illustrate how and why processes and policy lines become sticky due to locked-in effects. Positive feedback effects, which are conducive to self-reinforcing institutions or policy lines, ultimately amount to processes of *institutional development* and *policy evolution.* There are significant elements that contribute to institutional development over time. First, individual and organizational adaptations to existing arrangements may make reversal unlikely (Pierson, 2004: 147), which means that over time actors tend to adapt to the existing institutional arrangements. Second, the concept of *asset investment* (Pierson, 2004: 148) provides insight into how the investment of particular assets – such as relationships, knowledge and privileges to name just a few – into an institution helps to explain institutional persistence 'as actors in each society invest in a particular institutional arrangement, they have incentives to protect their investment by opposing change' (Gourevitch cited in Pierson, 2004: 148). Along the same lines, it has been claimed that the positive possibility of path-dependence and policy solutions outliving their usefulness is that lessons may be drawn from past experience, which may lead to new strategies being put forward (Armstrong and Bulmer, 1998: 56). Hence, *institutional learning* emerges as lessons are drawn from past experience, and the lessons learnt further feed into institutional development and policy evolution. The focus on the dynamics of institutional stability and policy continuation reveals how particular institutional structures and policy lines actually become entrenched over time and how the lock-ins produced by them further reinforce these institutions and policies by extending the existing institutional arrangements and policy lines. Policies and institutions can have positive feedback effects, which in turn lead to self-reinforcing processes and path-dependent courses of action. Consequently, the lock-ins of certain institutional arrangements or policies explain how these become embedded over time and how they are prone to yield institutional development and policy evolution over the long term. The feedback effects generated by Eastern enlargement on the current accession process underscore the persistence of policy mechanisms and templates over time. Institutional and policy structures are hard to change once they have made inroads in the enlargement process and have become stable.

Conclusion

The founding Treaties were silent with respect to the protection of human rights, particularly due to an essentially economic focus of the European integration process and the agreement that Member States have the sole responsibility for human rights matters at the national level. However, over the last 50 years, the EU has developed a human rights role and identity, which have been more prominent and robust in EU external policy dimension. This external human rights remit took a life of its own during the Eastern enlargement process, when the EU intervened in a wide range of human rights matters in the candidates, despite lacking a similar mandate in relation to the Member States. The Europeanization of the CEECs' institutions and policies, therefore, captures the extent to which these countries were transformed according to an EU script. At the same time, the Europeanization of the CEECs' human rights provision had to rely on the EU's creative and innovative application of the accession criteria, given that there are no EU human rights templates and standards. Yet, the feedback effects of EU human rights conditionality, as applied to CEECs, on the EU itself have not been researched so far. Given the 'policy of bifurcation' regarding EU internal and external human rights roles, policy feedback here is conceptualized as policy development due to entrepreneurial actions (in EU internal dimension) and as policy continuation in line with a historical institutionalist framework (in EU external dimension). These two conceptualizations of feedback processes will provide the explanatory narrative for the feedback effects triggered by the EU's intervention in child protection in Romania before 2007.

Notes

1   For an overview of the early developments, see Pierre Pescatore (1981)'The Context and Significance of Fundamental Rights in the Law of the European Communities', *Human Rights Law Journal*, 4(2): 295–308; Ulrich Scheuner (1975) 'Fundamental Rights in European Community Law and in National Constitutional Law', *Common Market Law Review*, 12(2): 171–191; Samantha Besson (2006) 'The European Union and Human Rights: Towards a Post-national Human Rights Institution?', *Human Rights Law Review*, 6(2): 323–360.

2   'Third country' here refers to non-EU countries which conclude various types of agreements with the European Union. The term does not refer to Third World countries.

3   'Affirming as the essential objectives of their efforts the constant improvement of the living and working conditions of their people' (Preamble of the Treaty of Rome).

4   According to the Single European Act Preamble, the Member States were 'determined to work together to promote democracy on the basis of fundamental rights

recognized in the constitutions and laws of the Member States' and that they would 'display the principles of democracy and compliance with the law and with human rights to which they are attached' (*Official Journal of the European Communities*, No. L 169/1 of 29 June 1987).

5   Article F TEU (2) provides that: 'the Union shall respect fundamental rights, as guaranteed by the European Convention for the Protection of Human Rights and Fundamental Freedoms signed in Rome on 4 November 1950 and as they result from the constitutional traditions common to the Member States, as general principles of Community law' (*Official Journal of the European Communities*, No. C 191/1 of 29 July 1992).

6   Article 6(1) TEU provides that 'the Union is founded on the principles of liberty, democracy, respect for human rights and fundamental freedoms and the rule of law, principles which are common to the Member States' (*Official Journal of the European Communities*, No. C 340 of 10 November 1997).

7   Article 2 TEU states that 'the Union is founded on the values of respect for human dignity, freedom, democracy, equality, the rule of law and respect for human rights, including the rights of persons belonging to minorities' (*Consolidated Texts of the EU Treaties as amended by the Treaty of Lisbon*, 2007).

8   The Council of Europe membership conditions state that 'the people's representatives must have been chosen by means of free and fair elections based on universal suffrage; freedom of expression and notably of the media must be guaranteed; rights of national minorities must be protected; and the state must sign the European Convention on Human Rights within a short period' (Winkler cited by Smith, 2003: 115).

9   The Copenhagen political conditionality states that an applicant country has to have 'achieved stability of institutions guaranteeing democracy, the rule of law, human rights and respect for and protection of minorities' (European Council, 1993).

10   European Council (1997) *Presidency Conclusions*, DOC/97/24, Luxembourg, 12–13 December.

11   The Preamble of the Europe Agreement with Romania reads 'Recognising the need to continue and complete, with the assistance of the Community, Romania's transition towards a new political and economic system which respects the rule of law and human rights, including the rights of persons belonging to minorities, operates a multi-party system with free and democratic elections and provides for economic liberalization in order to establish a market economy' (*Official Journal of the European Communities*, No. L 357/174 of 31 December 1994).

2

European Union accession conditionality and human rights in Romania

The Commission has no competence to monitor prisons in the Member States and then it starts becoming difficult if you start monitoring things externally for which you don't have an internal mandate. And I know that Member State X can say 'well Commission, why are you looking so strenuously into those prison conditions in these candidate countries when we are not really sure you should?'

(Commission official)

Introduction

The end of the Cold War afforded the former communist states with the opportunity of re-uniting with Europe. Unlike the other Central and Eastern European Countries (CEECs), Romania's efforts to join the European Union (EU) had been marred with setbacks due to its turbulent post-communist transition, which impacted on its rapprochement with the EU. Romania's progress towards EU membership was slow and at times uncertain, which made Romania, along with Bulgaria, one of the accession 'laggards' (Noutcheva and Bechev, 2008). Respect for human rights and minority protection in Romania constituted one of the main hurdles towards Romania's prospects of meeting the accession political criteria. By deploying a wide array of instruments and mechanisms, the European Commission in particular intervened in a wide range of human rights and minority protection matters in order to support Romania's efforts to meet the accession criteria and be in line with European and international standards. However, as the Romanian case clearly demonstrates below, the EU's intervention in human rights issues in the CEECs went well beyond the accepted EU *acquis* on and mandate in human rights in relation to Member States. Despite acting in an uncharted territory, the Commission's application of human rights conditionality in Romania sought to bring about radical institutional and legislative transformations in the field of human rights provision and standards.

This chapter explores the breadth and depth of the changes and developments engendered by the EU in Romania before 2007. The first section provides an overview of the key events and processes shaping Romania's accession negotiations with the EU, by highlighting the distinctive accession path pursued by one of the Eastern enlargement 'backmarkers' (Papadimitriou and Phinnemore, 2008:34). Section two, on the other hand, examines the wide-ranging scope of EU intervention in Romanian human rights protection. Although some of the policy areas targeted by EU accession conditionality were problematic and sensitive, they were not as visible and prominent as the issue of child protection in Romania, which is examined in depth in Chapter 3. Nevertheless, even these lower level interventions established a precedent for EU action in areas such as prison conditions or minority protection, over which the EU does not enjoy an internal mandate in relation to its Member States. The second section, therefore, examines the magnitude of EU interventions in a wide spectrum of human rights areas in Romania for which the EU lacks an internal competence and *acquis*.[1]

Romania and EU accession

Romania's communist past and its turbulent post-communist transition shaped the direction and pace of its prospects of re-joining Europe and its political and economic values. The end of communism in Romania and the political elites' lack of commitment to liberal and democratic values, along with a protracted transition to market economy, anticipated that Romania's 'return to Europe' was going to be a contentious and arduous process. Studies on Romania's post-communist political and economic development (Gallagher, 1995, 2005; Verdery, 1993; Mungiu-Pippidi, 2002; Phinnemore, 2006) illustrated that the dynamics of the relationship between the EU and this ex-communist state was to a certain extent determined by the failure of Romania's political elites to make a clean break from the communist legacies. For this reason, Romania's prospects for EU membership and its capacity to align its institutions and laws with the European ones was regarded with deep suspicion by Brussels. Indeed, Romania's nationalist version of communism had been more repressive and brutal than the versions of communism in the other CEECs. In the same vein, the demise of communism in Romania in 1989 was accompanied by bloodshed, which led to allegations of a coup orchestrated by second-rank Communist Party elite (Ratesh, 1991). Instead of following the model of non-violent regime change, or the so-called velvet revolutions, experienced by its neighbours, the Romanian revolution had the ingredients of 'a secretive Leninist coup d'etat by men who were irrevocably tarnished by their association with the former regime both through the office they had held and the methods by which they had achieved power' (Light and Phinnemore, 2001:21). It is not surprising, therefore, that the path to EU membership followed by the successive Romanian governments was problematic due to, *inter alia*, various anti-Western influential elite groups who had a sway on the pace and direction of economic and political reforms in Romania.

The fall of communism in Europe indicated that all former communist states would be competing to rejoin the European family of democratic states. For this very reason, the Union devised instruments to facilitate the EU institutions' engagement with the CEECs. Amongst the ex-communist states, Romania's position as a backmarker was peculiar, a fact highlighted by the EU's concern over the situation of human rights and minority protection in this country, which led to the inclusion of a human rights clause in the Europe Agreement signed with Romania in February 1993. The Europe Agreements signed with the CEECs were association agreements, which established institutional and political dialogues between the Union and its associated partners. Although all Europe Agreements had the same structure and general provisions, their specific content was tailored to the circumstances of each Eastern candidate. Therefore, from the outset of Romania's official engagement with the EU institutions, its human rights record received unparalleled attention amongst the CEECs, which is reflected by the 'improved conditionality' via the insertion of an 'automatic suspension' clause with respect to human rights violations in Romania (Papadimitriou, 2002). The EU's employment of improved conditionality in relation to Romania was not welcomed by the Romanian authorities; however, the Commission's reassurance that the human rights clause will be introduced in all future agreements with non-EU countries made it easier for countries such as Romania to accept this discriminatory approach to CEECs (Papadimitriou, 2002).

The former communist states applied for EU membership once the European Council had adopted the accession criteria in 1993, also known as the Copenhagen accession criteria.[2] The EU's commitment to accept new Eastern members was substantiated via the adoption of the pre-accession strategy, agreed by the Essen European Council in 1994, and which became coupled with the accession criteria. The Essen pre-accession strategy provided a roadmap regarding the shape and direction of the process of accession as devised by the EU institutions. Romania was amongst the first of the CEECs to submit an application for EU membership in June 1995. Yet, despite the CEECs' shared commitment to rejoin the European political and economic space, the EU struggled to reach a consensus over the 'method' of Eastward enlargement. Given the economics and politics of countries such as Bulgaria and Romania, the debate at the EU level centred on two potential enlargement routes: the differential treatment of Eastern candidates on the basis of their performance in meeting the accession criteria, and the 'regatta' option, namely the EU's employment of an all-inclusive approach in relation to CEECs. The EU opted for the latter, as the Luxembourg European Council meeting in 1997 made clear; yet it was the Commission's assessment of the CEECs' political and economic situation as part of Agenda 2000 for a Stronger and Wider Union (1997) that subsequently differentiated between the candidate countries' readiness for opening accession negotiations with the EU. On the basis of the Commission Opinion on each Eastern candidate, issued as part of Agenda 2000, the EU decided to open accession negotiations only with some of the CEECs. For instance, the Commission's Opinion on Romania's application provided a damning assessment of the country's progress towards democratic and economic transformation. Although the evaluation of the political criteria in relation to Romania was vague, the Commission raised significant concerns about the situation of minority protection and the broader protection of human rights, including child protection. Despite being denied a candidate country status in 1997, Romania remained on the EU's 'enlargement radar' till December 1999, when the Helsinki European Council decided to open accession negotiations with all remaining CEECs, including Romania and Bulgaria. To cut a long story short, Romania came late in the accession negotiation process and therefore had a lot of catching-up to do to fulfil EU accession demands.

Extent and depth of EU intervention in the Romanian human rights provision

The EU's intervention in the human rights provision in Romania was not limited only to the notable area of child protection, but it included a wide range of human rights and minority protection issues. Child protection was a highly politicized and sensitive accession condition, and the EU's role in this area was extensive and politically visible, particularly due to the issue of international adoptions. However, the extent of EU intervention in Romania's human rights provision went well-beyond the child protection case. Even if the EU's policy of conditionality was uneven in terms of the instruments employed and the changes forged, it went, nevertheless, beyond the EU's internal remit in relation to the EU Member States and established a precedent in and familiarity with human rights areas for which the Commission had hardly any expertise in or mandate to intervene internally. The breadth and depth of EU interference in human rights protection in Romania, during accession negotiations, is outlined below.

The human rights conditionality applied in Romania illustrates that uneven political pressure was exerted on human rights areas monitored before 2007. The political salience and visibility acquired by certain human rights matters was a function of both the degree of rights violations, on the one hand, and of the influence of non-governmental organizations (NGOs) and international community on the Romanian government, on the other. The instruments employed by the Union to transform the human rights provision included financial and technical assistance, while the compliance with the main European and international instruments acted as a yardstick to measure progress. The amount of financial assistance and technical expertise deployed for each human rights area concerned depended on the severity of the rights violations and, above all, on the political weight and visibility acquired by the respective policy sector.

Social rights

The broad spectrum of social issues was at the heart of the EU human rights conditionality as applied in Romania. Amongst the social policy sectors addressed by the EU, the situation of the people with disabilities in residential care and the mental health care system stands out by far. Both policy sectors still bore the communist legacy of providing care to people with physical disabilities and those with mental health problems (Mundt *et al.*, 2012). The Commission requested extensive legislative and institutional changes in order to tackle the violation of rights in these areas and to modernize how care was provided to people with disabilities and with mental illnesses. The Commission's bold intervention in these areas, however, lacked the necessary expertise and *acquis* to guide developments on the ground. The EU's demands with respect to social matters, which are mainly matters of national competence, are controversial due to the political sensitivity that these areas entail and the broader perception that EU institutions lack jurisdiction to impose structural changes with respect to these areas. Nevertheless, the Commission's role consisted of applying a specific template of reform to all human rights areas, which included the adoption of a new legislation in conformity with international law and instruments, the establishment of new institutional structures and regular EU evaluations of the actual situation on the ground.

Social issues found various routes of getting onto the Romania's accession agenda. The question of people with disabilities had been on Romania's accession agenda since the Commission's first report on *Romania's Progress towards Accession* in 1998, while the problem of people with mental illnesses became an accession condition on Romania's accession agenda only in 2005, after an Amnesty International Report was published highlighting the abuses taking place in a psychiatric hospital.[3] The question of people with mental health issues was placed on Romania's accession agenda in the autumn of 2005, after Romania had already concluded the accession negotiations. Mental health as a human rights issue is highly controversial within the EU due to the variety of mental health systems and legislative frameworks in place in Member States. There was no EU *acquis* on mental health when this policy sector became an accession condition for Romania and there was little expertise on and tradition of involvement in this area even at the level of Directorate General (DG) Health and Consumers (SANCO).[4] Furthermore, mental health was not an accession condition for the countries that joined the Union in 2004. No wonder, therefore, that the Romanian authorities reacted with disapproval of having to meet a new and difficult accession condition within a short time span, particularly given that the Commission lacked an internal legal competence in this area.[5] According to Commission officials, there was pressure from lobby groups and NGOs on the Commission to make mental health an accession condition for Romania in order to delay Romania's accession to the EU. For instance, the Irish NGO, Focus on Romania (FoR), contacted the Commission and some MEPs, for example Mairead McGuinness, asking the Commission to employ mental health as a binding condition for Romania's accession in order to forge change in this area.[6] According to the Commission, the small but powerful lobby by FoR aimed to delay Romania's accession on the grounds of human rights violations[7], and it particularly endeavoured to achieve this by asking the Commission to impose the safeguard clause on mental health and abandoned children.[8] In other words, the issue of mental health was employed as a tool by those who intended to postpone Romania's planned accession to the EU in 2007. The emergence of the mental health issue on Romania's accession agenda illustrates how various vested interests can influence the EU agenda and, subsequently, why EU institutions need to react to these influential groups.

The Commission's role in addressing the issue of mental health had to consider two aspects underlying its intervention: the EU's lack of *acquis* and expertise in mental health, on the one hand, and the proposal of a set of recommendations and measures that could be delivered within the time-frame prior to Romania's accession to the EU, on the other. At the same time, the Commission had to grapple with the pressure from various lobby groups which attempted to place new issues on Romania's accession agenda and hence to curtail its prospects of joining the EU. As a Commission official put it: 'certain NGOs, certain lobby groups ... some of them had hidden agendas, they didn't like very much the idea of Romania's accession to the EU so they tried to explore different sectors which were difficult for Romania ... because it's clear that to deal with issues like mental health, it takes years to improve ... they [lobbies] also knew that the Commission necessarily cannot do very much, as there's no *acquis* basis'.[9] By intervening in mental health in Romania, the Commission had to strike a balance between the demands imposed on candidate countries such as Romania, on the one hand, and what these countries could deliver realistically within the given timeframe before joining the EU, on the other.

The Commission's role in the area of persons with disabilities and mental illness was guided by the concrete situation at country level, namely the actual conditions in institutions, along with the legislative and institutional framework in place.[10] The main problems faced by people with disabilities and mental illness living in care institutions were, first, the poor conditions in these institutions and, second, the legislation which protected their rights.[11] The communist model of institutional care along with a legislation that did not focus on rights led to a wide range of abuses and the violation of human rights. The patients living in residential institutions or who were treated in psychiatric institutions were physically and sexually abused by the staff working in these institutions. Additionally, the treatment of people with mental illness was still carried out in a communist fashion: they were treated together with people with learning difficulties, although the former could be cured.[12] The evaluation of the situation in care institutions was based on the Commission's own visits to assess the underlying problems faced by the patients living there.

The EU had no expertise in addressing disability-related matters, including the protection of the rights of disabled people. Yet, the Commission's role relied on the employment of Poland and Hungary: Assistance for Reconstructing their Economies (PHARE) funding to assist the Romanian government with the implementation of the *Strategy for the Integration of the Disabled* (2004), which involved institutional reform via the closure of big residential institutions and the creation of alternative, community-based services for people with disabilities (Ministry of Labour, Social Solidarity and Family, 2005: 3). The PHARE grant scheme[13] funded projects developed by local authorities' departments responsible for social assistance – the so-called General Directions for Social Assistance and Child Protection – and implemented either by these authorities alone or in partnership with NGOs (Ministry of Labour, Social Solidarity and Family, 2005: 4). The creation of alternative, community-based services had as a main objective the welfare of people with disabilities and their families (Ministry of Labour, Social Solidarity and Family, 2005: 6). The EU financial assistance was channelled towards supporting the revamp of the system and care services. Apart from the institutional overhaul, the EU also intended to forge broader societal changes, by shifting social attitudes to and perceptions of people with disabilities. To this end, the European Commission Delegation in Bucharest played a key role in raising awareness of the plight of this group of people by carrying out self-awareness campaigns, whereby members of the EC Delegation went through Bucharest in wheelchairs to raise awareness of the difficulties encountered by people in wheelchairs in accessing public places and transport.[14] According to Commission officials, this kind of public awareness campaign was effective in reaching its targets, despite the allocation of small EU funding for it.[15]

The overhaul of mental health followed a similar pattern of transformation. The situation in psychiatric institutions and facilities was assessed via peer review missions organized and run by the Commission. The peer review visits were carried out by Commission officials, mental health experts from Member States and Romanian officials, and they had the main goal of assessing the conditions in psychiatric institutions in order to evaluate the main underlying problems in this area. Hence, the reviewers drafted their own reports and made recommendations regarding the changes that should occur in psychiatric hospitals. The peer review reports drew attention to the main shortcomings of the mental health system, namely that people with mental illness and people with learning difficulties were treated together in psychiatric hospitals, even if the latter constituted a different category of patients.[16] Subsequently, the biological model of mental illness employed in these hospitals rendered rehabilitation difficult (Prot-Klinger, 2006: 11). The reviewers made clear recommendations about what should change and how: for instance, they suggested that community psychiatry via community-oriented centres had to be developed as a more effective way of helping patient–community relations (Prot-Klinger, 2006: 11). Yet, the Commission had less than two years to support the Romanian authorities to address the mental health provision and, therefore, the measures adopted did not always produce the anticipated outcomes. Indeed, the Commission allocated financial assistance as grants for project-funding under PHARE – about €3 million[17] – for mental health and supported twinners from Member States to train Romanian authorities on how to address the situation of mentally ill people. For instance, PHARE supported project funding to develop community mental health services in 2006, while a PHARE Twinning Light Project[18] was funded for the Action Plan for Implementing the Mental Health Reform Strategy (Ministry of Public Health, 2007: 16).

The EU's intervention in sensitive policy areas such as mental health had to consider the mental health provision, along with the level of its protection, in the Member States. Given that mental health is a problematic and sensitive human rights area also in the Member States, the conditionality applied in Romania in relation to mental health had to reflect the level of protection attained in the Member States and the competence division in this area.[19] In spite of the significant shortcomings in mental health and the short timeframe underpinning the Commission's intervention in this area, the Commission concluded that some substantial progress had been achieved and, above all, that the reform in mental health was on the right track. The Commission's actions in mental health have also provided unique opportunities for learning by doing and hence for the development of invaluable expertise in this area. However, social policy areas such as disabilities and mental health are sensitive and highly politicized national policy sectors which require a longer time span for the structural changes to bear fruit and for the situation on the ground to improve substantially.

Civil and political rights

The Commission sought to elicit changes also in relation to civil and political rights, particularly addressing violations such as ill-treatment in custody and prison conditions. Given the Commission's lack of expertise and mandate in these areas in relation to Member States, and particularly the lack of an EU *acquis* to act as a benchmark, the Commission's role regarding prison conditions and ill-treatment by the police in Romania had to rely on the Member States' experts to carry out the assessment of the situation at local level. The Commission's active engagement in transforming these sectors was often regarded as evidence of Commission overstepping its jurisdiction.[20] Notwithstanding this, the Commission's extension of competence in relation to candidate countries was permitted by the Member States, as long as the same competence would not be exerted in relation to them.

The situation concerning prison conditions in Romania faced two sets of shortcomings: first, the treatment of inmates, and second, the concrete living conditions in prison cells. For instance, the most serious problem regarding prison conditions was severe overcrowding (European Commission, 2002: 31), which was also connected with minors being detained in the same cells together with adult inmates, which violated international and European legislation in this area. The living conditions in Romanian prisons were poor due to low food quality, limited medical care and unhygienic conditions. At the same time, the ill-treatment of detainees by prison staff was harshly criticized by the Commission. For instance, the Commission referred in its reports to the use of excessive physical violence and disciplinary measures against inmates, such as depriving inmates of food parcels and the use of chains for restraint (European Commission, 2002: 32). The European Parliament also raised concerns about cases of ill-treatment by law-enforcement personnel where many of the victims were Roma (European Parliament, 2005: 9). Various vulnerable social groups were subject to ill-treatment by the police, and this was an alarming situation as Romania had no provisions for punishing such actions (European Commission, 1997: 16).

As in the case of other human rights violations, the Commission lacked in-house expertise regarding the evaluation of prison conditions and treatment of inmates. To this end, the Commission's assessment of the ill-treatment by the police relied on cases of degrading treatment by the police reported by human rights organizations in Romania (European Commission, 2000: 22) and the evaluations carried out by the Council of Europe's Committee for the Prevention of Torture. For instance, a damning report published in 2003 by the European Committee for the Prevention of Torture raised awareness in Brussels of the conditions in police detention facilities and of the detainees' lack of information about their rights, along with their subjection to ill-treatment. Yet, at the heart of the problem was the total absence in the Romanian Criminal Code of any legislative sanctions against the police, which amounted to a systematic violation of human rights by the police, namely the use of physical violence to extract confessions without there being any safeguards to prevent it from happening. The plight of Romanian inmates highlighted deeper deficiencies regarding the powers of law enforcement bodies and the lack of criminal sanctions for the abuses committed by police officers. In this respect, the Commission requested two key changes: the public accountability of police officers and demilitarization of the police force (European Commission, 2001: 25). These changes were further substantiated by the revised Criminal Code in 2004.

The EU allocated financial support via PHARE to improve the living conditions in prisons. For instance, the funding was employed to refurbish prison cells, to finance various workshops in prison to help inmates learn new skills or for the acquisition of new medical equipment, which were employed to improve the health of prisoners.[21] The financial support was not as substantial as in the case of high-profile human rights areas such as child protection; however, it generated the involvement of national authorities in addressing the shortcomings in this policy area. The Commission also employed the twinning mechanism – as part of the PHARE package – and peer review to assess the conditions in prisons. Twinners, who were prison reform experts from Member States, worked alongside Romanian civil servants in the part of the Justice Ministry that dealt with prisons. The Commission, therefore, had to resort to the employment of expert evaluations due to its lack of technical know-how and EU guidelines in this area.

The assessment of the conditions in prisons and detention centres relied on the Council of Europe's own assessment and standards, on the one hand, and the evaluation carried out by the Commission itself, on the other hand. For instance, the Council of Europe's Committee for the Prevention of Torture evaluated the pre-trial detention and prison conditions in Romania (between 1998 and 2004) and published several reports with its main findings. The evaluations carried out by the Committee for the Prevention of Torture were employed to shed light on the situation in prisons and to indicate that the conduct of the Romanian police breached the Council of Europe norms and standards of human rights protection. The Commission's monitoring, therefore, relied both on the Council of Europe's evaluation of prison conditions and the Commission's own field visits to prisons or assessment questionnaires sent to prison administrations. The peer review visits[22] to detention centres and prisons were conducted by the Member States' experts on these areas and Commission staff, while the evaluation of the situation at grassroots level was guided both by the Council of Europe standards and assessors' common sense.[23] The Commission's evaluation of the concrete changes on the ground proved patchy; however, the employment of the Council of Europe's own assessments ascribed a certain level of legitimacy to the EU's approach to prison conditions.

As in the case of other controversial human rights sectors, the Commission's intervention in relation to prison conditions had to find grounds to justify its intrusive role in relation to the Member States. Indeed, the Commission's significant leverage with respect to candidate countries was politically sensitive and, at times, contested due to the perception that the Commission was overstepping its legal boundaries and powers vested in it by the Member States. The contentious aspects surrounding the Commission's role in areas such as prison conditions revolved around questions regarding the breadth and depth of the Commission's actions, given that conditions in prisons constitute a problematic sector also in the Member States, a fact often raised by the Council of Europe's own monitoring of this human rights area in the Member States.[24]

Another human rights area that raised the Commission's concern in its reports was freedom of expression and freedom of the press. The communist legacy of media control, and the attempts of the post-communist governments to employ media outlets to their own political advantage (European Commission, 2000), signalled the need to address these policy sectors as part of the political conditionality. There were several problems related to freedom of expression that triggered the Commission's involvement and raised concerns about Romania's legal provisions for and the practical impact of freedom of expression. More specifically, there were three kinds of shortcomings highlighted by the Commission: first, the punishments in the Criminal Code for accusations of slander and offence to authorities; second, the independence of the media; and third, the interference of authorities with freedom of the press. The changes sought by the Commission focused on three aspects: adoption of new legislation, the need to curtail political pressure over the media, and, finally, the practices and rules underpinning freedom of expression had to be in line with the standards employed at the European level, as enshrined in the European Convention on Human Rights. First, the Commission asked for a reversal of the burden-of-proof situation: according to Romanian legislation, the burden of proof was weighed against journalists since the accused was obliged to prove the absolute truth of public statements, while, according to the case law of the European Court of Human Rights (ECtHR), the responsibility for the burden of proof lay with the plaintiff to demonstrate that a misrepresentation of the truth had taken place. The Commission recommended that Romanian legislation be amended in order to be in line with Member States' legal practices and the standards provided by the case law of the ECtHR (European Commission, 2001: 26). The independence of the press was an issue of significant concern for the Commission: the number of genuinely independent media outlets was small and ownership was highly concentrated, resulting in a high degree of self-censorship (European Commission, 2003: 26). Additionally, many media companies were heavily indebted to the state: hence, the operation of some of the media outlets was dependent on the good will of Romanian authorities (European Commission, 2003: 26). Moreover, according to the European Parliament, many media organizations faced a precarious economic situation, which enabled the national authorities to exert pressure on them (European Parliament, 2004: 4). Indeed, media organizations would become easy targets for various political vested interests, which consequently, interfered with the freedom of the press. Due to the constant EU pressure regarding freedom of the press and expression, the political sway on the media abated and newspapers became less politicized. Similarly, the economic viability of the media improved as well: a new legislative measure provided for more transparent and objective criteria for the acquisition of advertising space by public institutions (European Commission, 2005a: 16). Therefore, it was crucial for the EU to ensure that the media were not subject to political control and interests, and that both legally and concretely freedom of expression was protected.

Another human rights area in which the EU intervened was the trafficking in human beings. The EU *acquis* indirectly related to trafficking in human beings is the legislation covering police cooperation and the fight against organized crime, which was also assessed in the Progress Reports as part of Chapter 24 on *Cooperation in the Field of Justice and Home Affairs* of the *acquis* criteria. There are a number of EU legal instruments applied in the EU and which border on trafficking in human beings. For instance, the Council Framework Decision 2002/629/JHA on combating trafficking in human beings, provides for measures aimed at ensuring approximation of national legislation regarding the definition of offence, prosecution, penalties and protection and assistance to victims. The Council Directive 2004/81/EC on the residence permit issued to third-country nationals who are victims of trafficking in human beings or who have been the subject of an action to facilitate illegal immigration, who cooperate with the competent authorities, is the main piece of EU legislation that is directly related to the issue of trafficking. All Member States are required to apply this Directive to developing country citizens who are victims of trafficking, irrespective of whether they enter a Member State territory illegally. This Directive establishes the legal obligation for Member States to provide for reflection period and residence status to victims of trafficking.

The crux of the problem in Romania was human trafficking via illegal border crossing, given that Romania was a country of transit for and sometimes origin of trafficking. The EU had to address the type of human trafficking occurring in Romania, while at the same time attempting to tackle the underlying causes of this practice rather than deal with its effects. The main form of trafficking was in women and girls for the purpose of forced prostitution (European Commission, 2000: 22), and children and persons with disabilities, who were trafficked in order to be exploited as street beggars (European Commission, 2003: 24). The main reasons for this form of trafficking were economic and social uncertainty, widespread poverty and domestic prostitution rings (European Commission, 2001: 25). According to data from the International Organisation for Migration, as many as twenty thousand women were trafficked from Romania each year, and, therefore, the Romanian authorities had to eliminate human trafficking as part of the accession conditionality. The Commission criticized the Romanian authorities for lacking sufficient legislative tools for prosecuting and punishing traffickers and protecting the victims of trafficking (European Commission, 2001: 25).

The Commission employed two instruments to promote change in this human rights area. First, it denunciated, via its monitoring reports, the slow progress achieved in this area due to administrative, institutional and financial shortcomings. For instance, the institutions set up to tackle the problem of trafficking were under-staffed and had limited financial resources. At the same time, Romanian institutions dealing with the issue of trafficking suffered from poor inter-institutional coordination, for example, with regard to keeping records of the victims of trafficking or helping them to reintegrate into society. Secondly, the Commission recommended that Romania ratify international instruments on trafficking in human beings, such as the UN instruments, and adopt the relevant EU *acquis* on this area. For instance, in 2002 Romania ratified the UN Convention against Transnational Organised Crime and the Protocol on Preventing, Countering and Punishing Trafficking in Human Beings, especially Women and Children (European Commission, 2003: 24). The Commission also requested that Romania join regional cooperation initiatives on human trafficking. Hence, in 2003, Romania signed the *Statement for Protection of the Witnesses and Trafficking of Children*, a Stability Pact Task Force within the framework of regional cooperation initiatives. The EU employed regional and EU tools to secure the Union's external borders, given Romania's prospective membership, and encourage regional cooperation in tackling cross-border human trafficking.

The cultural and legal communist legacies were, perhaps, most obvious in areas such as the right of private ownership and gay rights. Even if the protection of these human rights is enshrined at the level of the European Convention on Human Rights, there is no EU legislation covering these sectors *per se*. The right of ownership was guaranteed by the Romanian Constitution adopted after 1989. However, the legal and financial instruments related to property illegally confiscated during communism were still not in place. The shortcomings underlying the restitution of property were manifold. First, there were three types of properties: buildings, agricultural lands and the property confiscated from churches. Second, some of the buildings could not be restituted in kind, and hence a fair compensation and criteria for how to calculate this compensation had to be established. Ultimately, the legislative and institutional structures in order to deal with these complex issues had to be set up. The Commission strictly monitored the developments in this human rights area and put pressure on Romanian officials to forge changes in order to solve the underlying problems of restitution of property. Of course, the solution to addressing fairly and legitimately the restitution of confiscated properties was not always easy, especially as there were no yard-sticks or guidelines in this area. For instance, controversial aspects, such as how to compensate fairly owners whose properties could not be restituted in kind, were questions that both the Commission and Romanian authorities had to grapple with. All Romanian post-1989 governments attempted to find solutions to the property restitution issue by providing equal opportunities to all parties concerned, namely both owners and tenants. Despite the lack of expertise in this area, the Commission employed the annual assessments in the Progress Reports to signal the human rights violations and demand specific measures to be implemented. For instance, according to Commission officials 'we had a very, very strong instrument: annual reports ... and in the annual reports, in the first chapter of the Copenhagen criteria: we never hesitated to highlight what we thought was wrong and what needed to be corrected'.[25] The Commission repeatedly made reference to the number of cases taken to the ECtHR and the rulings of the Court which also stressed the legislative obstacles concerning restitution of property. Romanian citizens sued the Romanian state in relation to the restitution of nationalized properties at the ECtHR and the vast majority won substantial financial compensations for their cases. The success of the ECtHR rulings led to a gradual increase in the number of cases brought to the Strasbourg Court. For instance, the number of cases filed annually with the ECtHR gradually increased from 6,400 in 1998 to 61,300 in 2010 (European Court of Human Rights, 2010).

The EU played a crucial role regarding the legal status and protection of gay rights in Romania. Gay rights had been a moot issue at the societal and political levels due to the entrenched conservatism of the Romanian traditional society. Indeed, sexuality constitutes an area where Romanian churches have worked together against the post-communist regime to define acceptable and unacceptable sexual behaviour for society (Turcescu and Stan, 2005). In the 1990s, according to Romanian law (Article 200 of the Criminal Code), homosexual acts were deemed to cause 'public scandal' and thus considered a criminal offence, punishable by prison sentence. Homosexual relationships in Romania were punished with prison terms of up to 5 years and, due to this, Romanian authorities were heavily criticized by European bodies for failing to recognize and protect gay rights. This matter was highlighted by the Commission from its first *Opinion on Romania's Application for Membership of the EU* in 1997. In 2000 the Romanian parliament adopted legislation that amended the Criminal Code in order to decriminalize homosexuality: hence, homosexual relations were no longer considered a criminal offence. This legislative change brought Romanian law in line with European standards: this meant that homosexuality was decriminalized and that sexual offences were to be governed by the same legislation irrespective of sexual orientation (European Commission, 2001: 23). The new law was regarded as a clear victory for gay rights campaigners and the broader human rights provision in Romania despite the still strong opposition to this law manifested by the Romanian Orthodox Church. However, the Commission had to persuade the Romanian government about the need to enforce gay rights legislation, the key incentive being EU membership.[26] Gay rights advocacy groups and NGOs such as ACCEPT actively lobbied the main EU institutions to raise awareness of the plight of the gay community in Romania. Indeed, the gay community was well-organized and their EU lobbying eventually paid dividends, because, as a result of the Commission's pressure on the Romanian government, homosexuality was decriminalized.

Some human rights areas required mainly legislative changes in order to be on a par with the European standards, namely the Council of Europe norms. The Commission-driven actions relied heavily on learning by doing, given that the Commission lacked the specific expertise required. The Commission's intervention went beyond the existing EU *acquis* as there is no EU *acquis* on pre-trial detention, Ombudsman or legal aid system. The EU demanded the provision of legal aid and protection of human rights during the pre-trial detention period. For instance, according to the Commission, the Ombudsman was not an effective institution of human rights protection. Its remit was limited, it was regarded with suspicion by other public institutions, it was under-staffed and there was lack of public awareness of what this institution stood for (European Commission, 2000: 22). All these factors contributed to the Ombudsman's lack of impact on human rights protection in Romania. According to the Commission, in criminal cases legal assistance is deemed mandatory for certain categories of defendants who have insufficient means to employ a lawyer. Under Romanian legislation there were several criteria allowing for legal aid; however, few requests were granted in practice and the remuneration of lawyers providing legal aid was very low. Limits to the right to legal representation were deemed by the Commission to constitute significant human rights violations (European Commission, 2003: 25). In other words, the EU's leverage to redress various matters of human rights violations entailed the establishment of an institutional and legislative framework that would place Romania on a par with the Member States.

The Commission also requested changes in relation to pre-trial detention, particularly with respect to the legal protection of those held in custody. There were several problems outlined by the Commission regarding pre-trial detention. First, there was an excessive use of custody and pre-trial detention (European Commission, 1998: 11). Hence, compared with European standards the pre-trial arrest warrants could be issued too easily by prosecutors.

Second, another problem was the pre-trial detention period: this period for a person arrested on remand could go up to half of the maximum term provided for the crime alleged, while up to 30 per cent of the persons in penitentiaries were detained on remand (European Commission, 1999: 17). However, judicial review was applied both during pre-trial detention and during the judicial phase. At the Commission's request, the Council of Europe's Committee for the Prevention of Torture carried out an investigation in 2003, as mentioned above. As is the case with all policy sectors where the EU lacks legislation and policy templates, the Commission pleaded for Romania's alignment with the European standards embraced by the Member States, and subsequently the implementation of the relevant institutional and legislative adjustments to render this possible. Indeed, the Commission demanded two key changes regarding pre-trial detention. On the one hand, Romania had to adopt international instruments – such as the Council of Europe instruments – on human rights protection and, on the other hand, the Romanian legislation had to be amended in order to be in line with European rules and practices. In 2004 Romania signed Protocol 14 of the European Convention on Human Rights: this protocol amended the system of control provided for in the Convention. The adoption of these international instruments was intended, first, to enhance the respect for the rights of the detainees by aligning Romanian rules and practices to the European ones, and second, they provided a legitimate international system of control and monitoring of Romanian practices in this human rights area. In brief, the Commission had to ensure that the prospective Member States provide a degree of human rights protection matching the standards in place in the Member States and across Europe.

Minority protection

One of the most contentious human rights sectors in which the EU intervened and sought change was the protection of national minorities, particularly the case of the Roma. The EU, however, has no tradition of involvement with minority protection internally, as protection of minorities is part of the national competence of EU Member States and there are no Treaty provisions that give clear and explicit authority to EU institutions in this area. However, Article 13 TEC of the Treaty of Amsterdam[27] granted the Community powers to combat discrimination based on sex, racial or ethnic origin, religion or belief, disability, age or sexual orientation. Based on this Treaty provision, two directives have been enacted in the area of anti-discrimination: the Racial Equality Directive, 2000/43/EC,[28] and the Employment Equality Directive, 2000/78/EC.[29] These two directives constitute the EU *acquis* in the area of anti-discrimination and they have to be transposed by Member States and candidate countries into national legislation. The Racial Equality Directive is explicitly related to Roma discrimination, and covers most of the areas where members of this community can be discriminated against. The Employment Directive focuses on discrimination in relation to access to employment and is aimed at a wider range of social categories, including the Roma. Moreover, both Directives provide for the establishment of an institution in charge of the promotion of equal treatment and assistance provision to victims of racial discrimination.

The Commission's role in relation to the Roma question in Romania, however, went well beyond the anti-discrimination *acquis* due to the complexity of the plight of the Roma community. Romania has the largest Roma minority in Europe and, thus, addressing the problems faced by the Roma constituted one of the key challenges for the Commission and also for the Romanian government. The Roma question was complex due to several factors. First, the violation of rights experienced by the Roma community ranged over a wide spectrum of issues: from socio-cultural issues like access to education, to legal and economic matters, such as housing and ID documents. Second, the Roma community itself was not homogenous and did not always speak with one voice, and therefore, how to engage effectively with the Roma communities proved extremely difficult. Last but not least, the expected effects of the solutions to the problems faced by this minority were regarded as being long term. Therefore, the successful tackling of the plight of the Romanian Roma was deemed to include national coordinated and targeted actions addressing the myriad of structural problems faced by this minority.

The key problem faced by the Roma was generalized discrimination which was underpinned by the entrenched prejudices of the majority population. According to the Commission's evaluation of the plight of the Roma, the discrimination against this minority affected all aspects of life: housing, employment, education, access to health services or justice. The effects of this widespread discrimination amounted to huge educational and income disparities between the Roma and the majority. Above all, according to the Commission, the Roma question was an enormous problem also because the public opinion silently agreed with the existing situation, as a Commission official put it.[30] The EU aimed, however, to support the Romanian authorities to root out the most salient impediments faced by the Roma in terms of the economic situation, the political representation of the Roma and the cultural attitudes and prejudices of the majority population towards them. To be effective, the EU instruments targeted both the Roma communities and Romanian majority. Thus, the Commission developed a detailed and highly intrusive policy in this area in terms of the changes sought – both legislative and institutional – and particularly concerning the improvement of living conditions of the Roma.

The EU approached the Roma question in Romania on different levels and the reforms demanded by the Commission exerted certain influence on the pace of accession negotiations.[31] Given the Commission's lack of examples of best practice and policy templates in this area, along with the multi-dimensional character of the Roma question, the Commission's approach focused on the institutional infrastructure, legislative framework and implementation of Roma policies. For instance, at the governmental level, the Commission specifically requested that the Romanian authorities address the situation of the Roma both in institutional and legislative terms by establishing structures focusing on Roma community.[32] In policy terms, the Romanian government was urged to design action plans or strategies in order to tackle these issues concretely. The participation of Roma representatives – either as a Roma inter-service group or as an inter-ministerial group to deal with Roma issues horizontally – at a governmental level was particularly requested.

Both the European Parliament, via its rapporteur, and the Commission demanded that a national strategy addressing the Roma question be elaborated and implemented by the government together with the Roma community (European Commission, 1999: 19; European Parliament, 2000: 6). The development of a national strategy on the Roma had also been identified as a priority in the 1999 Accession Partnership (European Commission, 2000: 24). Given the cross-cutting nature of the Roma question, a National Strategy for Improving the Situation of the Roma, adopted in 2001, targeted key areas such as health, education and employment. The Strategy had been elaborated both by the government and the Roma organizations and it covered a ten-year period, setting a plan of measures for the first four years. The Strategy aimed to address most of the shortcomings outlined by the Commission, namely changing negative perceptions and cultural attitudes, improving living conditions, and encouraging Roma participation in all aspects of society. The implementation of the Strategy was to be secured by Roma NGOs together with local authorities.

The Roma issue was cross-sectoral and, therefore, required coordinated action across all governmental departments. To this end, at the Commission's behest a governmental agency – the National Agency for Roma – was set up at the central level in 2005. The National Agency for Roma is the only institution of its kind in Europe; its main roles are to ensure the participation of the Roma in the decision-making process at the governmental level and to monitor the implementation of Roma policies at the local level.[33] In accordance with its legal remit, the National Agency for Roma has, first, to elaborate the government's policy and measures in the field of Roma protection, and, second, to coordinate, monitor and evaluate the effectiveness of the measures included in the Roma Strategy in achieving their objectives (National Agency for Roma, 2006: 9). Hence, by acting as the Roma focal point at government level, the Agency is responsible for policy coordination and the mainstreaming of the Roma question at the level of ministries, given that these governmental bodies are in charge of implementing the Roma Strategy. Additionally, an institution specifically overseeing anti-discrimination policy was set up in 2002. The National Council for Combating Discrimination was initially viewed as a facade institution created due to the EU's pressures to transpose the institutional provisions of the Racial Equality Directive.[34] The main role of this institution is to investigate and sanction all forms of discrimination that are brought before it (National Council for Combating Discrimination, 2005: 2).

The main instruments employed by the Commission to address the plight of the Roma were financial funding via PHARE and the adoption of international instruments on minority protection. The PHARE support was targeted at providing assistance to three main aspects: funding of public awareness campaigns, financial assistance with the implementation of the National Strategy for Improving the Situation of the Roma and, lastly, project funding. According to the European Commission Delegation in Romania, the public awareness campaigns proved to be the most successful instrument in terms of raising awareness of the problems faced by the Roma and making the Roma question visible at the societal level.[35]

The Roma question, however, was extremely complex and, therefore, it was not clear which policy sectors had to be prioritized initially. Yet, one of the main sectors targeted by PHARE was education. After the adoption of the Roma Strategy in 2001, PHARE financial support was channelled towards assisting with the implementation of the Roma Strategy, with a particular focus on the educational sector of the Strategy, namely improving access to education for disadvantaged groups, especially the Roma (European Commission, 2003: 9). The reasoning behind the provision of financial assistance for education was to help create Roma role models from youngsters who had not experienced segregation in schools.[36] Financial assistance for education involved three aspects: de-segregation in schools, training of staff and teachers regarding discrimination against the Roma, and the creation of Roma teachers and instructors who would act as role models for Roma pupils. All levels of schooling were targeted, namely primary, secondary and high-schools, and the main framework employed by the Commission when allocating funding was the creation of partnerships between local authorities and Roma communities. For instance, the overall objective of PHARE 2001 project – called *Access to Education for Disadvantaged Groups, with a Special Focus on Roma*[37] – was to support the implementation of the Ministry of Education and Research strategy for improving educational access for disadvantaged groups. The project was part of the Ministry's main objective to achieve the goals of the National Strategy for Improving the Situation of the Roma and targeted geographical areas with a high percentage of Roma population and high risk of exclusion regarding educational access.

The EU allocated funding for the access to education of disadvantaged groups also via PHARE 2003, which was implemented from 2004 to 2007. PHARE 2003, worth €9 million from the EU and €2.33 million from the Romanian government, did not target the Roma minority *per se*, yet most of its components, such as the Second Chance programme or the inclusion of children with special educational needs in mainstream schools, were relevant for the Roma community. For instance, the objective of the Second Chance programme was to provide an opportunity to complete the lower secondary education to those students who either did not attend or who had dropped out school (PHARE Implementation Unit for Access to Education for Disadvantaged Groups Project, n.d. a: 8), while the special educational needs programme targeted people with disabilities, people with learning difficulties and people from disadvantaged groups, including minorities (PHARE Implementation Unit for Access to Education for Disadvantaged Groups project, n.d. b: 8). However, supporting education was also a complex goal due to the fact that education was deeply intertwined with health or social assistance issues, and, therefore, an integrated approach had to be developed and implemented across various policy sectors.

Apart from the educational sector, Commission action also focused on the health sector, which was also supported by PHARE via a Twinning Light project in 2006. Members of the Roma community had limited access to health care because of the general discrimination suffered against them. Therefore, twinners from the Member States evaluated the access of the Roma communities to medical assistance and, based on their findings, they worked together with the Ministry of Public Health on the training of Roma health mediators (Ministry of Public Health, 2007: 33). The role of health mediators involved facilitating communication between Roma communities and medical staff, on the one hand, and educating the Roma on health issues, on the other hand (Ministry of Public Health, 2007: 79). The training and use of Roma health mediators as role models proved a successful policy that had positive impacts on the access of the Roma to health care.

One of the main objectives of the Commission's policy towards the Roma in Romania was to ensure that Romania adhered to the main international instruments targeting the protection of minorities. To this end, Romania became party to the Council of Europe Framework Convention for the Protection of National Minorities, which is the main instrument on minority protection at the European level. As State Party to this Convention, the Committee of Ministers of the Council of Europe concluded in 2002 that Romanian authorities had to speed up the social integration of the Roma and address the main problems faced by this minority: discrimination and a poor socio-economic situation (European Commission, 2002: 37). At the Commission's request, Romania also signed in 2000 the Additional Protocol No. 12 to the European Convention on Human Rights prohibiting discrimination on any grounds (European Commission, 2001: 22) and ratified it in 2006.

Despite the Commission's holistic approach to this policy sector, the actual progress on the ground was uneven or, as was often the case, longer time was needed for the EU intervention to bear fruit. For instance, there was more progress in education than in the housing sector as the latter was deemed to be a competence of the Romanian government.[38] Hence, the results regarding the Roma progress were mixed and there were still cases of Roma discrimination at country level, particularly in rural areas. Comparisons with the situation of minority protection in the Member States were often employed to gauge the Roma question in Romania. According to the Commission, 'with the Roma we needed to make sure that they were not more discriminated against than they are in the EU 15: Roma have difficulties everywhere in the world ... so we had to see that Romania is at least on the same "insufficient" level as the EU 15 are'.[39] How to address effectively the Roma question, therefore, was a contentious matter at the EU level due to the way the old Member States themselves discriminated against this minority at the national level. Thus, given the size of the Roma community in Romania and the complexity of their predicament, on the one hand, and the problems faced by the Roma across Europe, on the other hand, the Commission concluded that the level of progress achieved in this area was substantial and significant.

The situation of the Roma involved socio-economic, political and cultural matters that had to be addressed coherently and effectively. Given the wide range of obstacles faced by this minority, it was deemed that the Commission could not have solved the plight of the Roma within such a short-time span. Yet, the Commission funded public awareness campaigns on the discrimination faced by the Roma and, unlike other human rights sectors, the financial aid channelled to this human rights area was deemed to have a long-term effect[40]. What the Commission endeavoured to achieve was to support the Romanian government in its actions to tackle the problems faced by the Roma community, while conceding that solving the Roma question was a long-term process.

The most challenging aspect to transform regarding the Roma question, however, was the shift in the engrained cultural attitudes of the majority population towards the Roma. In spite of the Roma policies and action plans adopted by the Romanian government, it was fundamental to achieve the attitudinal shift of the majority population towards the Roma. This cultural shift was regarded to be a long-term process due to the majority's embedded prejudices and racist views towards this minority and was unlikely to have been achieved before Romania joined the EU. The process was likened by Commission officials to the desegregation of the blacks in the USA.[41]

Another area of minority protection extensively monitored by the Commission was the Hungarian minority. Unlike the Roma, who were discriminated against on a large scale and were not socially integrated in the mainstream society, the Hungarian minority was not discriminated against and their main problem was one of cultural identity. The key advantage enjoyed by the Hungarian minority was its organizational and political clout in making their voice heard at the European level, given that the Hungarian government was a close ally of the Hungarian community in Romania (Kelley, 2004). For instance, the European Parliament was vociferous, due to Hungary's influence, in demanding that Romanian authorities take into account the expectations of the Hungarian minority in accordance with the principles of subsidiarity and cultural and administrative self-governance, and that they ensure adequate funding for the improvement of education standards (European Parliament, 2006: 5). Furthermore, the European Parliament urged Romania to comply with the basic European principles regarding the protection of minorities, to adopt strategies for integrating minorities, to recognize their legitimate rights and to introduce legislation against discrimination pursuant to Article 13 TEC and the EU Charter of Fundamental Rights (European Parliament, 2001: 8).

The Romanian authorities had to adopt legislation targeting the administrative and educational sectors in order to reflect the provisions of the Council of Europe on minority protection. In 1999 an Education Law was adopted, thus creating the legal framework for establishing multi-cultural universities and giving the right to national minorities to study in their mother tongue at all levels and forms of education for which there was sufficient demand (European Commission, 1999: 18). The new law of local administration (1999) provided that civil servants working directly with the public had to speak the language of an ethnic minority in areas where the minority represented at least 20 per cent of the population (European Parliament, 2001: 9). It has been claimed that both the Education Law and the law providing for minority languages in dealings with local authorities illustrate the role of ethnic minority mobilization and minority representation in the coalition government in forging these crucial legislative changes (Kelley, 2004: 153–154). According to the Commission, the protection of the Hungarian minority had been addressed by the time of Romania's accession to the EU due to their being better organized, if compared with the Roma, and their being an active part of the coalition government throughout the EU negotiations period. As mentioned above, the problems faced by this minority were significantly different to the ones faced by the Roma.

As far as international instruments are concerned, Romania was party to the Framework Convention for the Protection of National Minorities under the auspices of the Council of Europe: the Convention was signed by Romania in 1995 and entered into force in 1998. Also, Romania signed the European Charter for Regional or Minority Languages in 1995, although it was not ratified until 2008 and entered into force the same year. Furthermore, it has been claimed that Romania had to comply with the Council of Europe norms on minority protection in their maximalist version.[42] It has been shown that the role of other international institutions, such as the High Commissioner for National Minorities (OSCE) or the Council of Europe, were less able to influence the domestic developments in this area due to the lack of linkage to tangible consequences, such as EU membership (Kelley, 2004: 143). In brief, the institutional infrastructure and international monitoring of minority protection regarding cultural rights were in place mainly due to the Hungarian minority's involvement in mainstream politics.

Conclusion

Human rights protection was at the heart of EU accession negotiations with Romania. The communist institutional and policy legacies, along with the failure of post-communist governments to reform the human rights provision, signalled that radical transformations had to occur in all human rights sectors before Romania could join the EU. The Commission intervened in a wide array of policy issues, imposing conditions and demanding radical changes, although it lacked the necessary expertise and EU *acquis* to guide its actions. Indeed, Commission actions demonstrated a process of learning by doing, whereby Commission officials acquired first-hand experience in addressing rights violations in ex-communist states. The Commission's role in transforming the human rights provision in Romania was even more challenging due to contentious aspects regarding the standards or degrees of protection to be achieved: indeed, candidate countries were not expected to eclipse the Member States in terms of the level of human rights and minority protection. The comparative approach adopted by the Commission was also intended to provide a level playing field in terms of human rights standards across Europe, including in the candidate countries. As the Romanian case demonstrates, the EU applied an extensive human rights conditionality, which, undoubtedly had unintended consequences on the EU institutions' role and scope in human rights.

Notes

1   The human rights developments forged by the EU in Romania involved the Commission's engagement with human rights issues for which the EU did not have internal competence or *acquis* – either primary *acquis* in terms of Treaty provisions or secondary legislation. However, there are limited Treaty provisions and secondary legislation, for instance the anti-discrimination legislation, which are indirectly related to aspects of human rights protection. The international

human rights conventions ratified by all Member States are part of the Justice, Freedom and Security *acquis* and are deemed to be part of the indirect *acquis* on human rights.

2 To join the EU, a new Member State must meet three criteria: political – stability of institutions guaranteeing democracy, the rule of law, human rights and respect for and protection of minorities; economic – existence of a functioning market economy and the capacity to cope with competitive pressure and market forces within the Union; acceptance of the Community *acquis* – ability to take on the obligations of membership, including adherence to the aims of political, economic and monetary union (European Council, 1993).

3 In May 2004 Amnesty International published a report on the situation in a big psychiatric institution – 'Poiana Mare'. According to this Report, 17 patients died of malnutrition and hypothermia in 2004, and the living conditions in the hospital were deplorable, while the patients' needs for primary medical care were not being met (Amnesty International, 2005:8).

4 According to a Commission official 'Mental health as such: there wasn't any EU policy on mental health at that time, no *acquis communautaire* in this field really, because the Commission is very much tied to whether there is a basis in the *acquis*'. Author's interview with a Commission official in DG Enlargement, Brussels, May 2008.

5 According to a Commission official 'Romania and Bulgaria were not so happy because they said 'Hey, there's a clear discrepancy here between the treatment of us and the others [the countries which joined the EU in 2004]. ... And also, we really didn't have competence: so why should the Commission ask these?'. Author's interview with a Commission official, DG Enlargement, Brussels, May 2008.

6 According to the 'Letter to Jonathan Scheele' from Focus on Romania (2005) Commission internal document, 12 December.

7 According to Enlargement Directorate-General (2006) 'Explanatory Note: Focus on Romania', Commission internal document, ELARG/A/3/KT D92006, Brussels, 17 February.

8 According to the 'Letter to Mr Rehn' from Focus on Romania (2006), Commission internal document, 6 April.

9 Author's interview with a Commission official, DG Enlargement, Brussels, May 2008.

10 According to a Commission official, 'What usually guides DG Enlargement work in any area is that we look if [sic] there's any legislation in place, what kind of legislation it is and then, of course, the administrative structures: is there a competent ministry, are there officials working on this issue, and of course, under the political criteria, also what are the living conditions in the institutions ... we followed certain international standards etc., but it was clear that we were looking at the legislation, we were also visiting the institutions to see what the situation on the ground was'. Author's interview with a Commission official, member of the Romania team, DG Enlargement, Brussels, May 2008.

11 Author's interview with a Commission official, member of the Romania team, DG Enlargement, Brussels, May 2008.

12 For instance, people with learning difficulties cannot be 'cured' and as such, they are part of the Authority for Handicapped Persons, while people suffering from

mental illnesses can be given treatment and hence they are under the responsibility of the Ministry of Health. Author's interview with a member of the of the PHARE team in the EC Delegation in Romania, Brussels, May 2008.

13   For instance, the PHARE grant scheme contracted for 2005 was worth €16 million (Ministry of Labour, Social Solidarity and Family, 2005: 7).

14   Author's interview with a member of the PHARE team in the EC Delegation in Romania, Brussels, May 2008.

15   Author's interview with a member of the PHARE team in the EC Delegation in Romania, Brussels, May 2008.

16   For instance, people with mental health problems were to be treated in psychiatric hospitals (under the responsibility of the district health department, part of the Ministry of Health), while people with learning difficulties were to be looked after in social care institutions (under the responsibility of the Authority for Handicapped Persons, part of the Ministry of Labour and Social Solidarity) (Katschnig, 2006: 31).

17   Author's interview with the task manager for human rights in the EC Delegation in Romania, Bucharest, July 2008.

18   'Twinning Light' is a mechanism to address carefully circumscribed projects of limited scope which emerge during the negotiation process (European Commission, 2002).

19   As a Commission official put it: 'you always need to make comparisons with the other EU countries because it's not the idea that a candidate would be better than the Member States themselves [in terms of mental health provision]'. Author's interview with Commission official in the Romania team, DG Enlargement, Brussels, June 2008.

20   Author's interview with the Commission task manager dealing with prisons in the Romania team, DG Enlargement, Brussels, May 2008.

21   Author's interview with the task manager for human rights in the EC Delegation in Romania, Bucharest, July 2008.

22   According to Commission officials, an underlying problem of the visits carried out by the Commission was the bias of Romanian authorities towards showing the best prisons and not how most of them were. Author's interview with the Commission task manager dealing with prisons in the Romania team, DG Enlargement, Brussels, May 2008.

23   As a Commission official put it: 'so we took a German judge and we went to see how detention facilities worked in prisons, and in the police context we took a police officer to see how detention cells were being organized in a police station. There you are relying heavily on the interpretation of the experts that you bring with you: the Commission has no expertise or experience in these areas but I guess if you see some cells very overcrowded, very filthy, with no light, no water, then you think probably that this is not in accordance with the European norms, whatever they are.' Author's interview with the Commission task manager dealing with prisons in the Romania team, DG Enlargement, Brussels, June 2008.

24   As a Commission official put it 'overcrowding is not a non-issue in other parts of the EU and then you have this problem between the Commission being asked to monitor something which we don't have the competence for. And if you take experts that say "Well, I've seen prisons in other countries; ok, it's not perfect, but it's kind of in the range of acceptable", and as long as you bear in mind that

Romania comes from a very low development GDP compared to, for instance, Finland or Luxembourg, it's not really fair to compare them'. Author's interview with the Commission task manager dealing with prisons in the Romania team, DG Enlargement, Brussels, May 2008.

25 Author's interview with one of the heads of the Romania team, DG Enlargement, Brussels, June 2008.

26 Author's interview with a Commission official, DG Enlargement, Brussels, May 2008.

27 Article 13 TEC provides that: 'Without prejudice to the other provisions of this Treaty and within the limits of the powers conferred by it upon the Community, the Council, acting unanimously on a proposal from the Commission and after consulting the European Parliament, may take appropriate action to combat discrimination based on sex, racial or ethnic origin, religion or belief, disability, age or sexual orientation'.

28 The Racial Equality Directive implements the principle of equal treatment between people irrespective of racial or ethnic origin by giving protection against discrimination in employment and training, education, social protection, social advantages, membership and involvement in organizations of workers and employers and access to goods and services, including housing. The Directive contains definitions of direct and indirect discrimination and harassment. Moreover, this Directive provides for the establishment in each Member State of an institution to promote equal treatment and provide independent assistance to victims of racial discrimination (Council Directive 2000/43/EC of 29 June 2000, 'Implementing the Principle of Equal Treatment between Persons Irrespective of Racial or Ethnic Origin', *Official Journal of the European Communities,* 19 July 2000).

29 The Employment Directive implements the principle of equal treatment in employment and training irrespective of religion or belief, disability, age or sexual orientation in employment, training, and membership in organizations of workers and employers. This Directive includes identical provisions to the Racial Equality Directive on definitions of discrimination and harassment or rights of legal redress and the sharing of the burden of proof (Council Directive 2000/78/EC of 27 November 2000, 'Establishing a General Framework for Equal Treatment in Employment and Occupation', *Official Journal of the European Communities,* 2 December 2000).

30 Author's interview with one of the heads of the Romania team, DG Enlargement, Brussels, June 2008.

31 According to a Commission official: 'We always said: we have a certain leverage – because we can say if you don't do this or that, accession may be more difficult – but there are limits: we told Romania, as we told other countries, to do a lot regarding the Roma'. Author's interview with a member of the 'Coordination' unit in DG Enlargement, Brussels, May 2008.

32 Author's interview with a Commission official in DG Enlargement, Brussels, May 2008.

33 Author's interview with the head of the National Agency for Roma, Bucharest, July 2008.

34 Author's interview with the Commission team leader for minorities and civil society in the EC Delegation in Romania, Bucharest, July 2008.

35   Author's interview with the Commission team leader for minorities and civil society in the EC Delegation in Romania, Bucharest, July 2008.

36   Author's interview with the Commission team leader for minorities and civil society in the EC Delegation in Romania, Bucharest, July 2008.

37   There were several PHARE projects targeted at promoting access to education for disadvantaged groups, such as PHARE 2003, yet not all PHARE projects targeted at disadvantaged groups focused on Roma children in particular.

38   Author's interview with a Commission official in DG Enlargement, Brussels, May 2008.

39   Author's interview with a Commission official, member of the country desk in the Romania team, DG Enlargement, Brussels, June 2008.

40   Author's interview with one of the heads of the Romania team, DG Enlargement, Brussels, May 2008.

41   Author's interview with the head of the EC Delegation in Romania, Brussels, May 2008.

42   Author's interview with a member of Romania's chief negotiator's team, Brussels, September 2008.

3

Child protection in Romania and European Union accession

Romania in a way suffered a lot because of this 'black sheep' label because of the children's situation, but in a way, Romania received so much financial support and assistance that now Romania is a model of how it has transformed and reformed its child protection. (Commission official)

Introduction

European Union (EU) leverage over the reform of child protection in Romania was unprecedented within the context of Eastern enlargement. The Romanian children's case, including the issue of international adoption, acquired a high profile[1] and unparalleled political salience within Romania's accession agenda. The overhaul of the child protection sector was an accession condition that all the Central and Eastern European Countries (CEECs) had to address within the context of the political criteria for accession to the EU. However, it was only within Romania's accession context that child protection became a highly politicized and contentious area as part of Eastern enlargement. A wide range of actors, such as adoption agencies, members of the European Parliament (EP) and EU Member States, attempted to influence the pace and direction of the changes forged by the Commission in child protection in Romania before 2007. The international adoption issue and the situation of children in care institutions received extensive international media coverage, something which did not occur in the case of other Eastern candidate countries. At the same time, the political stakes regarding the Romanian children's case were high, and the EU had to find effective workarounds (Jacoby et al., 2009) to transform child protection before Romania became a Member State. The EU developed and employed a wide range of instruments to transform child protection, alongside extensive monitoring and strict scrutiny undertaken by the Commission. Evidence of the transformative actions triggered by the EU in relation to Romanian children's issue is provided in this chapter. Child protection is examined here in the light of the EU's extensive intervention in an area where it lacked EU *acquis* and expertise. However, the Commission's creative role in crafting

EU conditions to uphold children's rights and the extent of the developments generated by the EU in practice underscore the scale of the transformations undergone by child protection in Romania before 2007. This chapter, therefore, explores the underlying problems in child protection, the developments that occurred and the EU instruments employed to support these transformations. The EU managed to induce substantial legislative and institutional transformation which made the Romanian childcare a model in terms of its radical overhaul, along with the principles and institutional framework underpinning child rights provision in a former communist state.

Child protection post-1989: key problems

Child protection in Romania after 1989 faced a wide range of acute legislative, institutional and administrative deficiencies. The fall of communism exposed the appalling conditions of Romanian orphanages and the huge number of children cared for in these institutions (Latianu, 2001; Jerre, 2005). The Western media, in particular, covered widely the plight of children living in large care institutions. In the early 1990s, therefore, international adoption had become the main rescue solution for the one hundred thousand institutionalized children (Morrison, 2004) and Romania was one of the main providers of children for inter-country adoption (ICA) worldwide (Selman, 2010). The legacy of the communist legislative system of childcare and the post-1990 laws adopted in this area made up a legal framework that facilitated and promoted the practice of international adoption by generating widespread corruption.

The childcare system in Romania was based on a communist law which gave the state total ownership of the rights of the child and greased the wheels of international adoption after 1989. Hoping to increase Romania's birth-rate, the communist regime adopted the Decree 770 of 1966, which prohibited abortion and contraceptives (Kligman, 1998), which eventually resulted in the births of many unwanted children, while high rates of maternal mortality produced a huge number of orphans (Ghetau, 1997). Therefore, the high number of child abandonment and hence institutionalized children was rooted in the communist childcare system and Ceausescu's pro-natalist policy. According to this policy, unwanted children were abandoned in *leagans* (baby homes for children under three years), and after three, they would go either to a *casa de copii* (children's home) or to a *camin spital* (home for the disabled) (Post, 2007: 23). These institutions provided accommodation for 100–400 children, which is why they are known as big, old-style institutions or orphanages. The state took responsibility for raising these abandoned children, and a popular saying during communism claimed 'the state wanted children, let the state look after them'. The main outcomes of this pro-natalist policy were a high rate of child abandonment, large institutions with improper living conditions, a child protection system inappropriate for child development, no experience in delivering services other than institutionalization and an acute lack of specialized staff (IMAS, 2004: 12). The key solution advocated by Romanian authorities to the shortcomings faced by child protection after 1989, particularly in the wake of international media coverage of children in institutions, was the promotion of ICA.

Nevertheless, the legislation underpinning the child protection system and ICA violated the main international instruments[2] on children's rights, i.e. the United Nations Convention on the Rights of the Child (CRC) (1989) and the Hague Convention on Protection of Children and Co-operation in Respect of Inter-country Adoption (Hague Adoption Convention) (1993). Romania had signed and ratified the CRC in 1990 and the Hague Adoption Convention in 1995; however, the principles and provisions in the two conventions were not reflected in the Romanian legislation or institutional framework. According to the CRC[3] and the Hague Adoption Convention,[4] international adoption is a childcare measure of last resort, which means that, in line with the principle of subsidiarity, ICA has to be considered after all domestic measures have been exhausted. Yet, in the Romanian case ICA had precedence over domestic adoption and other in-country solutions. The legal irregularities underpinning the ICA practice in Romania were unearthed by the findings published in a report in 2002 by the Independent Group for Inter-country Adoption Analysis (IGIAA), a group set up by the Romanian authorities and consisting of child rights experts (Jacoby *et al.*, 2009: 123). For instance, according to this report, the institutionalization law (11/1990) and abandonment law (47/1993),[5] according to which a child protected within residential care could be legally declared abandoned if parents had shown lack of interest in the child for a period of 6 months (IGIAA, 2002: 16–17), in practice facilitated the proliferation of the ICA practice as the main remedy for finding families for children in institutional care. By 'lack of interest' was meant a lack of evidence that the parents visited the child within a 6-month period; and, once declared abandoned, the child became eligible for adoption (IMAS, 2004: 23). Additionally, the entire childcare system was still underpinned by Law 3/1970, a communist law which promoted institutionalization as the prevalent child protection method for all disabled, orphaned or abandoned children (IGIAA, 2002).

The post-1990 legislative framework led to the emergence of a Romanian international adoption market which was offer-driven, according to which Romania was a supplier in the activities of agencies specializing in international adoptions (IGIAA, 2002: 23). For instance, according to UNICEF, more than ten thousand children were internationally adopted between January 1990 and July 1991 (European Parliament, 2009: 26). The law adopted in 1997 further enhanced the legal framework for the emergence of a

Romanian international adoption market and therefore rendered Romania the main supplier[6] of children for ICA in the world (IGIAA, 2002: 23). This 1997 law set up a 'points system', which provided Romanian adoption non-governmental organizations (NGOs) with significant clout in terms of influencing the process of international adoption. According to this system, points were accrued by adoption agencies in return for the services they provided for children in care institutions and, based on their points, agencies would receive children for international adoption (Post, 2007: 50). The system established by this law included a database of children fit for international adoption and this database would be allocated to accredited agencies specialized in adoptions, which, via partner international agencies, would facilitate inter-country adoptions. In light of the provisions contained in the 1997 law, Romania was a supplier in the activity of agencies specializing in international adoption, while the Romanian Committee for Adoptions was assigned the obligation to authorize both Romanian and foreign agencies that operated in adoption (IGIAA, 2002: 23). Taking full advantage of the Romanian legislation, adoption agencies set up their own databases of children fit for international adoption whereby children would have 'price tags', with sums ranging from $6,000- to $30,000 (Jacoby *et al.*, 2009: 124), based on their age, health and physical features (Post, 2007). This system prioritized the best interest of adopters and not the best interest of children for three reasons: it generated financial gains without prioritizing the interests of the child first; it discouraged domestic adoptions and, above all, non-adoptable children were adopted (according to the 'US Report on International Adoptions', 2001, cited in Post, 2007: 85). Indeed, the vast majority of children living in institutions were neither orphaned nor abandoned by their parents:[7] they were cared for in institutions because of their families' poverty (European Parliament, 2001: 17). Due to this 'points system', adoption agencies would be paid hard currency for the children adopted by foreign families. In short, the international adoption system worked thus: first, international agencies would find clients, namely rich Western families willing to adopt a Romanian child; second, once the clients had been identified, the Romanian partner agency – from the list of accredited NGOs – would offer the child from the database; and, finally, the paperwork would be completed sometimes in less than 3 months by the Romanian agency, without the child – in most cases – being visited by the prospective adoptive parents (IGIAA, 2002: 24). Subsequently, the legislative system of childcare was channelled towards fostering the international adoption of Romanian children which was underpinned by corruption.[8]

Furthermore, the prevalence of corrupt staff in orphanages along with the lack of post-adoption monitoring further augmented the opportunities for illicit adoptions (Dickens, 2002) and the emergence of baby trade (Jacoby *et al.*, 2009: 117). What emerged in Romania was a system of private adoptions, whereby a form of ICA emerged in which individuals or mediating bodies outside the formal structure of the Hague Adoption Convention's Central Authority proposed a match, which is not approved by the Hague Adoption Convention system (Hayes, 2011: 289). Therefore, private ICA was promoted as the best solution for addressing the plight of children living in large residential institutions, particularly as Western families were willing to lend a helping hand in the light of the media coverage of the appalling conditions in Romanian orphanages. From 1990 to 2000, ICA was poorly regulated[9] and infringed the main international instruments by prioritizing ICA at the expense of domestic adoptions and due to the lack of post-adoption monitoring mechanisms.[10] According to the EP's rapporteur for Romania, ICA from Romania was 'child selling ... children being smuggled out of the country [...] it was no surprise to me when Romania was named by the UN as one of the top eleven countries as a source of human trafficking'.[11] For instance, the level of ICA peaked in 2000, when 3,035 children were adopted internationally, while only 1,219 children were adopted nationally (National Authority for the Protection of Child's Rights, www.copii.ro).

Apart from this legislative framework facilitating children's institutionalization via abandonment and thus promoting inter-country adoption,[12] the entire child protection system was deeply corrupt. According to the EU and other international actors, there was an entire corrupt network supporting the international adoption of children in pursuit of financial profit: these were the adoption agencies and their international counterparts, the Romanian Committee for Adoptions, managers of childcare institutions, local judges and the international lobby.[13] Adoption facilitators had resorted to procuring children directly from biological families usually in exchange for money (Roby and Ilfe, 2009: 663) and hence 'paper orphans' were regularly manufactured (Graff, 2008: 63). Corrupt local intermediaries and authorities could manipulate domestic legislation and international conventions, as the weak institutional oversight provided a propitious framework for rendering international adoption a profitable business. Indeed, ICA from Romania resembled a child-selling market and child trafficking was at the heart of the Romanian children dossier (Post, 2007: 52). Furthermore, ICA was plagued by widespread corruption because of the sheer lack of transparency of the flow of money incurred from processing ICA and the paperwork required: indeed, there was no legal control of the fees paid for ICA as this was private money and there were no legal instruments to control the money raised through international adoption.[14] For instance, foreign families would pay large amounts of money to adoption agencies, which would bribe and persuade mothers to abandon their children, who would thus become adoptable. Put bluntly, international adoption agencies were doing match-making with countries: by facilitating 'adoption tourism, agencies would go into orphanages simply to look for children'.[15]

The practice of ICA was largely driven by the deplorable conditions in old-style institutions, which bore the imprint of the communist system of care. The material conditions in childcare institutions were extremely poor, despite the Commission's provision of humanitarian aid since the early 1990s (European Commission, 1999, 2000). The reasons behind the poor living conditions in these institutions were two-fold: on the one hand, the available funds were mismanaged by childcare administration; while, on the other hand, the entire institutional infrastructure, which included a large number of staff,[16] was ineffective and hence detrimental in meeting childcare standards. Due to the deplorable living conditions in care institutions in the early 1990s, EU aid consisted of mainly heating, refurbishment programmes and medical and nutritional assistance for childcare institutions (Transtec, 2006: 14). Thus, emergency humanitarian aid was channelled to the most deprived institutions. Furthermore, according to the European Parliament's own assessment of the children's situation, children in these institutions were also subject to 'physical and psychological cruelty, food deprivation, sexual abuse and improper medical care' (European Parliament, 2001: 17).

Due to the lack of radical reform of the system, financial mismanagement and Romania's precarious economic situation, the abominable situation of children in residential care reached a tipping point in the late 1990s. In 1999 the child protection system reached the point of total meltdown when, due to dramatic food shortages, living conditions in institutions worsened dramatically and hence the so-called childcare crisis ensued. This crisis determined the Commission to exert significant pressure on the Romanian government to give top priority to child protection (European Commission, 1999: 16). According to the Commission's task manager for children's rights 'something had gone terribly wrong and children's homes lacked food, had debts and salaries of staff were months in arrears' (Post, 2007: 24). One of the reasons for the humanitarian crisis was the lack of coordination between the central government and local authorities: for instance, social services had been decentralized yet the central authorities failed to provide the necessary funds to local social services (UNICEF, 2004; Lambru and Rosu, 2000: 147; Latianu, 2001: 100). Additionally, given that child protection was not under the responsibility of one central agency, oversight and control functions were shared by many agencies (Jacoby *et al.*, 2009: 121). Therefore, the mismanaged decentralization of social services yielded unexpected financial shortcomings at the local level, which required urgent external humanitarian assistance. Indeed, due to the humanitarian nature of the crisis, the Commission's support at that time was mainly material: it was aimed at making sure that care institutions had heat and food, which, however, constituted a turning point in the Commission–Romanian authorities relations with respect to child protection.[17]

The childcare crisis of 1999 had three major consequences (IGIAA, 2002: 24). First, the crisis fed the campaigns of international adoption agencies that promoted themselves as the only ones capable of ensuring the best interests of the child via international adoption; second, it led to a fall in public support for the government in power at that time; and, third, it obliged the European Commission (EC) to grant emergency humanitarian aid consisting of food and basic items for institutionalized children, which had been granted via the cancellation of a Poland and Hungary: Assistance for Reconstructing their Economies (PHARE) programme initially supporting the institutional reform of the child protection system. The childcare crisis in 1999 brought to the fore the complexity and interlinkages of the problems that marred the system: the financial and administrative shortcomings exacerbated the legislative loopholes and the outdated, communist institutional infrastructure of childcare. Therefore, Romania had a short timeframe at its disposal to eradicate the structural deficiencies in its child protection before it could join the EU.

Romania's accession agenda and EU *acquis* on children's rights

Romania's accession agenda

Child protection systems in all CEECs violated children's rights when these countries had opened accession negotiations with the EU. Yet child protection in Romania was largely viewed as a specific Romanian problem and, hence, it became exclusively associated with Romania's EU accession agenda. The children's question in Romania also gained a particularly high profile status due to the political pressure exerted by the EP's rapporteur for Romania, Baroness Emma Nicholson, on this issue and the international media coverage of the conditions in Romanian orphanages. Additionally, child protection in Romania drew the Commission's attention also due to lobbying actions at the EU level by pro-ICA groups and organizations.

Hoping to gain access to EU financial assistance that could be employed to sustain ICA from Romania, adoption agencies such as the French Solidarité Enfants Roumains Abandonnes (SERA) lobbied the Commission regarding the situation of institutionalized children. Directorate General (DG) Enlargement was pressured by SERA's leader, Francois de Combret, an influential investment banker, to make the plight of institutionalized children an issue for Romania's EU accession in 1997 (Post, 2007: 37). For this reason, the situation of children in institutions was mentioned in the Commission's Opinion on Romania included in Agenda 2000: for a Stronger and Wider Union (1997), which was not the case for other former communist states. [18] SERA's framing of ICA as the only rescue solution for Romanian children in institutions did not get onto the Commission's agenda; instead, the Commission's Opinion only mentions the huge number of orphans cared for in residential institutions (European Commission, 1997: 54). However, the Commission's Opinion drew attention to the situation of institutionalized children as an EU enlargement matter. When lobbying the Commission, SERA would employ an 'emotionally loaded' strategy, which involved painting a bleak image of the plight of Romanian children in care institutions, while ICA was framed as the best childcare measure available to them. For instance, De Combret would send critical letters to the Commission complaining about the EU's failure in addressing the appalling conditions of children in care.[19] Meanwhile, the extensive coverage of the plight of Romanian children by the international media further facilitated the mentioning of the Romanian children's case in the Commission's Opinion in 1997.

Yet, the EP rapporteur for Romania played a key role in placing child protection on Romania's accession agenda prior to Romania's opening of the formal EU accession negotiations in 2000. According to Commission officials, Emma Nicholson's active support of child protection as an EU accession condition and her bold position regarding ICA ensured that the children's question was intimately linked to Romania's accession agenda after the Helsinki European Council (December 1999), when Romania became a candidate country. Indeed, the EP rapporteur's pro-active role contributed to the political salience acquired by this human rights area within the political conditionality applied to Romania. For instance, in 2000 Romania's ability to meet the political criteria was dependent on Romania's resolution of the childcare crisis (European Commission, 2000: 19); while in 2004 the accession negotiations came close to a halt at the EP rapporteur's suggestion due to the international adoption question. The prominence attached to the Romanian children's issue at the Commission level was reinforced by the creation of a special position – the task manager for children's rights in the Romania team in DG Enlargement – in order to 'monitor Romania's child protection from a human rights perspective in the framework of Romania's future accession to the EU' (Post, 2007: 11). However, while other former communist countries also faced similar problems in their child protection systems, it was only child protection in Romania that became a politicized and controversial accession condition within the Eastern enlargement context. As the task manager for children's rights in the Romania team put it:

> So if this issue [child protection] existed in most of the former communist countries, mainly due to poverty and lack of assistance for families, how come the European Commission only dealt with the Romanian children? Why did other country teams did not have a task manager for children? (Post, 2007: 19)

EU *expertise and* acquis *on children's rights*

When child protection and the broader provision of children's rights became an accession condition in relation to Romania's accession agenda, EU institutions had to admit their lack of expertise and experience of involvement in this area. Indeed, there is no clear EU competence in relation to children in the EU Treaties and the primary responsibility for addressing most issues facing children rests with the Member States at national level. The predominant focus in the EU Treaties has been on the 'citizen-as-worker'. It was the Treaty of Amsterdam that included the first significant provisions on children at the Treaty level. Article 29 TEU provided for intergovernmental cooperation to tackle 'offences against children' – which is the first ever mention of children at the Treaty level – while Article 13 TEC included a 'non-discrimination' clause enabling the Union to take action on equality grounds, particularly age. Additionally, Article 137 TEU provided a legal basis for combating social exclusion and thus tackling child poverty. However, there were no clear and specific legal bases in the Treaties to enable EU institutions to address explicitly issues pertaining to children's rights at the time of Romania's accession negotiations. The situation in Romania required that the Commission employ international instruments on children's rights and utilise the Member States' experts to support the Romanian government to reform the system.[20] Indeed, the issue of international adoption, child protection and children's rights constituted an uncharted territory for the Commission and the EU as a whole. The lack of necessary expertise was even more compelling given the complexity underpinning the translation of CRC principles into effective and concrete policy measures. Therefore, the magnitude of the task to transform child protection in Romania that the Commission had embraced, in other words, was truly huge.

Did the EU have a children's rights *acquis* when children's rights became an accession condition for Romania? According to the EP's rapporteur for Romania, children's rights have always been in the 'Justice and Home Affairs' chapter of the *acquis communautaire*, as are women's rights and the rights of the workers.[21] This was the rationale behind the EP rapporteur's placement of children's rights on Romania's accession agenda. However, for the Commission the answer was not that clear-cut: there is no EU children's rights *acquis*, and this became evident when the Commission started monitoring child protection in Romania. The availability of EU *acquis* to act as guidance was paramount due to the complexity and the abstract nature of CRC principles, given that the CRC constitutes the main international instrument which all Member States have adhered to. Children are represented in the CRC as independent and autonomous rights-holders and their freedom and well-being as rightful entitlements, as the CRC establishes a direct relationship between a child and the State. Yet, the CRC offers limited concrete guidance about the implementation of its provisions, and it is widely contended that EU Member States have been slow in complying with the CRC principles at the domestic level (Kilkelly, 2001). Therefore, the Commission's role in transforming child protection in Romania in line with the CRC principles relied heavily on acquiring the necessary expertise in this area in order to promote a comprehensive and coherent children's rights agenda as part of EU accession conditionality.

The Copenhagen political criteria, particularly human rights and minority protection conditions, unlike the *acquis* criteria, are not negotiable as such by candidate countries: they have to be fulfilled before formal accession negotiations are opened.[22] Yet, the candidates' compliance with child rights criteria became a moot issue due to the Commission's lack of know-how and experience in addressing child rights matters. The Commission Directorate Generals, in particular DG Justice, Freedom and Security (JLS) and DG Employment, Social Affairs and Equal Opportunities (EMPL), had no expertise on children's rights when this issue got onto the accession agenda in relation to Romania. This became obvious when DG Enlargement requested the support of these DGs to provide guidance on the children's question in Romania.[23] The main Commission officials in charge of the Romanian children's case, the so-called Romanian children dossier, had no expertise on and knowledge about 'orphanages and child protection' (Post, 2007: 15). Due to the Commission's lack of legal mandate in this area inside the EU and given the fact that children's rights is not an EU issue *per se*, even at the Commission level there was little agreement on whether the CRC, having been ratified by all EU Member States, could be deemed as part of the indirect *acquis*.[24] Therefore, from the outset the issue of children in Romania caused a lot of stir at the EU level, particularly if one takes into account the violation of children's rights also in the old Member States, a fact well-documented across Europe by the Council of Europe (Commissioner for Human Rights, 2010).

EU instruments to forge change

The EU had no specific instrument or mechanism targeted at addressing children's rights matters in candidate countries. The Commission had to rely on its potential to improvise and, therefore, devise instruments tailored to tackle the violation of children's rights, which would be backed up by the EU's active leverage exerted as part of accession conditionality (Vachudova, 2005). The Commission supported financially and technically the Romanian government to reform the childcare system and adopt new legislation in line with the international instruments on the rights of the child. The financial and technical assistance was accompanied by the pressure exerted by the Commission, and particularly the EP's rapporteur Emma Nicholson, on Romanian authorities to implement the necessary changes in the field of childcare. For instance, during the childcare crisis the Commission's active leverage was so great that the accession negotiations came to a halt due to Romanian government's indecisiveness in tackling the problems faced by the child protection system on the ground.[25]

The Commission had a clear objective in relation to the childcare situation in Romania: to 'support the government in transforming the entire child protection system from a child protection system which was designed to provide children to families – rich families from Western Europe – to a child protection system that was designed to place at the forefront of the system the interests of the child'.[26] Lacking any specific instruments for child rights *per se*, the Commission had to employ creatively the instruments at its disposal, whilst reacting effectively to the changing circumstances on the ground. For instance, the PHARE financial assistance started being deployed for the reform of the childcare system rather than as humanitarian aid in late 1999. However, the financial support had to revert back to humanitarian aid in 2000 due to the childcare crisis. The Commission endeavoured to support the government in various ways to reform the childcare system and, therefore, kept the Romanian authorities focused on the children's issue. The main instruments employed by the Commission were, first, the financial and technical assistance provided under the PHARE programme for the reform of the system; second, Member States' legal experts on family law for the new legislation and the international instruments on children's rights. The Commission's monitoring and evaluation via the annual reports constituted a significant instrument for ensuring that Romanian authorities kept their commitments as part of the accession negotiations process.

Poland and Hungary: Assistance for Reconstructing their Economies (PHARE)

The main financial assistance for child protection was channelled via the PHARE programme both as part of pre-accession and formal accession negotiations. Between 1990 and 2000 more than €160 million was provided as EU aid to prop up the old system and provide humanitarian aid (Jacoby *et al.*, 2009: 120). In 1999 alone the Commission allotted, via PHARE, €25 million to support the development of alternative care services at the local level (Delegation of the European Commission in Romania, 2005: 2–3). The financial support provided under the PHARE programme continued after Romania became a candidate country[27] and it was targeted at supporting various aspects of the reform of the Romanian childcare system. The EU financial assistance, delivered as part of PHARE, was coupled with the 'root-and-branch' reform of the system. More specifically, the key objective of PHARE was two-fold: on the one hand, the de-institutionalization of those children already in the residential care system by providing substantial funding to local authorities in charge of childcare and social assistance; and the prevention of institutionalization and abandonment via the provision of modern alternative care services, on the other (National Authority for Child Protection and Adoption, 2004: 2). It should be noted that there were other international donors, such as the World Bank, US Aid or UNICEF, which contributed financially to the reform of the system, yet the EU's financial support was the most substantial. Additionally, Romania's main aim was to join the EU: thus, meeting the Commission's accession conditions in relation to child protection was the top priority on government's agenda.

The main component of the PHARE programme was support through grant schemes for projects. A grant scheme – Children First – was set up by the Commission to fund projects which were aimed at creating alternative childcare services by the local Departments for Child Protection in counties. The Commission sought to support local authorities, rather than children's NGOs, as it was deemed that it was the role of the state to finance social assistance and child protection and, therefore, to provide alternative care services. The reasoning behind this decision was two-fold. First, it was the local authorities' responsibility to provide childcare services: local authorities could have worked in partnership with NGOs, yet, while there were not NGOs all across Romania, there were institutions and children in care in all Romanian counties.[28] Second, local authorities had to forge the deinstitutionalization of children at the local level, so, by financially assisting their efforts, the Commission in practice supported the reform of the child protection system. The Commission's policy also promoted an anti-abandonment approach to childcare, which was further reinforced by the Commission's anti-ICA position. The Commission's anti-ICA stance reflects the rights and principles enshrined in the European Convention on Human Rights (ECHR), according to which ICA is an extreme measure due to two factors: first, it is the state's duty to promote and facilitate contact between children and parents and work for the reunification of parent and child; and, second, the state has the obligation to establish adequate child protection measures meant to target child abandonment and family support (Bainham, 2003).

The Commission funded three Children First programmes as part of PHARE 1999, PHARE 2001 and PHARE 2002.[29] All Children First grant schemes included three elements: first, the setting up of the Children First fund – the grant component – to fund local projects on child protection at the local level; second, the public awareness campaigns, both regarding the changes that were taking place and child rights *per se*; and third, the technical assistance for the grant scheme, intended to assist local authorities in the selection and monitoring of the projects funded under Children First. The overarching objective of all Children First grant schemes was the closure of large institutions or orphanages and the creation of modern child protection services, such as networks of foster carers, family type homes, and mother and child centres. The rationale behind project funding was to forge the implementation of the best practice, thus the Commission only funded the best projects at the county level in terms of attaining the objectives of Children First.[30] The EU project funding was coupled with the revamp of the system and therefore with its transformation from a communist childcare system to a modern, rights-based system of child protection. Furthermore, EU funding was particularly channelled to support the development of alternative care services, namely family type environments, and hence to facilitate the de-institutionalization of children (National Authority for the Protection of Child's Rights, 2005: 3). The Commission's decision to both finance local authorities directly, rather than NGOs working in childcare, and channel the funding towards the actual reforming of the system rather than supplying funding as aid, was a fundamental decision in the Commission's approach to child protection in Romania.

All Children First programmes funded under PHARE coupled the prevention of child abandonment via the closure of large, old-style institutions. For instance, the Children First 1 programme consisted of two components. The first component supported the creation and development of community-integrated child welfare projects at local level, which allowed the development of a wide range of services focused on preventing child abandonment and institutionalization by targeting key areas, such as the prevention of child abuse, abandonment or neglect; the prevention of the institutionalization of children in difficulty and children with disabilities; the protection of children in need or with handicap in family type care and the de-institutionalization of children in residential care (Transtec, 2006: 17–18). The second component of Children First 1 was the restructuring of the residential care institutions. This component addressed the reform of residential institutions by reorganizing them into community child welfare services according to the rationale that children should be placed and kept in residential care only for medical and social reasons and in their best interests (Transtec, 2006: 18). The PHARE 1999 Children First 1 programme supported the closure of twenty-nine big institutions, which represented 30.85 per cent of all institutions closed in the counties where PHARE 1999 projects were implemented and 27.1 per cent of all institutions closed nationwide (National Authority for the Protection of Child's Rights website, www.copii.ro). Furthermore, the apartments and family type homes for children built as part of the Children First 1 programme constituted 85.53 per cent of all the newly established family type homes in the counties where the programme was run, and 83.12 per cent of all such homes nationwide (National Authority for the Protection of Child's Rights website, www.copii.ro).

The Children First 2 (PHARE, 2001) continued the same trend of reform initiated under the PHARE 1999 programme, namely providing assistance to local authorities in order to close big old-style institutions and develop a wide range of alternative childcare services. The overall objective of PHARE 2001 Children First 2 was to support the government with the implementation of the National Strategy for the Protection of Children in Need (2001–2004) by financing the development of alternative services. The structural changes had to be accompanied by public awareness campaigns, such as '*Casa de copii nu e acasa*' [An orphanage is a house not a home] (2001)[31], which included TV spots and billboards throughout the country, aimed at preventing child abandonment. The awareness campaigns aimed to inform citizens about the importance of a family environment for raising a child, the effects of child abuse and institutionalization, and also about the childcare services available for the prevention of abandonment and institutionalization (National Authority for Child Protection and Adoption, 2004: 2). The campaigns were targeted both at the general public and at the professionals working in the system. The public had to be made aware of all the alternative services available and that the placement of children in institutions was not a good solution, while professionals working in the system had to become familiar with the scope of the reform and its implications. To this end, the CRC principles, such as the child's right to be raised by his/her parents, the right to maintain contact and personal relations with his/her parents, the right to freedom of expression and the right to be informed, to name just a few, were prioritized during the national training sessions (National Authority for the Protection of Child's Rights, 2006: 16).

Children First 3, funded under PHARE 2002, followed the same process of structural reform. The projects financed by Children First 3 were the ones that targeted the closure of old-style institutions, such as the homes for children with disabilities and any other large, old-style institution with more than 100 children (Transtec, 2006: 24). The public awareness campaign of Children First 3 was aimed at preventing institutionalization by informing the public about alternative care services, such as maternal centres, foster care and national adoption, and the available access to social assistance. Children First 3 funded projects that led to the closure of thirty large, old-style institutions (Transtec, 2006: 25). Overall, the EU's Children First scheme helped close more than ninety old-style institutions, while setting up scores of the newer type of residential institutions (Murray, 2006: 2, see Table 3.1). Likewise, more than 50 per cent of the children listed as abandoned in Romanian hospitals in 2005 were returned to their parents, while substantially fewer children were abandoned (Murray, 2006: 3). The reform of the system meant that more and more children were cared for by foster families (family care) or in residential care, as provided by modern, apartment-like units (see Table 3.1).

Technical assistance as part of PHARE was provided via twinning projects: twinners from Member States trained Romanian civil servants in the Ministry of Labour and Social Assistance on child welfare know-how

Table 3.1 Romania: number of children in child protection system from 1998 to 2011

Date	Number of children in public and private residential care	Number of children in family care (extended family, foster care, foster families)
31/12/1998	38597	17044
31/12/1999	33356	23731
31/12/2000	57181	30572
31/12/2001	49965	37553
31/12/2002	43234	43092
31/12/2003	37660	46568
31/12/2004	32679	50239
31/12/2005	28786	47723
31/12/2006	26105	47871
31/12/2007	25114	48172
31/12/2008	24437	47159
31/12/2009	23696	45550
31/12/2010	23183	43817
30/06/2011	22742	43518

Source: Romanian Office for Adoption (www.adoptiiromania.ro).

and CRC principles underpinning child protection. They drafted their own reports on the level of progress achieved in practice and made recommendations to the Commission. Twinning projects involved a process of learning regarding the practices and ways of doings things consistent with the protection of children's rights and international instruments. All in all, the financial and technical assistance provided by the Commission via the PHARE programme aimed to support the Romanian authorities to undertake some radical changes which required strong political will and financial backing. To this end, EU financial assistance sought to bolster the Romanian government's commitment to reforming the child protection irrespective of the costs incurred in achieving it.

Member States' legal experts

The Romanian legislation was lagging behind the reform of child protection in the early 2000s. At the same time, the Romanian government was pressured by pro-adoption lobbies in the USA and Europe to lift the moratorium on ICA, which had been imposed at the Commission's behest in 2001. Therefore, the Romanian authorities had to adopt a new legislation on child protection and children's rights that would reflect the changes that had already occurred in this area in Romania. Yet, given that the Commission itself had no expertise on this area, an Independent Panel of Experts on

Family Law – made up of child rights experts from the Member States – was set up by the Commission as this is the common institutional practice when the Commission lacks the required expertise.[32] The Independent Panel of Experts on Family Law had the mandate to advise the Romanian government on the new legislation by employing as yardsticks the CRC and ECHR, which would have ensured that the Romanian legislation on children's rights would be on a par with the Member States' legislation.[33]

From 2003 to 2005, the Independent Panel of Experts on Family Law provided their expertise and know-how on the drafting of the Romanian children's rights legislation. The Panel would meet regularly with the Romanian officials in charge of drafting the new legislation in order to discuss the proposed draft legislation and amend it in case it did not reflect the international provisions on children's rights. The Panel had the final say over the new Romanian legislation before it could be passed. Indeed, the Panel had to provide legal advice on four drafts of legislation, namely the law on the rights of the child; the law establishing a legal framework for adoption; the law on the organization and funding of the National Authority for the Protection of Child's Rights and the law regarding the establishment of the Romanian Office for Adoptions. All four pieces of legislation became part of the new package of legislation on children's rights, which entered into force in January 2005. The complexity of the Panel's mission was significant: the Panel had to ensure that the primary legislation drafted by Romanian authorities was underpinned by an effective institutional and administrative infrastructure crucial for the implementation of the new legislative framework on child protection. The role of the Panel in providing expert advice on the new legislation was even more demanding due to the constant international pressure exerted by pro-adoption lobbies on Romanian authorities and the European Commission. In brief, the new Romanian legislation on children's rights was the outcome of the advisory role played by European experts at the Commission's request.

International instruments

The Commission acted as an indirect factor for the compliance with the CRC and ECHR. All candidate countries, and particularly Romania, encountered challenges in complying with European and international instruments for the protection of children's rights. By employing its borrowed *acquis* (Jacoby *et al.*, 2009: 120), i.e. the CRC, the Commission forged the transposition of key child rights principles into Romania legislative provisions and institutional structures. Additionally, Romania had to adopt some of the CRC optional protocols, such as the UN Optional Protocol on the Sale of Children, Child Prostitution and Child Pornography. Moreover, the moratorium on ICA was imposed on Romania's international adoption practice particularly due to its failure to respect its obligations under the Hague Adoption Convention and the CRC. In brief, the Commission's active leverage ensured that Romania respected its international obligations derived from the main international conventions on children's rights to which it was a State Party.

Entrepreneurs as push factors

The former Commissioner for Enlargement Günter Verheugen and the EP's rapporteur for Romania Baroness Emma Nicholson of Winterbourne were the key actors at the EU level who acted as push factors for the developments in child protection in Romania. Verheugen and Nicholson spoke with one voice in terms of the policy line advocated for the children's question in Romania and, most importantly, they supported each other's approach regarding the transformations in Romania (Iusmen, 2012b). Their entrepreneurial actions were particularly salient with respect to the pressure to reform the child protection sector and ban international adoption. Their key positions in the EU's institutional structure, namely the Commissioner in charge of the enlargement process and the Parliament's representative in charge of Romania's accession process, afforded them the opportunity to leave their mark on the pace and direction of the Romanian children's case (Iusmen, 2012b). The European Parliament, through its rapporteur, also monitored and assessed the situation of human rights in Romania. Based on the Commission's reports and on her own evaluation of Romania's human rights performance, the EP's rapporteur would draft her own reports. Emma Nicholson was the longest serving EP rapporteur for Romania – from 1999 to 2004 – and she was the lynchpin of the reform in child protection and of the moratorium on international adoption. Indeed, due to her bold stance on the issue of ICA, Emma Nicholson's name became widely associated with the moratorium on ICA and the ensuing reform of child protection. It has been claimed that some officials in the Commission and some members of the European Parliament did not approve of Emma Nicholson's strong involvement in the Romanian child protection reform and her alliance with Commissioner Verheugen (Post, 2007: 60).

Emma Nicholson reported to the Foreign Affairs Committee of the Parliament on the progress in human rights in Romania. Nicholson's role was of such a high profile – in pressuring Romanian authorities to reform the childcare system and ban international adoptions – that, at times, the direction and pace of the reform process were regarded as the outcomes of her bold political interventions at the domestic and EU level. For instance, she explicitly requested that Romanian authorities 'tackle root-and-branch reform of child health and development within the proper legal framework, including the suspension of international adoption to address trafficking directly' (European Parliament, 2001: 9). According to Nicholson, there were three major obstacles to Romania's accession to the EU: institutionalized children, including the international adoption practice; the corruption linked to adoption and the need to reform public administration (Post, 2007: 72). The EP's rapporteur also played a crucial role in raising awareness of children's rights and the CRC provisions at the Parliament level. Indeed, due to the Romanian case, children's rights and ICA were for the first time debated at the level of the Parliament. Nicholson's reports were extremely detailed and they gained large amount of debating time, and, consequently, 'people became keenly interested in all the topics ... [she] placed in the reports: the debates were very large and were considerable in terms of depth and knowledge expressed.'[34] The EP rapporteur's firm attitude in relation to the Romanian children's case and her strong commitment to its root-and-branch reform, including the ban on international adoption, have led to a substantial revamp of the entire sector of child protection before Romania joined the EU in 2007.

The Verheugen–Nicholson partnership worked on three levels (Iusmen, 2012b). First, both the Commission and the EP's rapporteur pressured the Romanian government to reform the child protection system and ban international adoptions. Second, once the Romanian government had banned inter-country adoptions, both the Commissioner and Nicholson defended the Romanian government's position from the criticisms of and pressure exerted by pro-adoption lobbies, either from Europe or the USA (Iusmen, 2012b). Third, they both had to defend the Commission's or, respectively, the Parliament's position – regarding the changes taking place in the Romanian child protection – either at higher levels in the Commission or in relation to other MEPs. For instance, Nicholson would criticise, during Parliament hearings, the pressure exerted by the French NGO SERA on the Parliament in general and on the Commission in particular in order to allow international adoption from Romania (Post, 2007: 55). The employment of the membership conditionality (Vachudova, 2005) allowed these two EU entrepreneurs to induce radical changes in child protection and ICA, although some of these policies, such as the moratorium, were not welcomed by all EU Member States (Post, 2007).

The Enlargement Commissioner who followed Verheugen, Olli Rehn, and the new EP rapporteur for Romania Pierre Moscovici no longer attached a salient role to child protection, and divergent opinions began to emerge between the Commission and some members of the Parliament regarding the transformations in the childcare system in Romania, particularly with respect to the ban on ICA maintained by the new legislation (Iusmen, 2012b). The EP's new rapporteur for Romania endorsed a different approach to international adoptions and to children's rights in general. For instance, Pierre Moscovici advocated the idea of setting up an international commission in order to examine the pipeline cases and, furthermore, he urged the Romanian government to authorize international adoptions if necessary in accordance with the Hague Adoption Convention (European Parliament, 2005, 2006). Moscovici was lobbied by American adoption groups in 2005 – after the new legislation on children's rights entered into force in Romania – to set up an international committee to review adoption cases (Post, 2007: 229). The new EP rapporteur's support for this type of committee and the authorization of the pipeline cases were also obvious from his Reports presented to the Parliament. In short, the role of EU entrepreneurs like Emma Nicholson and Günter Verheugen, who advocated a comprehensive policy approach to the changes needed in the children's case, was crucial in forging the reform of Romanian child protection. Their role and authority were even more compelling due to the international pressure exerted on Romanian authorities and the EU in relation to the ban on international adoption. The effectiveness of the two entrepreneurs in eliciting radical developments in Romania depended on their partnership, cooperation and firm stance regarding the EU's approach to the Romanian children's case as part of EU accession requirements.

EU intervention and transformation of child protection

The Romanian child protection system underwent a set of radical changes from 1999 to 2005: a moratorium was placed on international adoptions in 2001, the system was reformed via the closure of old-style institutions and the creation of alternative childcare services and, on 1 January 2005, a new legislation on children's rights entered into force (Iusmen, 2012b). The legislation, which was based on the international and European instruments on children's rights, reflected the substantive progress achieved in this sector. The EU-driven changes occurred within a short time span, yet EU actions to overhaul child protection could only matter when there was real support from the Romanian government (Jacoby *et al.*, 2009: 128).

Reform of child protection system

The Commission and the EP's rapporteur requested three crucial changes in this area: first, the closure of old-style institutions and creation of alternative services; second, the support of families in order to prevent abandonment; and third, new legislation that should put children's rights and the best interest of the child at the heart of the child protection system. However, these changes occurred gradually, often following a chaotic path of transformation due to the unstable domestic political context. Therefore, the reform of the Romanian child protection system involved several stages, but the radical changes were enacted due to the coming to power of President Emil Constantinescu and the centre-right Democratic-Convention (DC) in late 1996 (Jacoby *et al.*, 2009: 118). First, due to the DC government the system was decentralized and this process of decentralization started in 1997. At the heart of the children problem was the centralized communist model of child-care, with large institutions which acted as orphanages hosting hundreds of children. The decentralization of the child protection system started in 1997 when the Department for Child Protection (DCP) was created as an independent governmental structure in charge of overseeing the work of county-level DCPs. The DCP had to coordinate and supervise the development of policies on child protection, although it lacked a clear, rights-based focus. As the responsibility for child protection shifted from the central to the county level, each county established its own DCP to deliver and finance child protection services. Yet, the decentralization process – involving a radical shift of responsibilities and a new institutional infrastructure – was poorly coordinated, which was one of the key reasons for the childcare crisis in 1999. Second, therefore, the reform of the system entailed shifting the priority from 'institutional' care to 'family' care (National Authority for the Protection of Child's Rights, 2006: 9). Hence, a significant number of institutions were closed down and alternative services were set up using PHARE funds.

The Commission promoted a rights-based approach in relation to the reform process in Romania and therefore it urged the Romanian government to adopt a national strategy on child protection (European Commission, 2000: 20). A rights-based approach involves the integration of rights standards into every aspect of decision making and, therefore, it demands that the impact of issues and decisions upon individuals must be seen and examined through the lens of rights with its predilection for envisioning the entitlements of individuals and the duties of states, as opposed to alternative paradigms such as a needs-based approach (Darrow and Tomas, 2005; Jonsson, 2003) or, as is commonly the case with children, a welfare-based approach (Santos Pais, 1999; Eekelaar 1992). The National Strategy on the Reform of the Child Care System (2000) had as key priority the reduction in the number of institutionalized children and children at risk of being institutionalized (European Commission, 2000: 20), which was in line with the CRC principles. The Romanian government eventually adopted in 2001 a revised National Strategy on the Protection of Children in Need (2001–2004), which had to be implemented at a national level while the reform of child protection was closely monitored by the Commission. The National Strategy was supported by PHARE funds and focused on three main aspects: the closure of old-style institutions, the de-institutionalization of children and the creation of suitable child protection measures, which was in line with the Commission's requirements from the Romanian government. The Commission contended that only a root-and-branch reform of childcare system would secure Romania's EU membership, because otherwise, 'by aiding the system as it then was, you were merely sticking a plaster [on] and you needed more than [a] sticking-plaster solution'.[35] Furthermore, new professions were created, such as the profession of foster carer, and networks of foster carers and professional carers were set up, as part of the provision of alternative care services.

The closure of old-style institutions was accompanied by the development and implementation of modern child protection services, such as family type modules, day care centres, maternal centres, recuperation centres or foster care networks. These alternative services were meant to help institutionalized children find new homes or return to their natural families. For instance, day-care services (targeted at children from troubled families) ensure maintenance, recovery and development of child's capacity to overcome any situation which may lead to child's separation from his/her family, while family-type services ensure care for the child who is temporarily or permanently separated from parents and these services are provided via extended family or foster parents (National Authority for the Protection of Child's Rights website, www.copii.ro). Residential-type services provide protection and care for the child who is temporarily or permanently separated from his/her parents as a result of application of the placement of the child according to the law. These placement centres include 'family type modules or homes', 'maternal centres' and 'emergency reception centres' (National Authority for the Protection of Child's Rights website, www.copii.ro). For instance, family-type homes provide children with accommodation, care and education with the scope of helping their socio-professional integration when they leave these homes, while maternal centres – which accommodate single mothers – provide residential services for mothers and children or pregnant women who are in a risk situation with regard to the separation of the child from his/her family.

The development of alternative childcare services emerged primarily due to the substantial financial and technical assistance provided by the Commission. For instance, by the end of 2005, over 170 large institutions had been closed down, while a range of new services had been set up (National Authority for the Protection of Child's Rights, 2006: 11). The number of children in institutions dropped from 57,060 (in 2001) to 27,188 (in 2006) according to the statistical data from the National Authority for the Protection of Child's Rights (National Authority for the Protection of Child's Rights, 2006: 13). With regard to the special protection services for children separated from their parents, at the end of June 2006 there were one thousand one hundred functioning public placement centres and three hundred and ninety-three private placement centres, while the public placement centres comprised of four hundred and thirty-nine apartments, three hundred and forty-two family type homes, one hundred and thirty-six modular institutions and one hundred and eighty-three classic-type institutions (National Authority for the Protection of Child's Rights website, www.copii.ro). Indeed, the reform of the child protection system in Romania provides the 'most dramatic example of a country engaged in large scale movement of children from institutions to foster care and group homes' (Dillon, 2003: 202). The development of family-based alternative care, such as fostering or guardianship, was the key target of the reform of child protection in Romania before 2007. According to aggregated data on family-based care for countries in Eastern Europe, Romania has the highest number of children placed in family-based alternative care (see Table 3.2), which underscores the scale and extent of child protection reform. In its final Progress Report in 2006, the Commission approved of the improvements in child protection: a significant reduction in the number of institutionalized children was signalled along with the improvement of the living conditions in the remaining institutions (European Commission, 2006c: 39).

Table 3.2 South-Eastern Europe: children in family-based care (with foster parents or guardians: absolute numbers and rates per 100,000 children 0–17 years old) in 2000, 2005 and 2007, at the end of the year

	Number of children in family-based care			*Rate (per 100,000 children 0–17 years)*		
	2000	2005	2007	2000	2005	2007
South Eastern Europe						
Bulgaria	–	4,074	5,964	–	302	462
Romania	26,917	47,723	46,160	537	1,100	1,132
Albania	–	–	–	–	–	–
Bosnia & Herzegovinia	3,783	3,311	3,296	402	368	378
Croatia	4,376	3,774	3,574	470	437	425
Montenegro	–	–	–	–	–	–
Serbia[a]	–	2,700	3,350	–	187	241
TFYR Macedonia	1,126	1,157	1,126	206	235	238

[a] Foster care only

Source: TransMONEE database (2009) as cited in UNICEF study 'At home or in a home? Formal care and adoption of children in Eastern Europe and Central Asia' (UNICEF, 2010b).

Moratorium on ICA

Romania violated the key international instruments on children's rights and ICA (European Commission, 2001) and, therefore, within the Eastern enlargement context a moratorium on ICA was placed in 2001 by the Romanian government at the Commission's behest. The EU's position was that Romania had to reform its legislation on international adoption in order to be in line with the European practices on ICA, whereby under the ECHR provisions ICA is an extreme measure of childcare (Bainham, 2003; Kilkelly, 2009). What is striking here, nevertheless, is that the EU imposed condition-ality in a policy sector where it had no *acquis* or experience of intervention, i.e. the ICA policy, and therefore the Commission had to craft a policy line that would successfully address the concrete situation on the ground. One of the key reasons for the implementation of a moratorium on ICA was that the reform of the child protection system and a ban on international adop-tions were mutually exclusive: namely child protection could not be reformed if children did not become part of the system as they were adopted inter-nationally. At the same time, although EU-receiving countries accounted for 40 per cent of all ICA from Romania, it was deemed inappropriate for EU Member States or prospective states to *send* children for international adoption (Selman, 2010). The moratorium – particularly advocated by the EP's rapporteur – was imposed as a 'mechanism to end practices that were incompatible with Romania's international obligations under the United Nations Convention on the Rights of the Child and which risked opening opportunities for trafficking in children and other forms of abuse' (European Commission, 2001: 24). Despite ascribing an extreme interpretation to CRC and Hague Adoption Convention provisions, the moratorium on ICA proved the only feasible solution to curb the corruption underlying ICA and, there-fore, provide the incentives for the reform of the system.

The moratorium on ICA decimated the business of international adoption agencies, which, therefore, went to great lengths to determine the Romanian government to resume ICA. Pro-adoption lobbies started contacting the Commission and the EP's rapporteur requesting that Romania lifted the ban on ICA. Yet the Commission's official position on the moratorium was clear: the EU was not against ICA as such, but against the corruption and bad prac-tices in child protection (Post, 2007: 108). The Commission had to provide moral support to the Romanian government to implement what was right for children and resist the pro-ICA lobbies' pressure. The outcome of the ban on ICA was that the number of abandoned children dropped significantly due to two factors: there were no longer financial gains involved, on the one hand; and the development of alternative care services, on the other hand.[36] For instance, according to official data, there was a sharp decrease in the number of Romanian children entering the USA due to ICA from 783 in 2001 to

57 in 2004 (European Parliament, 2009: 26), while the number of domestic adoptions increased significantly from 2001, as the ratio of ICA to domestic adoption had been reversed (see Table 3.3).

Table 3.3 Romania: number of international and national adoptions, 1998–2008

	1998	1999	2000	2001	2002	2003	2004	2005	2006	2007	2008
Domestic adoptions	840	1710	1291	1274	1346	1383	1422	1136	1421	1294	1300
Inter-country adoptions	2017	2575	3035	1521	407	279	251	2	0	0	0
Total	2857	4285	4326	2795	1753	1662	1673	1138	1421	1294	1300

Source: National Authority for the Protection of Child's Rights statistics (www.copii.ro).

International adoptions were banned on paper; however, in reality, the so-called exceptional cases or pipeline cases meant that a certain number of children were still adopted internationally, as their international adoption had already been judicially approved before the moratorium entered into force. However, the approval of the pipeline cases by the Romanian government was highly criticized by Commission officials and Emma Nicholson in particular. For instance, once the moratorium was in place, there were 1,200 children – the pipeline cases – who had already been selected for international adoption and who were destined for the US, which meant that adopting families had already paid the fees to Romanian adoption agencies. Therefore, after international adoptions had been banned, the Romanian government was under intense pressure to either lift the moratorium or proceed with the adoption of the pipeline cases.

The moratorium on international adoptions was in place from 2001 to 2005, when the new legislation on children's rights entered into force. Throughout this period, significant pressure was exerted on Romanian authorities to lift the ban. For instance, US families lobbied politicians in the Congress in order to render Romania's accession to NATO also conditional on the adoption issue. According to Commission officials, the Romanian child protection was one of the issues that were even on the NATO accession agenda (Post, 2007: 125). The USA employed various channels to pressure the Commission in relation to the adoption issue. For instance, within the 'EU–US Informal Dialogue' on enlargement context, the US Deputy Secretary of State for European Affairs would make strong pleas for the Commission's support to reopen adoptions (Post, 2007: 128). At the same time, the American pro-ICA lobby would pressure the Commission – via various politicians in the Congress – in relation to the Commission's and the Member

States' position on the Romanian moratorium on international adoptions. To this end, the Commission adopted within the EU–Romania Association Council context – according to which once a year both the EU and Romania gave their formal position on EU accession – the *EU Joint Position Association Council* (2002). The Commission had to negotiate the various positions of the Member States in relation to the moratorium in Romania and, at the same time, to get the Member States to embrace the Commission's position (Post, 2007: 121). Eventually, the EU Joint Position, which included the position of the EU Member States, reflected the Commission's stance on international adoption according to which a new legislation had to be passed before ICA could be resumed (Post, 2007: 121).

The Romanian government would approve the adoption of the exceptional cases provided that the adoption of these children was guaranteed by certain high-rank politicians. For instance, the then President of the Commission Romano Prodi was one of the top politicians who guaranteed for the adoption of some of these exceptional cases of Romanian children, which was radically at odds with the policy line advocated by Verheugen and Nicholson. It has been claimed that Romano Prodi regularly called the Romanian Prime Minister to allow 36 exceptions to the moratorium for Italy, and Prodi's cabinet also contacted the Romanian ambassador in Brussels regarding the same issue (Post, 2007: 151). For instance, according to the Government Memoranda – regarding exceptions to the moratorium distributed to the press in 2004 – behind each child whose adoption had been authorized as an exceptional case, despite the ban on ICA, was the name of a foreign politician who had lobbied for his or her adoption. This foreign politician was described as a personal guarantor for the quality of adoption (Post, 2007: 181). Yet, the then President Prodi's name was mentioned as the most important lobbyist in the Memoranda (Post, 2007: 183). Indeed, the anti-ICA policy line advocated as part of enlargement policy generated a deep rift within the Commission, as some Commission officials advocated a more lenient position in relation to the regulation of ICA in Romania (Post, 2007).

Prior to the new legislation entering into force in 2005, the Romanian government authorized, via an emergency ordinance, the adoption of 105 children by Italian families – the so-called 'Italian deal' – on the grounds that these children constituted exceptional cases. An emergency ordinance is a governmental decision with the status of law that does not require parliamentary approval before implementation, yet the Parliament grants its approval ex post. The 'Italian deal' was deemed to be the outcome of the pressure exerted by Italy, namely the then Prime Minister Silvio Berlusconi, on the Romanian government. Indeed, some old EU Member States, like Italy, were pressuring the Romanian government to authorize measures on ICA that were against the Commission's anti-ICA policy in relation to Romania. The 'Italian deal' put a strain on the accession negotiations between Romania and the Commission as the then Enlargement Commissioner Verheugen did not approve of the authorization of the exceptional cases. However, in spite of the way in which the Romanian government dealt with the exceptional cases, the Commission contended that the overall effect of the moratorium was positive and that the Romanian government had been subjected to intensive political pressure from those who were eager to adopt Romanian children. In brief, the Commission, together with the EP's rapporteur Emma Nicholson, strongly supported the moratorium on ICA, and, therefore, endeavoured to defend the Romanian government's anti-ICA position against the international pressure exerted by adoption lobbies, both adoption agencies and politicians, to lift the ban on ICA.

New legislation and institutional structures

A new legislation on children's rights had to be passed to take stock of the significant reform undergone by the child protection system. The Commission explicitly requested – after the moratorium on ICA had been imposed – that the Romanian government adopt new legislation on childcare and international adoption, along with the development of the necessary administrative capacity to ensure its effective implementation (European Commission, 2002: 30). To meet this EU demand, in 2004 Romania adopted legislation on child welfare and child adoption, which was primarily the outcome of the legal work carried out by the Independent Panel of Experts on Family Law with Romania authorities.

The Independent Panel of Experts on Family Law aimed to ensure that the new Romanian legislation was in line with the practices of the EU Member States regarding international adoption. The new Romanian legislation on children's rights (272/2004) and adoption (273/2004) – which was based on the CRC provisions – entered into force in 2005 and maintained the moratorium on ICA by limiting it to extreme exceptions: Romanian children could be adopted abroad only by their relatives up to the second degree of kinship.[37] Foreign couples could adopt Romanian children as long as they were permanent residents in Romania (law 273/2004). The new legislation on children's rights and child adoption, which was welcomed by the European Commission (European Commission, 2005b), was highly innovative and revolutionary and was recommended as a model even for some West European states. According to a member of the Independent Panel of experts 'the legislation is pushing very far the application of the UN Convention of the Rights of the Child and it contains a number of provisions by which the other EU Member States could be inspired'.[38] However, the USA-based pro-ICA lobby was highly critical of the new legislation that maintained the ban on ICA. Yet, the Independent Panel of Experts' stance on the new Romanian legislation was that it mirrored the practices of the

Member States as no EU Member State expatriates its children.[39] Advancing a legal rather than a political argument, the European child rights experts in the Independent Panel followed the provisions in the international instruments on children's rights and the positions of key international child rights bodies, such as UNICEF (2010a) and the CRC Committee (Mezmur, 2009; Herczog, 2009). At the same time, the ICA policy template promoted by the EU in Romania followed the child protection model of the Member States, where a wide range of childcare services are targeted at supporting biological families to keep their children, while family-based care alternatives are rendered available on a large scale and ICA is a measure of last resort. By relying on the technical advice provided by child rights experts on the new Romanian legislation, the Commission embraced a strict anti-ICA policy and legislation in Romania as part of the EU accession process. Indeed, the EU contended that Romania's legislation on ICA and children's rights complied with the key international instruments and, therefore, the EU wholeheartedly supported the new legislation on children's rights within the enlargement context (European Commission, 2005b).

The new legislation on children's rights – which entered into force on 1 January 2005 – put the 'best interest of the child' at the heart of the Romanian system of childcare and is based on three kinds of rights: protection rights, development rights and participation rights. *Protection* rights are reflected by the provisions of the new law, such as children's right to be protected against economic exploitation (Article 8); any form of violence, abuse and neglect (Article 85); sexual exploitation and sexual abuse (Article 99); any form of corporal punishment and any other form of degrading treatment (Article 28 and 90). *Participation* rights provide children with a say in relation to those matters concerning their lives, which reflects Article 12 CRC. *Development* rights include provisions such as the right to education, the right to health care or the right to social security. According to Law 272/2004, children have the right to receive education which would allow them to develop their capacities and personality in non-discriminatory conditions (Article 47), children have the right to be brought up by their parents (Article 30) who are responsible for the upbringing of their children (Article 31) and the child has the right to a living standard which would enable his/her physical, mental, moral, spiritual and social development (Article 44). The new law also mentions the responsibility of professional groups, such as teachers, medical staff, the church and the police, for identifying and notfying the authorities of the risk situations that children or their families may face (Article 43). The new law assigns parents the primary responsbility for children's upbringing, while the local community and state support are subsidiary. This change constitutes a radical shift from the old child protection law, which assigned the state the primary responsibility for child upbringing.

By focusing on the prevention of institutionalization, the new law obliges local authorities to provide services supporting families facing economic hardship in order to prevent parents from institutionalizing their children due to poverty-related reasons. The role of the community in the protection of children's rights involves community members – such as neighbours, education institutions, medical institutions, the police, professionals from the local public administration institutions, i.e. the Social Assistance Public Service – taking note of the possibility of families being at risk in their community (Article 5 of 272/2004 law). To this end, the local public authorities, such as local councils or county councils, have the duty to support parents in fulfilling their legal obligations by developing and ensuring diversified and accessible services which correspond to the child's needs. The role of the state is complementary: the state observes the protection of children's rights by means of specific activities carried out through state institutions and public authorities with competence in this field (Article 5 of 272/2004 law). These legislative aspects are in line with the ECHR provisions, whereby states are obliged to support the birth family or to seek the reunification of the child with the family (Bainham, 2003: 7). Law 272/2004 contains also specific provisions regarding the situation of children leaving the child protection system and who face the risk of social exclusion. For instance, children are helped to integrate into society and in the labour market by benefiting from special protection even after turning 18 and even if they do not study for a degree for a period of 2 years (Article 51 of 272/2004 law). The four fundamental principles behind Romania's children's rights law reflect the CRC core principles, namely the best interests of the child, the right to life and development, non-discrimination and the right of the child to express his/her views in all matters affecting him/her (National Authority for the Protection of Child's Rights, 2006: 16). The four principles are fundamental to ensuring that children's rights are protected.

The new legislation was revolutionary in terms of its contents. Not only was the new legislation based on the CRC and ECHR provisions, which are the main instruments embraced by all EU Member States, but it also codified the latest conventions on children's rights. Indeed, this was one of the most advanced legislative frameworks on children's rights in Europe as the European experts – who advised the Romanian government – drew on the latest conventions on the rights of the child, such as the Convention on Contact concerning Children (part of the Council of Europe) if the parents are separated or divorced. Furthermore, some of the provisions of the new legislation were extremely ambitious given that even the legislation of some of the old Member States does not include them, for instance the fact that children under two are not admitted to institutions unless there are medical grounds for their admission.[40] Additionally, the new legislation forbids the placement of children under 2 years of age in residential-type services. Therefore, it has been claimed that, at least on paper, this new legislation is one of the best bodies of legislation on children's rights in Europe.[41]

The new legislation on international adoption, i.e. Law 273/2004, regulates the adoptions regime in Romania. The new law is based on the CRC provisions, namely Article 20 CRC and Article 21b CRC, as it places the best interest of the child (Article 2), and the preservation and continuity of the child's ethnic, religious, cultural and linguistic identity (Article 2) at the heart of the adoption process. This means that when selecting the adoptive family, aspects related to the cultural, ethnic and linguistic identity of the child would have to be considered. Thus, national adoptions and particularly adoptions from the same geographical area as the child's are the top priority according to the new legislation (Article 26). Apart from the geographical-local aspect, the relatives or extended family of the child have priority in the selection process (Article 26). Moreover, the child's biological parents – where applicable – have to give their consent for adoption (Article 12) and, in accordance with the principle of child participation (Article 12 CRC), the child's needs, opinions and wishes have to be taken into account when processing adoption (Article 27 of 273/2004 law). In summary, there are a number of fundamental principles underpinning the Romanian law on adoptions, such as the best interest of the child, the principle of bringing up the child in a family environment, the principle of preserving the child's ethnic, cultural and linguistic origin or the principle of informing the child and taking into account his/her opinion (Romanian Office for Adoptions, n.d.: 8). One of the core principles guiding the new adoption policy is the provision of a family for a child rather than a child for a family, which was the case before. Last but not least, the Romanian adoption legislation reflects the Hague Adoption Convention provisions regarding the hierarchy of childcare solutions, according to which in-country family solutions have to be prioritized (Hague Conference on International Law, 2008: 29–30).

The authorization and the procedure of international adoption have to follow the prescriptions of the Hague Adoption Convention and the CRC. Unlike the previous legislation, and crucially important from the EU's perspective, the new legislation provides for post-adoption monitoring structures and measures (Article 44 of 273/2004 law): the Romanian Office for Adoptions, which authorizes the adoption, has to provide information on the development of the child for at least 2 years. Equally important, and in line with the Hague Adoption Convention provisions, Romanian adoption agencies have to prevent any financial gains or other benefits that can result due to ICA: apart from the adoption fee, no other donations or sponsorships are to be received by the institutions processing international adoptions (Article 67 and 68 of 273/2004 law). The Romanian legislation was amended in November 2011 and, respectively, in April 2012: the amendments were intended to speed up the process of domestic adoption and also to allow

Romanian citizens living abroad to adopt children from Romania, provided that within 2 years' time after the child has been declared adoptable no eligible family, including the child's extended family, is found for the child. These amendments of the legislation reflect the situation after 2007, when many Romanian citizens chose to live in other European countries and wanted to adopt Romanian children (Panait, 2011).

The new legislation, however, was not welcomed by everybody, either in the Commission or outside the EU. This new legislation was controversially debated both in Europe and outside Europe, particularly in the USA, where there was the most powerful lobby for international adoption. According to Commission officials, the US families adopting children from Romania lobbied the Congress to intervene in Romania and at the Commission level in order to lift the ban on international adoptions, which was upheld by the new legislation.[42] For instance, the Washington based Helsinki Committee – an independent US government agency that monitors countries that participate in the Organisation on Security and Cooperation in Europe – virulently criticized the EU and more specifically Baroness Emma Nicholson, who was held responsible for Romania's ban on ICA, upheld by the new legislation. For instance, the press release of the Helsinki Committee for 2005 read:

> 'The Romanian government was told by the European Union to ban inter-country adoptions as the price for membership, and they capitulated. That the EU should demand such a policy is appalling. That the Romanians should accept it is equally troubling ... Romania has denied thousands of children a loving home and a caring family, and the EU is at fault for letting politics get in the way of helping children'
>
> (quote in Post, 2007: 236).

There were dissenting opinions regarding the new package of legislation even in the European Parliament: for instance, some French and Belgian MEPs questioned the Commission's anti-ICA approach, claiming that the new legislation was not adequate for Romania's child protection (Post, 2007). Furthermore, some NGOs like the Irish Focus on Romania[43] (FoR) continued to pressure the Commission on the children's question even in 2006. According to the FoR's letters sent to the Commission and its lobby at the Parliament level, the situation of Romanian children was still inadequate in terms of childcare and this was partly due to the EU-imposed ban on ICA.[44] Yet the Commission supported the Romanian government and the new legislation despite the dissenting views coming from either outside or within the EU, which is clearly reflected in the EC Delegation press release (2005) entitled 'The EU supports Romania's legislation on adoptions'.[45] The European Parliament became the main EU venue targeted by adoption lobbies. For instance, adoption agencies such as SERA and Amici dei Bambini (Friends of Children) petitioned or contacted Members of the

European Parliaments (MEPs) to employ accession conditionality to lift the ban on ICA. Political pressure, therefore, was exerted by the use of the accession conditionality stick to undo the new legislation on ICA. Due to the fact that MEPs were subject to pro-adoption lobbies, the Parliament adopted a Written Declaration in July 2006 on the issue of international adoption in Romania. According to this Declaration, the Parliament was calling on the Romanian authorities to 'take due account of the Parliament's opinion and to consequently resume without delay consideration of pending cases, in the best interest of the children, and to authorize international adoption where appropriate' (quote in Post, 2007: 257). A clear inter-institutional rift had emerged between some MEPs and the Commission with respect to the restrictive legislation on ICA in Romania.

The main supporter of the Romanian legislation on children's rights, Baroness Emma Nicholson, however, was no longer the EP's rapporteur for Romania when the new legislation entered into force in January 2005. Nicholson's bold support of the new Romanian legislation, nevertheless, made her the main target of the pro-ICA lobby, which continued to vilify her as 'the bête noir who is running a personal campaign to ban all adoptions', and she was portrayed by this lobby as 'some sort of viceroy of Romania whose powers over the government as well as the European institutions exceeds those of any elected official in existence' (Nicholson, 2006b). However, even at the Commission level the new legislation, which upheld the ban on international adoption, was not widely endorsed by everyone. For instance, at higher levels in the Commission there was a lack of consensus regarding the changes that were implemented in Romania. The then Commissioner for Freedom, Security and Justice Franco Frattini disapproved of the approach taken in Romania by the Commission and did not consider foster care as a good solution: thus, he deemed that ICA between the EU Member States should be rendered possible as a measure of child protection, which does not reflect, however, the provisions of international instruments on children's rights.[46]

The new legislation established a new, reformed institutional infrastructure. For instance, in 2001 the National Authority for Child Protection and Adoption in Romania (ANPCA)[47] was established, under the General Secretariat of the Romanian government. The new package of legislation restructured this institution and, subsequently, two institutions emerged: the National Authority for the Protection of Child's Rights and the Romanian Office for Adoptions. After the new legislation entered into force, the decentralized child protection system became organized thus: the National Authority is in charge of child protection policies at the national level; while, as part of the reform process, the responsibility for delivering child protection services is delegated to local level, which means that the General Directorates of Social Assistance and Child Protection at the county level and Social

Work Services at the local level are in charge of childcare services (National Authority for the Protection of Child's Rights, 2006: 5).

The National Authority for the Protection of Child's Rights has been the main institution in charge of the protection of children's rights since 2005. This institution is now under the aegis of the Ministry of Labour, Family and Equality of Opportunities, which reflects the fact that the protection of children and their families is regarded as a social issue, as the Commission clearly stated in its Reports. The main role of this institution is to ensure that, both at central and local levels, children's rights are respected. At the governmental level, the National Authority for the Protection of Child's Rights has to ensure that all policies drafted by the government respect children's rights, while, locally, it coordinates directly the General Directorates of Social Assistance and Child Protection. The National Authority for the Protection of Child's Rights employs a rights-based approach to children's matters, whilst, at the same time, it endeavours to mainstream children's rights as a horizontal issue at the level of ministries. Thus, this institution has a fundamental role in ensuring that the new legislation is properly implemented and that subsequently, children's rights are respected.

Conclusion

EU application of human rights conditionality in child protection in Romania amounted to the EU's intervention in uncharted territory. Nevertheless, the EU's active leverage in children's case in Romania has generated an unprecedented legislative and institutional overhaul of this sector before 2007. As shown above, the EU, particularly the Commission and the EP's rapporteur for Romania, crafted and implemented a policy line on children's rights which was highly contested both within and outside the EU for banning international adoption from Romania. The Commission's intervention was even more controversial due the EU's lack of expertise on and experience in addressing children's rights matters. Yet, the highly intrusive policy applied by the EU in relation to child protection in Romania generated a significant body of know-how and experience in children's rights which did not exist before at the Commission level. Child protection in Romania was radically transformed from a communist system to a modern one based on the key international and European instruments on children's rights. The Romanian government's commitment to reform child protection influenced the pace and direction of accession negotiations, as the children's question was an unduly examined issue, compared with other areas in Romania and, particularly, the child protection in other CEECs. As shown here, the pro-active role of EU actors such as Commissioner Verheugen and EP rapporteur Nicholson played a fundamental role in pushing the radical reforms in this policy sector before 2007. Indeed, the EU was *the* major catalyst for the structural reform of child protection in Romania as part of the enlargement process.

However, even if the transformation of children's sector in Romania had not been effective and far-reaching, the 'feedback' effects of such intervention were significant. The experience of EU intervention in child protection in Romania created a precedent in terms of the extent and depth of EU action in this policy area. The accumulation of EU know-how on and broader experience in children's rights will have had far-reaching implications and consequences for the EU's current enlargement policy and, crucially, for the EU's internal approach to children's rights. Thus, it can be claimed that in light of the expertise and practical knowledge garnered at the Commission level in relation to this human rights sector – due to the Romanian children's case – the normative perspective on EU involvement with children's rights has shifted from a 'terra nova' stance to one of 'déjà vu'.

Notes

1   According to a Commission official, 'in order of high-profile, probably there was the child protection issue, secondly the Roma, thirdly the disabled'. Author's interview with the head of the EC Delegation in Romania, Brussels, May 2008.
2   According to Commission Regular Reports, the 'Commission expressed concern with regard to legislation and practices on inter-country adoption that allowed considerations other than the best interest of the child to influence adoption decisions' (European Commission, 2001: 24).
3   According to Article 21b CRC international adoption is a last resort measure, which is in line with the need to preserve the child's cultural and ethnic background (Article 20 CRC). The key focus of the CRC provisions in relation to ICA is on the preservation of the child's biological family and, to this end, it is the state's responsibility to develop and implement policies designed to support family preservation (Vite, 2008: 25).
4   The Hague Adoption Convention provides the minimum safeguards to protect the rights of children affected by ICA by achieving cooperation between states and recognition of adoptions that take place in line with the Convention's provisions. By constituting an implementing instrument of the CRC (Selman, 2009; Smolin, 2010), the Hague Adoption Convention provides that 'due consideration' has to be given to possibilities for domestic placement (Article 4). The Hague Conference on Private International Law adopted guidelines on how to interpret the Hague Adoption Convention provisions contending that 'in-country permanent family or foster care should be preferred to international adoption' (Hague Conference on International Law, 2008: 29–30).
5   According to documents consulted by Commission officials, the so-called abandonment law had been adopted when Romania's right to get the US Most Favoured Nation Clause was discussed in the US Congress: 'the US had made improvement of the situation of the Romanian children a condition for this trade agreement and it was in that context that Romania adopted the abandonment

law ... Thus, under the disguise of wanting to improve the living conditions of institutionalized and disabled children, the US Congress pushed for an abandonment law, a law that rendered children adoptable' (Post, 2007: 66).

6   The adoption system set up by the previous legislation was demand-driven – if a family expressed their wish to adopt, a child would be identified through different methods – while the system set up by the legislation adopted in 1997 was offer-driven, respectively there would be a database of children fit for international adoption (IGIAA, 2002: 23).

7   It has been shown that the Romanian children adopted by foreigners were neither orphaned nor abandoned by their families, they were in fact being sold by their parents due to poverty-related reasons (Dillon, 2003: 249).

8   As a Commission official put it: 'an abominable system which the nearest I've seen is a kind of a frequent flyer airline system: the more you flied [*sic*] the more points you got, the more money you gave in donations, the more points you got and the points bought children'. Author's interview with Commission official in DG Enlargement, Brussels, May 2008.

9   There was no monitoring of or investigation into what happened to all the children who were adopted internationally between 1990 and 2004 due to an unregulated system with no post-adoption monitoring (see Nicholson, 2006a: 64–77).

10   According to EP rapporteur for Romania: 'it was important to look at the paperwork, and these children had no paperwork: there were thirty thousand children who left Romania and they left no trace behind: almost nothing. Nobody knows where they left; that isn't inter-country adoption, that's child selling'. Author's interview with Emma Nicholson, the EP's rapporteur for Romania, Brussels, May 2008.

11   Author's interview with Emma Nicholson, the EP's rapporteur for Romania, Brussels, May 2008.

12   There was a strong correlation between the number of children abandoned and the number of children adopted by foreign families: the more children were abandoned the higher was the demand for children for international adoption. Author's interview with the secretary of state for the Romanian Office for Adoptions, Bucharest, July 2008.

13   For instance, the then secretary of state for Child Protection – Cristian Tabacaru – had a privileged relationship with adoption agencies and NGOs, such as the French NGO SERA. Author's interview with Commission official the EC Delegation in Romania, Brussels, May 2008.

14   Author's interview with the secretary of state for the Romanian Office for Adoptions, Bucharest, July 2008.

15   Author's interview with Commission official, member of the Romania team, DG Enlargement, Brussels, May 2008.

16   According to an interviewee 'you had in some of these institutions more staff than children there'. Author's interview with one of the heads of the PHARE team in the EC Delegation in Romania, Brussels, June 2008.

17   According to a Commission official: 'one of the turning points was in 1999 when there was a visit to an orphanage near Giurgiu and we were, at that time, providing food aid for the orphanages, but it was all dry food, and the fresh food was to come from the government and the county council: they had plenty of dry

food but no fresh food whatsoever. You had a clean place, but with not enough food ... It was clear that the whole system was falling apart and that led to a big push for the entire revision of the whole regulatory system'. Author's interview with Commission official in DG Enlargement, Brussels, June 2008.

18   For instance, according to the Commission official overseeing children's rights in Romania, De Combret led a psychological 'war' with the Commission and 'had incited the Commission into making the children an issue for Romania's accession' (Post, 2007: 37)

19   Author's interview with Commission official in DG Enlargement, Brussels, May 2009.

20   As a Commission official put it, 'I would say that in childcare we have little or no expertise – our expertise is at the level of principles but at the level of the practice we frankly have no expertise, so there we practically relied on the technical assistance of different Member State experts who came in for quite a long period'. Author's interview with Commission official in DG Enlargement, Brussels, May 2009.

21   Author's interview with Emma Nicholson, the EP's rapporteur for Romania, Brussels, May 2008.

22   Author's interview with one of the heads of the Romania team in DG Enlargement, Brussels, May 2009.

23   According to the task manager for children's rights in the Romania team in DG Enlargement, Roelie Post, there was no expertise on children's rights at the time of Romania's accession process. As she put it in her book: 'I contacted DG Justice to see if they held expertise on the matter [children's rights legislation]. But that was not the case as the Commission had not dealt with this issue before. So I would have to do without the support of a line DG' (Post, 2007: 95).

24   Author's interview with the task manager for children's rights in the Romania team, DG Enlargement, Brussels, June 2008.

25   As a Commission official put it: 'That [the situation of child protection] involved putting quite a lot of political pressure on the government in the sense of 'if you really want to be at the negotiating table with us' ... respect for children's rights was one of the pillars of our democracies, either the government would find enough budget to look after these children or we would ... But the consequence of us finding the money instead of the government was that we would not be opening negotiations with them: there was a fair amount of pressure put there'. Author's interview with Commission official in DG Enlargement, Brussels, May 2009.

26   Author's interview with a Commission official, one of the heads of the PHARE team in the EC Delegation in Romania, Brussels, June 2008.

27   According to Commission officials, the Commission spent €150 million on child protection in Romania between 2000 and 2007. Author's interview with a Commission official, one of the heads of the PHARE team in the EC Delegation in Romania, Brussels, June 2008.

28   Author's interview with the state secretary for the National Authority for the Protection of Child's Rights, Bucharest, July 2008.

29   Children First 1 was financed under PHARE 1999 programme (implemented from November 2001 to August 2003) and was worth €19 million. 'Children First 2' and 'Children First 3' were grant schemes components of PHARE

2001 and, respectively, PHARE 2002, with a combined budget of €21 million (National Authority for the Protection of Child's Rights, 2005: 1). These two grants had been implemented before Romania joined the EU on 1 January 2007.

30   Author's interview with the head of the EC Delegation in Romania, Brussels, May 2008.

31   The awareness campaign was worth €2.6 million (National Authority for Child Protection and Adoption, 2004: 2).

32   Author's interview with the task manager for children's rights in the Romania team, DG Enlargement, Brussels, June 2008.

33   Author's interview with a member of the Independent Panel of Experts on Family Law, Brussels, December 2008.

34   Author's interview with Emma Nicholson, Brussels, May 2008.

35   Author's interview with the head of the EC Delegation in Romania, Brussels, May 2008.

36   Author's interview with the secretary of state for Romanian Office for Adoptions, Bucharest, July 2008.

37   The 2005 legislation (law 274/2004) provided that children could be adopted internationally only by their grandparents living abroad. The legislation was amended in 2011 to include the provision that children can be adopted internationally by their relatives up to the third degree of kinship. In April 2012 new amendments were made to the legislation, according to which Romanian children can be adopted internationally if one of the three conditions is met: adoptive parents are Romanian citizens with usual residency abroad (but permanent residency in Romania), or they are related to the child up to the fourth degree of kinship, or one of the spouses is a Romanian citizen (Romanian Parliament, 2012).

38   For instance, the child rights experts who advised the Romanian government on the new legislation took into account the provisions in the latest conventions covering aspects on child rights available at that time. Author's interview with a member of the Independent Panel of Experts on Family Law, Brussels, December 2008.

39   Author's interview with a member of the Independent Panel of Experts on Family Law, Brussels, December 2008.

40   Author's interview with a member of the Independent Panel of Experts on Family Law, Brussels, December 2008.

41   Author's interview with a member of the Independent Panel of Experts on Family Law, Brussels, December 2008.

42   Author's interview with a Commission official, member of the Romania team, DG Enlargement, Brussels, June 2008.

43   'Focus on Romania' is a 'non-profit Irish voluntary organization which aims to focus world attention on the inadequate care of children and young adults in state institutions in Romania' (according to the 'Letter to Mr Rehn' from Focus on Romania (2006) Commission internal document, 6 April).

44   As the leader of Focus on Romania, John Mulligan, put it in a letter to the Commissioner for Enlargement Olli Rehn 'In short, a complete disaster area [child protection], where institutional care and human rights are concerned. Some of the blame for this has to be laid at the door of Brussels for the failure

over many years to impose real and enforceable conditions on Romania in the Adhesion and Accession phases of enlargement' (according to the 'Letter to Mr Rehn' from Focus on Romania (2006), Commission internal document).

45 'Following recent statements urging Romania to amend its child protection and adoption laws the European Commission would like to reiterate that, as mentioned in its Monitoring Report on Romania published in October 2005, the new legislation on children's rights and adoption, which entered into force on 1 January 2005, is fully in line with the UN Convention on the Rights of the Child and the European Convention on Human Rights and completes the reform on child protection. Similar to the practice in EU Member States, inter-country adoption is no longer foreseen as a child protection measure. The European Commission sees no need for change of the legislation' (from 'The EU supports Romania's legislation on adoptions' (2005) cited in Post, 2007: 239).

46 Author's interview with the task manager for children's rights in the Romania team, DG Enlargement, Brussels, May 2008.

47 The first institution in charge of children's issues was established in 1997 and it was called the National Committee for Child Protection, which was replaced the same year by the Child Protection Department within the government's executive structures. In 2000 this Department was turned into the National Agency for Child Protection, which in 2001 became the National Authority for Child Protection and Adoption, which included the Romanian Committee for Adoption (IMAS, 2004: 25).

4

Policy feedback effects

> I don't think we looked inside the Union, at our own human rights and implicitly children's rights record before. Each Member State has multiple human rights deficits and, in a sense, that hasn't been examined before. We have a multiplicity of defects in the human rights provision within the EU. Perhaps that's the new thing: we have started to look more seriously at our own failings as more and more imbalances of human rights came to light due to enlargement, as the EU got bigger.
>
> (Emma Nicholson)

Introduction

European Union (EU) intervention in children's rights in Romania was unprecedented within the context of Eastern enlargement. Awareness of children's rights was raised at the level of EU institutions, while substantial expertise and experience regarding child rights principles was accrued, particularly at the Commission level. In other words, there were propitious conditions for the emergence of new initiatives and actions to promote children's rights across EU policy sectors. Indeed, political and institutional circumstances at the EU level, along with the politicization surrounding the Romanian children's case, facilitated the onset of a range of feedback effects in the EU's internal and external policy dimensions. This chapter provides evidence supporting the feedback effects triggered by the Romanian children's case at the EU level. It is argued that the feedback effects amounted to the introduction of children's rights as an EU issue in EU internal policy, which generated policy development processes; while, in EU enlargement policy, elements of policy continuation have become entrenched. It is demonstrated that EU policy entrepreneurs seized the window of opportunity provided by the Romanian case to introduce children's rights as an overarching EU policy, developed and implemented particularly as part of the Area of Freedom, Security and Justice (AFSJ). Externally, children's rights have become a formal EU *acquis* accession condition and, consequently, a wide spectrum of issues pertaining to children is now strictly monitored in the current candidate countries. The Romanian children's case, therefore, acted as a catalyst for the establishment of children's rights, in line with the CRC principles, as an overarching EU policy sector.

Feedback effects: EU internal policy dimension

The Commission's intervention in child protection in Romania brought to the fore the 'bifurcated' nature of the broader EU human rights policy: externally the EU pursues an intrusive policy in the human rights provision of non-EU countries, while inside the Union, human rights constitute a matter of national competence of Member States. Given the scale and depth of the 'policy of bifurcation' (Williams, 2000, 2004) as substantiated by the Romanian children's case, it is contended that EU external human rights policy had unintended consequences and feedback effects on the EU's internal policy dimension. Therefore, policy feedback in the EU internal policy sphere is conceptualized as institutional and policy development, echoing Pierson's (1993) broader depiction of policy feedback, which occurs when policies – which are the effects of politics – in turn become causes, generating wide-ranging effects on actors' behaviour, institutions and on broader political processes. Yet, for the policy feedback to occur in the EU internal sphere, a set of favourable political and institutional conditions should be available in order to facilitate it. Therefore, EU entrepreneurs are well positioned to take full advantage of internal propitious circumstances and place new policy issues on EU agenda, by coupling what Kingdon (1984) describes as the three streams of problems, policies and politics, when a window of opportunity opens. Due to the EU's lack of general competence in child rights (European Commission, 2006b), policy feedback effects encapsulate soft law measures and new institutional infrastructure, which can, however, have far-reaching concrete effects at the EU and domestic levels.

Children's rights in Europe

The UN Convention on the Rights of the Child (CRC) (1989) constitutes the main international instrument for the protection of children's rights and is widely employed as the main child rights yardstick by both state and non-state actors. The CRC is regarded as the 'touchstone for children's rights throughout the world' (Fortin, 2009: 49) by providing a paradigm shift in thinking about children as both 'beings' and 'becomings' (Freeman, 2011: 27). The CRC merits include the breadth and extent of its detailed provision for the autonomous rights of children (Kilkelly, 2001: 308–326), which includes a series of civil, political, economic, social, developmental and cultural rights of children and young people. The Convention establishes children as rights-bearing subjects enjoying full humanity from birth, and, therefore, their well-being is a question of rightful entitlements (Veerman, 1992; Freeman, 2000; Archard, 2004). Above all, the CRC regards children as possessing individual and inalienable human rights. State parties to the Convention are required to incorporate the CRC within their own domestic law and ensure that all domestic law and policy fully reflect and uphold the rights and principles enshrined in the Convention. Nonetheless, the Convention is not directly enforceable on state parties, which means that states cannot be sanctioned for failing to comply with the Convention if they lack any implementing domestic legislation in that respect (Stalford, 2012: 34). At the European level, however, the enforcement mechanisms of the European Convention on Human Rights (ECHR) have been invoked in conjunction with the rights-based content of the CRC (Kilkelly, 1999) and thus child's human rights under the ECHR were interpreted in the light of the CRC standards and principles (Kilkelly, 2002). Indeed, the ECHR, despite not being originally drafted as a child-centred treaty, has developed 'the most extensive body of jurisprudence concerning children's civil rights of any of the regional human rights fora' (Van Bueren, 2007: 15–16).

All EU Member States have signed and ratified the CRC, yet the transposition of the CRC principles into national legislation and institutional structures varies significantly. The prevalent diversity of legal and cultural traditions concerning family matters and individual rights have shaped how Member States translated CRC principles into national legislation and institutional structures. For instance, in some Member States, established family or welfare policies have accommodated rights-based approaches; in others, children's rights have been addressed by policies more directly (Public Policy and Management Institute, 2011). Thus, certain EU governments deal with the protection of children's rights within broader welfare frameworks, while others have developed policy mechanisms specifically focusing on children's rights (Public Policy and Management Institute, 2011). The variety and fragmentation of institutional and policy structures focusing on child rights at the domestic level can influence state parties' capacity to comply with the CRC principles. It is not surprising, therefore, that the UN Committee on the Rights of the Child has often criticized in its reports the EU Member States' poor child rights record and the wide variation regarding the protection of rights across national policy sectors (Committee on the Rights of the Child, 2008).

The EU has addressed indirectly child rights matters since the mid-1990s, but without adopting a rights-based approach in line with the CRC or embracing a specific EU child rights policy. The emergence of issues impacting on the protection of the rights of the child has mostly unfolded randomly, and this evolutionary trend was generally characterized by isolated social and economic provisions with no explicit association with fundamental rights (Stalford and Drywood, 2011: 200). For instance, children were the indirect beneficiaries of employment equality legislation, which aimed at re-integrating women within the labour market, or of legislation covering immigration and asylum issues. The European Court of Justice's interpretations of labour mobility and free movement of persons (Stalford, 2000: 105–107; McGlynn, 2002: 388–389) had a pivotal role in the incorporation of children's matters in the regulation of the common market. Additionally, the Court's rulings[1] regarding cross-border family disputes, unemployment benefits and educational support provided children's entitlements under EU law. It was the Treaty of Amsterdam (1997) that, due to its provisions, 'provided the first significant impetus to the development of an EU children's policy' (Ruxton, 2005: 20). For instance, Article 13 TEC – which provides the basis for action to combat discrimination based on age – and Article 29 TEU – which makes offences against children a focus of common action in the field of police and judicial co-operation in criminal matters – augmented the type of actions relevant to children that the EU institutions could take. In other words, the expansion of EU competence to new policy sectors with each Treaty revision meant that child-related matters were addressed indirectly, although there was no direct reference to the CRC or the employment of a rights-based approach: children were objects rather than subjects of rights. Children were targeted via the rights enjoyed by their parents, and, therefore, child rights were subsumed into the broader area of human rights and fundamental freedoms. The EU was active in addressing the plight of those categories that had a direct bearing on the functioning of the common market, such as the youth, and, to this end, new initiatives such as the EU Youth Strategy have started emerging in the late 1990s. However, the EU had no specific child rights policy, the CRC principles were not mentioned in EU policy measures or legislation and, above all, EU institutions did not employ a rights-based approach to children. The Commission adopted a series of policy documents highlighting the EU's concerns regarding certain violations of child rights that had a cross-border aspect. For instance, some of these key initiatives include the Commission Communication on *Combating Child Sex Tourism* (1996), the *Joint Action to Combat Trafficking in Human Beings and Sexual Exploitation of Children* (1997), the Commission Communication on the *Protection of Minors and Human Dignity in Audiovisual and Information Services* (1997), the Commission Communication on the *Implementation of Measures to Combat Child Sex Tourism* (1999) and the Council Framework Decision on *Combating the Sexual Exploitation of Children and Child Pornography* (Decision 2004/68/JHA). What transpires from these policy documents and initiatives, however, is a patchy and indirect focus on children, whereby children's rights remained 'highly derivative and entirely dependent on their parents' decision to exercise those rights' (Stalford and Drywood, 2011: 202), while the EU's engagement with children's matters indicates a history of incoherence and uncertainty (Stalford, 2012: 25).

Stakeholders and advocacy groups had been voicing their support for an EU children's rights policy applicable inside the Union since the late 1990s. Indeed, a wide range of child rights organizations had lobbied Commission services to place the issue of children's rights on the EU's political agenda due to violations of children's rights across Europe (Grugel and Iusmen, 2013). Many children's rights networks and organizations have their head-quarters in Brussels and children's rights groups are particularly strong in Europe. Child rights advocacy and the emergent visibility and salience of child rights matters across Europe led to the inclusion of child rights in the EU Charter of Fundamental Rights (Article 24). Yet, the problems faced by children inside the Union and the role of EU institutions in various policy areas relevant to children were highlighted in the stakeholder study *How about us? Children's Rights in the European Union. Next steps* (Ruxton, 2005). The study constituted the outcome of the research and campaigning carried out by the European Children's Network, a coalition of networks and organ-izations campaigning at the European level for the interests and rights of children. The study indicated those areas where children's rights are violated and, therefore, where EU-level action is required. For instance, the author of the study identified violence, institutionalization and conditions in residen-tial care facilities, trafficking, asylum, discrimination and poverty and social exclusion as the principal children's rights challenges inside the EU (Ruxton, 2005), although in the majority of these areas the EU enjoys limited juris-diction. The report also mentioned the de-institutionalization process in child protection in Romania (Ruxton, 2005: 143), highlighting the progress achieved by Romanian authorities in this area and why the old EU Member States themselves should also tackle the situation of children in institutional care. The study concluded that EU institutions could do more to deal with children's matters inside the Union by advocating an integrated and compre-hensive EU child rights policy. Hence, the general contention was that children's rights are breached not only outside the EU, such as in the CEECs, but also inside the Union and, hence, action to uphold children's rights was needed at the European level. In brief, there was broad consensus across Europe that children face a variety of problems and that action at a supra-national level should be taken to complement the Member States' efforts to protect the rights of the child.

Conditions for policy development [2]

Child rights did not constitute one of the objectives of European integration over the last 50 years; although, at times, the Commission endeavoured to extend its policy remit to social matters (Cram, 1994), which had an indirect bearing on child rights issues. The Commission had attempted to develop a child rights policy in the EU internal dimension during the 1990s, before the Romanian case acquired high profile within the enlargement context. For instance, DG Employment, Social Affairs and Inclusion (EMPL) had begun addressing children's rights matters indirectly as part of family- and employment-related policies since the mid-1990s. To this end, under the Demography programme child-related matters were addressed as part of gender equality and employment policies, namely as subsidiary to other policy sectors. However, at Member States' behest, DG EMPL had to curtail its actions in the area of children's rights due to a lack of legal mandate in the Treaties.[3] Soft law instruments, such as the Open Method of Coordination (OMC), also addressed child rights indirectly, namely via the lens of social inclusion and social protection objectives. Although the OMC instrument did not employ a rights-based approach, it still endeavoured to target child-related matters by sustaining cross-national policy coordination, evaluation and the implementation of commonly agreed objectives regarding social inclusion and child poverty.

When fundamental rights gained high priority in the Hague Programme[4] – which included the key EU strategic guidelines for the area of freedom, security and justice for 5 years (2004–2009) – there was no direct reference to children's rights. Having been adopted by the Member States under the Dutch Presidency, the Hague Programme made no reference to children's rights, apart from the broad reference to boost the protection of fundamental rights inside the Union as part of the AFSJ. However, the intervention of the European Commission (EC) in the Romanian children's case, and particularly the individual involvement of EU actors such as the Commissioner for Enlargement Günter Verheugen and EP rapporteur for Romania Emma Nicholson in relation to the ban on ICA, had already raised significant awareness of children's rights inside the EU. For instance, due to the political visibility acquired by the Romanian case at the EU level, Commission internal services had started embracing children's rights as an area where they could also play an active role inside the Union.[5] This is why the first mention of children's rights as an area of EU internal policy – as part of the AFSJ – is in the Action Plan (2005) regarding the implementation of the Hague Programme: the objectives of the implementation plan include the 'protection and promotion of women and child rights', whereby the Commission proposed the adoption of a communication on the protection of the rights of the child in 2005 (Council of the European Union, 2005). The Action Plan had been drafted by those Commissioners whose portfolio covered AFSJ and who made up the Group of Commissioners on Fundamental Rights, Non-Discrimination and Equality of Opportunities. In short, the protection of children's rights was gathering momentum at the Commission level within the context of the policy objectives included in the Hague Programme.

Furthermore, the Commission's Communication *Strategic Objectives 2005–2009* (European Commission, 2005c) embraced discursively the protection of the rights of children 'against both economic exploitation and all forms of abuse, with the Union acting as a beacon to the rest of the world' (European Commission, 2005c: 9). Adopted by the first Barroso Commission (2004–2009), the *Strategic Objectives* provided a visible, yet declaratory, EU commitment to protect children's rights. In other words, there was a broad contention that children's rights could be addressed by the Commission as a stand-alone issue, by focusing on children as the subject of rights and not merely subsumed to the human rights area or touched upon indirectly as part of broader thematic sectors, such as social inclusion. According to Commission officials, it was expected that DG EMPL, due to its mandate covering social policy, would embrace the ownership for the development of an EU child rights policy for all Commission services.[6] At the same time, children's rights had been included in some of the key policy documents guiding EU external relations with non-EU countries, such as *The European Union's Role in Promoting Human Rights and Democratization in Third Countries* (2001) and *EU Guidelines on Children and Armed Conflict* (2003). In the context of EU external policy, DG External Relations (RELEX) had been advancing children's rights as part of its development and human rights promotion policies with non-EU countries since the early 2000s. Inside the EU, however, child rights policy was lagging behind, which pointed to a significant disjuncture between EU internal and external child rights commitments.

The political circumstances and societal context were propitious for the advancement of children's rights inside the Union. For instance, the public outcry generated by the case of Marc Dutroux[7] in Belgium provided an impetus for concerted EU action to tackle the commercial sexual exploitation of children (Manners, 2008b: 233). There was consensus across EU institutions regarding the need to introduce child rights also in EU internal policy dimension, particularly due to the political visibility acquired by the Romanian case and the violation of child rights inside the Union.[8] For instance, the Member States did not block the emergence of children's rights as a policy objective within the context of the implementation of the Hague Programme, whilst shared consensus emerged at the Commission level that child rights should be addressed as a cross-sectoral issue by all Commission services. At the same time, there was widespread awareness amongst European publics of the violation of children's rights both in the CEECs and Western Europe, particularly due to international media coverage of the appalling conditions in Romanian orphanages (Jacoby *et al.*, 2009). Put simply, the political circumstances inside the Union were advantageous for taking EU-level action to advance children's rights.

Meanwhile, there were disparate intergovernmental actions focusing on children's rights at the level of the Member States. For instance, the EU Member States began cooperating on children's issues in 2000 by setting up a Permanent Childhood and Adolescence Intergovernmental Group – *L'Europe de l'Enfance* – with the aim of mainstreaming children's rights in all EU policies (European Commission, 2006b: 14). The membership of *L'Europe de l'Enfance* consists of the Ministers of the EU Member States and high-level government officials in charge of policies regarding children at the national level and the meetings take place on an informal basis. The key aims of this intergovernmental group are to promote an improved under-standing of the living conditions of children in Europe and child policies, and the development of common approaches to fight transnational phenomena affecting children, for instance child trafficking and exploitation (European Commission, 2006b: 15). Although the decisions taken by this intergovern-mental group are not binding, they illustrate the emergence of cross-national initiatives taken by the Member States towards addressing children's issues at a European level.

Romania's anticipated accession to the EU in 2007 and the controversy generated by its moratorium on ICA further augmented the political salience acquired by children's rights at the EU level. As shown in Chapter 3, there was widespread disagreement at the level of EU institutions, particularly the Parliament and some of the Commission internal services, regarding the radical ban imposed on the ICA from Romania and the new Romanian legis-lation which maintained it. Therefore, the Romanian children's case provided a window of opportunity for raising awareness of children's rights issues within the broader EU context, particularly due to the conflicting approaches adopted by the key EU institutions in relation to it. For instance, the enforce-ment of the new Romanian legislation in 2005, which maintained the ban on ICA, generated controversy both at the Commission and Parliament's levels. At the Parliament level, various international adoption agencies lobbied members of the European Parliament (MEPs) and particularly the new EP rapporteur for Romania that followed Emma Nicholson, Pierre Moscovici, to block Romania's accession to the EU if ICA was not resumed; and a number of MEPs had attempted to block Romania's accession on grounds related to the ban on ICA, which was maintained by the new Romanian legislation. The clashing positions embraced by the Commission and the Parliament regarding the Romanian children's case generated a situation of 'attention gaining' (Princen, 2011) by mobilizing supporters or critics and raising interest for children's rights, which opened windows of opportunity for EU institutions to take action. Hence, the inter-institutional disagreements regarding the EU's role in the Romanian children's case heightened the urgency of adopting a formal and explicit EU policy that would spell out the Commission's role and scope in this area. Additionally, the Romanian case exposed the wide range of child rights violations, for instance in terms of institutional care and child abandonment, in the Member States (Ruxton, 2005). The Romanian case, therefore, both raised awareness of the problems faced by children in the

EU and also provided the political opportunity for EU institutions to initiate action in children's rights at the EU level.

It was Commissioner Frattini, however, who was well-positioned to seize the window of opportunity provided by the Romanian case. Being in charge of the policy area covering fundamental rights and freedoms, Frattini was strategically positioned at the EU level to employ an enlargement policy issue, i.e. the Romanian case, as a window of opportunity to introduce children's rights as an overarching EU policy issue. Frattini could justify his embrace of child rights matter as prompted by the EU's need to address the violation of children's rights inside the Union and as a response to stakeholders' lobbying. Indeed, Commission officials (in DG ELARG) who followed the Romanian case closely deem that the Romanian case acted as a catalyst for the emergence of children's rights as an EU internal issue and, therefore, Commission policy entrepreneurs had to initiate action quickly, namely to 'strike while the iron is hot' (Kingdon, 1984: 178). Thus, it has been claimed by the Commission officials who were involved with Romanian child protection that the children's question in Romania was one of the main triggers behind the Commission's Communication *Towards an EU Strategy on the Rights of the Child.*[9] The political visibility and salience acquired by the Romanian case created a propitious momentum to take up children's rights matters inside the Union. Commissioner Frattini had also followed closely the developments in the judicial system, along with the anti-corruption measures taken in Romania during pre-accession negotiations, which was part of his portfolio. Given his mandate, therefore, Frattini was familiar with the reform of the child protection system in Romania and the ban on ICA, of which he disapproved. According to Commission officials, in light of the awareness raised of the Romanian children's case and of the international adoptions issue at the EU level, Commissioner Frattini's initial intention was to hold an international conference on inter-country adoptions (Post, 2007: 220). Yet, instead of organizing this conference, Frattini placed child rights on the agenda of the Group of Commissioners on Fundamental Rights, Non-Discrimination and Equality of Opportunities in 2005 and requested all Commission services to conduct a review of their actions and activities regarding the protection of children's rights, which later led to the adoption of the Communication *Towards an EU Strategy on the Rights of the Child* in 2006. By setting the EU agenda 'from above' (Princen, 2007), Frattini pushed the rights of the child high up on the political agenda within the context of the Group of Commissioners on Fundamental Rights, Non-Discrimination and Equality of Opportunities, and, subsequently, embraced the ownership of children's rights as an issue of EU internal policy belonging to the area of justice, freedom and security. It was contended across Commission services that, due to the Commissioner Frattini's pro-active role, an enlargement issue led to bold action in EU internal policy dimension, which was not blocked by the Member States. Indeed, Commission officials who worked on the Romanian children's dossier share the view that the EU's recent policy developments in child rights constitute the spin-off from the enlargement policy applied in Romania.[10] Indeed, after the adoption of the Hague Programme, Frattini was committed to taking action in relation to child rights: 'I intend to focus on important issues such as the protection of women and children and the fight against racism and xenophobia' (Frattini, 2005: 1). Commission officials in DG Enlargement, for instance, contend that 'child protection is the best example in terms of the internal feedback of the human rights issues monitored in Romania: we didn't do anything in children's rights up until the early 2000s. Because of Romania we are developing now a policy – the strategy announced by the 2006 Communication – on children's rights throughout Europe.'[11] The same view is shared by the EP's former rapporteur for Romania, Emma Nicholson, who is convinced that EU intervention in child protection in Romania prepared the ground for the subsequent developments in children's rights at the Commission level.[12]

Communication Towards an EU Strategy on the Rights of the Child and key developments

Given the favourable political context described above, Frattini seized the opportunity to adopt an overarching Commission policy on children's rights. Therefore, the Romanian children's case provided Frattini with the window of opportunity to advance an EU children's rights policy, with the EU acting as 'a guardian angel' to all children (Frattini, 2008). It has been claimed that Frattini's embrace of children's rights was overshadowed by the limited legal basis to intervene in child rights in the area of justice, freedom and security: [13] this reinforces Frattini's entrepreneurship in children's rights being driven by his desire to accrue political capital via shaping the EU's public policy, given that children's rights have agenda-setting attributes due to their political appeal (Iusmen, 2013a).

The most concrete internal feedback effect triggered by EU intervention in children's rights in Romania and facilitated by the favourable political context at the EU level was the Commission's Communication *Towards an EU Strategy on the Rights of the Child* (Iusmen, 2013a) made public in July 2006 by Franco Frattini. At Frattini's request, between September 2005 and May 2006 all the Commission services had to provide their input into the drafting of the communication advancing the adoption of a 'Children's Rights Strategy' in the future. Several inter-service consultations and meetings were organized involving Commission staff from 15 Directorates-General – such as External Relations; Enlargement; Employment, Social Affairs and Equal Opportunities; Justice, Freedom and Security; Health and Consumers; Development; Education and Culture – but also representatives of UN agencies, such as UNICEF or International Labour Organization (ILO), the Council of Europe and NGOs active in children's rights (European Commission, 2006b: 5). Commissioner Frattini's actions were clearly driven by his commitment to make child rights an issue of EU internal policy. For instance, according to a Commission official: 'the Communication *Towards an EU Strategy on the Rights of the Child* was put in place in order to materialize this ambition [to take action on children's rights] of Frattini'.[14] The 'position paper' submitted by the Commission officials in the 'Romania team' on behalf of DG Enlargement – for the 2006 Communication – mentioned the EU's role in child protection in Romania, with a significant emphasis on the reform process steered by the Commission (Post, 2007: 220). Indeed, the radical overhaul of the Romanian child protection system is mentioned in one of the key documents – the Impact Assessment (2006) – accompanying the 2006 Communication *Towards an EU Strategy on the Rights of the Child*, as it is stated that 'over the years, the Commission has played a key role in encouraging reform and in funding the childcare sector in Romania where the progress achieved has been widely acknowledged' (European Commission, 2006b: 13).

The Communication constitutes the first initiative taken at Commission level to safeguard children's rights at level of EU institutions and in the Member States (European Commission, 2006a: 1–7). By promising to be a watershed document, the Communication set out an integrated and shared rights-based approach. The Commission also proposed to mainstream child rights in all EU legislative and non-legislative actions that may affect children (European Commission, 2006a: 7) and included measures intended to address children's rights as a self-standing issue and not simply subsumed into the general human rights category. Furthermore, the Commission acknowledges for the first time in EU internal policy that the CRC constitutes the definitive framework within which the EU will develop and implement its child rights actions. Thus, the CRC is now fully recognized as one of the EU children's rights standards, which was not clear or generally agreed prior to the Romanian children's question. The employment of the CRC as the main yardstick for the protection of children's rights both in the EU's internal and external dimensions fosters a wider coverage of children's issues by the Commission and hence more scope for EU intervention to address child rights.[15]

The Commission set up a new institutional infrastructure to support policy development, coordination and implementation focusing explicitly on child rights. New institutional structures, such as an Inter-service Group on Children's Rights (ISG), a Commission Coordinator for Children's Rights in DG JLS (now DG Justice) and a European Forum on the Rights of the Child, were established at the Commission level. The role of these structures is two-fold. First, the ISG and the Commission Coordinator for Children's

Rights are supposed to act as coordination and consultation mechanisms at the Commission level regarding all EU actions and policies relevant to children's rights and they are responsible for following up EU child rights policy. The European Forum on the Rights of the Child, which brings together key stakeholders, acts as an arena for exchange of good practice and contributes, together with the new Commission institutional structures, to the design and monitoring of EU actions relevant to children's rights. In addition, to further augment the visibility of children's rights at the Commission level, the unit on 'Fundamental Rights and Citizenship' in DG JLS was changed into 'Fundamental Rights and the Rights of the Child' in 2008 (Iusmen, 2013a). Apart from the institutional capacity-building, the Communication also led to the adoption of concrete measures and policy instruments on children's rights protection within the EU. For instance, a set of Hotlines and Helplines, such as the 116 000 Hotline for Missing Children or the 116 111 Child Helpline, which were included among the short-term measures of the Communication, have been implemented by some of the EU Member States (European Commission, 2010a).

The European Parliament in turn reacted to the Commission's Communication by adopting a report on 20 December 2007 – at the initiative of MEP Roberta Angelilli – according to which the Parliament strongly supported the Commission's initiatives towards the adoption of an EU Strategy on the Rights of the Child (European Parliament, 2007a). The Parliament's report was followed by the adoption of a Resolution on 16 January 2008 titled *Towards an EU Strategy on the Rights of the Child* which contained the key provisions in the December report. At the Parliament level, MEP Roberta Angelilli – who became the EP's rapporteur on the rights of the child – was the main supporter of the Commission's Communication in the Committee on Civil Liberties, Justice and Home Affairs (LIBE). For instance, Angelilli played a significant role in drafting the Parliament's response in relation to the Communication, prior to adopting the report in December 2007. According to the Parliament's report adopted in December 2007, the Parliament supported the Commission's determination to make children's rights 'a priority for EU action, to recognize children as fully fledged subjects of law, whose interest must be specifically taken into account in all policies and measures adopted at EU level, and to create instruments to promote their rights' (European Parliament, 2007a: 33). The Parliament recommended a more robust institutional and policy engagement on the part of the Commission with children's rights. Having the Parliament on board in relation to its child rights initiatives attached a degree of political legitimacy to and democratic approval of the Commission's child rights policy. At the same time, the Commission seemed to embrace an instrumental view of its role: namely, that its actions would have an added value in forging more effective actions on child rights across Europe. The Parliament's support of the Commission's child rights policy renders Commission actions legitimate to European citizens, whom the Parliament represents. Additionally, the Parliament attached a broad interpretation to the Commission's newly endorsed role, by advocating the creation of a new portfolio at the Commission level, namely a Commissioner for Human Rights, who would also be responsible in particular for the protection of children's rights and who would 'have responsibility for centralizing and coordinating all legislative, administrative, media and other activities relating to the protection of children's rights' (European Parliament, 2007a: 36).

The Parliament's Resolution of 16 January 2008 *Towards an EU Strategy on the Rights of the Child* provides for new initiatives and actions to be taken to further advance child rights initiatives and measures within the Union. For instance, in line with the Communication's provisions, the Parliament's Resolution highlighted the importance of incorporating and protecting children's rights in all EU policies affecting children directly or indirectly, namely mainstreaming, and of guaranteeing all children the right of 'participation' at the EU level in order to consider their opinions on all matters affecting them (European Parliament, 2008: 3). Furthermore, the Parliament called for the creation of an effective monitoring system, supported by annual reports and financial instruments, in order to ensure the implementation of the commitments set out in the Communication (European Parliament, 2008: 4). Therefore, the 2006 Commission Communication on child rights generated a snowballing effect, whereby EU institutions such as the Parliament quickly expressed their support for the EU's newly embraced role. The popularity of child rights matters at the level of EU institutions transformed what was initially perceived as a solely Commission attachment to children's issues to a broader EU commitment shared by the main EU institutions.

Children's rights as part of AFSJ and EU children's rights policy

Frattini's entrepreneurial actions in relation to children's rights generated developments at the EU level which further normalized and institutionalized the Commission's internal engagement with this policy sector (Iusmen, 2013a). The institutionalization of children's rights at the EU level was reinforced by the entry into force of the Lisbon Treaty in December 2009 and the binding aspect of the EU Charter of Fundamental Rights. The Treaty of Lisbon paved the way for major EU constitutional and legislative shake-up relevant for the protection of the rights of the child. There are two key aspects that enhance the EU's fundamental rights regime in relation to children's rights: the binding nature of the EU Charter of Fundamental Rights and the inclusion of child rights at Treaty level (Article 3 TEU). In addition to these constitutional changes, the prospective EU accession to the ECHR (Article 6(2) TEU) will further boost the fundamental rights framework for the protection of child rights. Article 24 in the Charter[16] contains explicit references to child rights, which echo the CRC provisions, such as child participation, protection and care for their well-being and the principle of the best interests of the child guiding all actions relating to children. Other Charter articles are also relevant for children, for instance Article 14 – right to education; Article 21 – non-discrimination; Article 32 – prohibition of child labour and protection of young people at work or Article 33 – family and professional life (McGlynn, 2002: 392–94; Ruxton, 2005: 21–22). The Charter's catalogue of children's rights has been described as a 'success story' as it entails an integrated construction of an EU child rights policy (McGlynn, 2006: 21). Furthermore, the binding nature of the Charter at the EU level means that EU institutions have an obligation to respect the rights, freedoms and principles set out in the Charter. In essence, the Charter becomes one of EU's main child-proofing instruments, along with the CRC. It is the Commission's role to oversee that the Charter provisions in relation to children's rights are respected both during policy-making and policy-implementation processes. Thus, the 'legal aims and effects of the Charter are to limit and to frame the powers of the EU institutions and not to expand such powers' (Piris, 2010: 153). To this end, the Commission adopted the Communication Strategy for the Effective Implementation of the Charter of Fundamental Rights by the European Union (2010), which sets out the strategy and methodology to be employed to ensure that the Charter is effectively applied throughout the decision-making processes. The monitoring of the effective implementation of the children's rights provision in the Charter involves both ideational, normative changes, such as a 'fundamental rights culture', and more concrete measures, such as a 'fundamental rights check-list' (European Commission, 2010b). These two provisions reinforce child-proofing in line with a rights-based approach at all stages of the legislative process. According to the methodology underpinning the effective implementation of the strategy, EU institutions have to consider children's rights during preparatory consultations and run impact assessments to examine how the proposed legislation affects children's rights. In a nutshell, the Charter has established the legal obligation for the EU to ensure that all its actions respect children's rights in line with the CRC provisions.

The Treaty of Lisbon enshrines for the first time the protection of children's rights[17] at the Treaty level, by listing it among the Union's objectives for its internal and external policies. These explicit provisions on child rights at the Treaty level are further accompanied by Treaty articles which have an indirect impact on the protection of children's rights: for instance, the Council and the Parliament are empowered to legislate on aspects related to combating the sexual exploitation or trafficking of children (Articles 79(2) d and 83(1) TFEU), while more generic Treaty provisions relating to citizenship (Article 20 TFEU) and non-discrimination (Article 19 TFEU) also enhance the adoption of more inclusive, child-sensitive EU laws and policies

(Stalford and Drywood, 2009). The Lisbon Treaty has extended the mandate of the EU to adopt binding legislative measures on cross-border matters pertaining to the AFSJ and indirectly impacting on the protection of children's rights. More concretely, the EU's legal competence covers policy matters identified by Articles 81 and 82(2) TFEU namely: (1) facilitating the mutual admissibility of evidence between the Member States in judicial procedures; (2) supporting the rights of people during the civil and criminal processes; (3) protecting victims of crime; and (4) measures relating to family law, including matters relating to child custody, where they have cross-border effects (Stalford and Schuurman, 2011). The provisions enshrined in the Lisbon Treaty have had a positive effect on the legitimacy and visibility of the EU children's rights agenda. At the same time, these constitutional changes make up the final dynamic, i.e. fundamental rights dynamic, of what Stalford (2012: 16–18) describes as the three dynamics that have driven and shaped the EU law and policy pertaining to children: the market integration dynamic; the social integration dynamic and, finally, the fundamental rights dynamic.

Yet child rights have further resurfaced as part of the Union's objectives regarding the AFSJ in the Stockholm Programme (2010–2014). Children's rights are high on the Stockholm Programme's agenda within the context of 'living together in an area that respects diversity and protects the most vulnerable' (European Commission, 2009: 7). The Commission's commitment to play an active role in children's rights internally was further reinforced by the current Commissioner's for Justice, Fundamental Rights and Citizenship (Viviane Reding) adoption of the Communication, An EU Agenda for the Rights of the Child (2011), setting out the actions the Commission intends to take in relation to children's rights as part of the Stockholm Programme. The EU Agenda for the Rights of the Child includes measures in areas where the EU can bring an added value, such as child-friendly justice, protection of children in vulnerable situations or regarding the issue of violence against children in both EU internal and external spheres (European Commission, 2011f). According to the Agenda, the approach adopted in relation to children is underpinned by two rights-based instruments: the UN Convention on the Rights of the Child, which has been signed and ratified by all EU Member States, and the EU Charter of Fundamental Rights, which now constitutes the EU's own bill of rights.

According to the state of play of the implementation of the objectives in the Agenda, so far the Commission has adopted a number of concrete legal and policy instruments augmenting the protection of child rights within the AFSJ. For instance, in May 2011 the Commission adopted a proposal for a Directive on Victims' Rights, raising the level of protection of vulnerable victims, including children, while in April 2011 a Communication on *EU Framework for National Roma Integration Strategies* was adopted aiming to promote a more efficient use of structural funds for the integration of Roma. A clear focus on the prevention of all forms of violence against children has emerged in relation to implementation of the *EU Guidelines on the Protection and Promotion of the Rights of the Child* (2007). At the same time, the Commission, under the leadership of DG Justice, has begun main-streaming the Council of Europe *Guidelines on Child-Friendly Justice* into the field of civil and criminal justice. Moreover, the justice-focused approach of the Agenda is further substantiated by the Commission's support for the development of training activities for judges at the European level regarding the optimal participation of children in judicial systems. To this end, the Commission adopted the Communication *Building Trust in EU-Wide Justice – A New Dimension to European Judicial Training* (2011), which includes the key objectives and measures to be implemented by the EU in order to train half of the legal practitioners in judicial cooperation in civil and criminal law in the EU by 2020. Therefore, there is a clear focus on the protection of children as belonging to vulnerable categories, which pertains to an enhanced protection of their rights within the AFSJ.

The focus on children's rights in the Stockholm Programme clearly prioritizes an emphasis on children's vulnerability and, hence, their need for protection. Indeed, there is a preference, on the part of the EU, for the pursuit of child protection issues to the exclusion of the more empowering aims of promoting child autonomy and participation (Cullen, 2004; Stalford, 2012). The Commission's endeavour to promote child protection measures inside the EU was also reinforced by the adoption of the Communication *Dial 116 000: The European Hotline for Missing Children* (2010) aimed at persuading Member States to render the 116 000 Hotline for Missing Children oper-ational at the national level. This Communication further augments the Commission's policy commitments in relation to children's rights origi-nating from the 2006 Communication *Towards An EU Strategy on the Rights of the Child*, while underpinning a 'softening up' process (Kingdon, 1984) in relation to the EU's role in children's' rights. By the same token, a signif-icant emphasis has been placed by the Commission on matters connected to illegal cross-border actions, such as human trafficking, sex tourism and child abduction, and sexual exploitation of children, such as child pornog-raphy. The legal initiatives and policy measures adopted to address these matters demonstrate a focus on child protection, based on the perception of children as experiencing the most vulnerable social and economic situations, which is consistent with what has been coined as a 'deficit-oriented' approach (Stalford, 2012: 224).

The institutional structures and policy measures established by the 2006 Communication have had mixed success in addressing the child rights issues they had been designed for. For instance, the mainstreaming of children's rights by the Commission Coordinator and the ISG was hailed as one of the key developments. However, despite the visible efforts taken by Commission officials in this area, the effective mainstreaming of children's rights is complex and requires considerable intra-institutional coordination and resources (Stalford and Drywood, 2009: 165–166), alongside effective leadership, to be able to successfully adapt and translate abstract ideas about children's rights into concrete policy measures. At the same time, the leading initiative of the 2006 Communication, i.e. the 116 000 Hotline for Missing Children, is fully operational only in seventeen Member States (European Commission, 2012) due to the Commission's lack of leverage to coerce Member States to render it operational. The consultation of key interests, whether pre-existing or engineered (Kohler Koch, 2007; Mahoney, 2004), was deemed crucial for the development of a comprehensive child rights policy. Yet tensions developed between DG Justice and the main child rights organizations in relation to how effectively the Commission develops and applies child rights principles inside the Union (Grugel and Iusmen, 2013). Child rights stakeholders' criticism was particularly voiced in relation to how the main consultation and policy advice tool (European Commission, 2006a: 8), i.e. the European Forum on the Rights of the Child, has been employed by the Commission, and particularly by DG Justice. A rift has emerged, therefore, between child rights stakeholders and DG Justice (Grugel and Iusmen, 2013). Representatives of children's rights NGOs, networks and EU institutions make up the bulk of the Forum, which is convened by the head of the Child Rights Unit (DG Justice). The Forum was expected to act as the focal point for the cooperation and consultation activities between the Commission (DG Justice) and child rights stakeholders regarding the development of child rights measures. However, the Forum meetings have not been effective in engaging children's NGOs in the policy process (Grugel and Iusmen, 2013:85), which raises doubts about the Commission's commitment to include child rights stakeholders in its policy-making process.

The worsening relationship between DG Justice and children's rights organizations emerged in parallel with rising tensions over the direction and content of the children's rights agenda inside the Commission itself (Grugel and Iusmen, 2013). For instance, DG Justice has set an agenda for the Forum which tends to reflect its own concerns, ignoring debates around EU external relations. Furthermore, tensions have emerged within ISG meetings, as they failed to prioritize strategic issues such as the effective incorporation of CRC principles into EU actions. As a result, Directorate General External Relations (DG RELEX) has decided to develop its own set of priorities and actions, such as the establishment of an external relations sub-group on children's rights (Grugel and Iusmen, 2013) in order to coordinate its own children's rights policies more effectively (European Commission, 2008c: 10). Subsequently, tensions between DG RELEX and DG Justice developed (Grugel and Iusmen, 2013), which also reflected to some degree a 'bifurcated' pattern of civil society engagement (Iusmen, 2012a: 146); namely, whilst DG RELEX has established a structured and inclusive relationship with children's NGOs, DG Justice has ended up alienating and disengaging civil society actors. This inter-institutional rivalry also stems from competing approaches or divergent policy frames (Rein and Schön, 1994; Rhinard, 2010) around the meaning of children's rights. Whilst DG RELEX tends to locate children's rights in the context of broader human rights issues, DG Justice has embraced a more limited approach (Grugel and Iusmen, 2013), by framing child rights measures as part of the AFSJ.

Child rights stakeholders have also been extremely critical in relation to the priority areas in EU child rights policy (EU Agenda) as part of the Stockholm Programme. For instance, there is an unbalanced focus on Europe of justice and Europe of protection, rather than Europe of rights, as the objectives in the Agenda suggest. Indeed, the Commission seems to prioritize a focus on children's protectionism at the expense of children's self-determinism. Certain policy issues, such as those focusing on justice and protection of vulnerable categories, prevail over actions that can empower children, e.g. via participation. These policy measures provide a dependency approach to children by proclaiming children's need for protection (their helplessness and hence dependency), particularly in relation to justice and vulnerability-related matters. Therefore, the Agenda advances mostly a 'needs-based' approach to children by sidelining a rights-based approach, which should have acted as a counterpoint to the former, and, above all, it would have reflected the focus on fundamental rights, as provided by Commissioner Reding's portfolio. Although some of the actions in the Agenda are framed in a rights-based language, the focus is on needs instead and particularly on how those needs can be met (e.g. Roma children, unaccompanied minors). The Agenda contents fail to provide a rights-based approach as they make no reference to 'dignity rights'; i.e. rights that could empower children and treat them as independent, autonomous rights-bearers. A rights-based approach requires the identification of the human rights claims of rights holders. Furthermore, a rights-based approach requires the application of child rights standards and principles to both the goal and process of policy development (Tun *et al.*, 2007: 33–34) being conceived both as a process and a product (Stalford, 2012: 29). Therefore, it serves to distinguish a rights-based approach to matters concerning children from traditional welfare approaches where children's voices remained, if not completely silent and marginalized, then subject to interpretation by the 'experts' (Tobin, 2009). The Agenda also fails to provide a holistic approach to children's rights, reinforced by an overarching action plan shared by all Commissions services, although it is intended to be implemented as *the* EU child rights policy. It is not surprising, therefore, that the measures included in the Agenda are tailored on the policy portfolio of Commissioner Reding. In the same vein, it has been shown that the Commission's endeavour to advance children's rights suffers from structural barriers (Stalford and Drywood, 2011: 214–215), such as insufficient collaboration between different Commission services, the lack of comparative statistical data and an ineffective engagement with child rights stakeholders responsible for service delivery at the grassroots level in the Member States.

Despite the policy development processes and emergent institutionalization of children's rights at the EU level, the EU still lacks legal competence to adopt hard law measures on the protection of child rights. The importance of the policy development process, however, resides in the institutional innovation, policy structures and political commitment to address children's rights by the Commission. There are now EU institutional structures and soft law mechanisms specifically designed and established at the Commission level for targeting the protection of children's rights across Europe. Soft law measures often prepare the ground for future binding legislation (Szyszczak, 2006; Wellens and Borchardt, 1989), while the institutionalization of current practices entrenches the EU's internal role and scope in the area of children's rights. The protection of children's rights has now become institutionalized at the Commission level due to the actions taken by EU policy entrepreneurs and the window of opportunity provided by Eastern enlargement via the Romanian children's case (Iusmen, 2013a). What had started as a discreet external policy matter, namely the transformation of child protection in Romania, has had knock-on effects at the EU level and further shaped the scope and function of the EU regarding the protection of child rights across Europe.

Feedback effects: EU external policy dimension[18]

Children's rights have become an entrenched accession condition that is strictly monitored in the current enlargement process. Feedback effects in relation to EU external policy, i.e. enlargement policy, therefore, are substantiated in line with historical institutionalist approaches (Bulmer, 1994; Pierson, 1993, 2004; Thelen and Steinmo, 1992), according to which path-dependency and locked-in effects are observed, which amounts to policy stability and embededness as part of EU enlargement processes. Therefore, the continuation of child rights policy as an EU accession condition does not entail only the temporal dimension of policies which, due to sunk costs, are hard to roll back by rendering any attempt of reform futile, but also the potential for the variation of path-dependent process. Indeed, the employment of the child rights as an EU accession condition is anchored in the experience acquired due to the Romanian children's case, yet its application in the current candidates has widened in scope by covering a broad spectrum of issues. The diversification of child rights policy was a reaction to the distinctive problems faced by children in the current candidates.

In terms of enlargement policy, child rights are now monitored in the current candidates both under the political criteria and as part of Chapter 23 under the *acquis* criteria. The lessons learnt at the Commission level due to the Romanian case are now employed in the current candidate states, while the children's case in Romania has fed concretely into the Commission's policy template in this area, particularly with respect to the category of 'children in crisis'. Indeed, in line with the EU internal policy focus, children's rights in enlargement policy are approached from a child protection perspective, given that mostly children who experience vulnerability in economic, legal and social terms are targeted. The children's case in Romania, therefore, established the Commission's institutional approach to children's rights matters, namely an enlargement policy template. The expertise and experience acquired at the DG Enlargement level is currently employed in the accession negotiations with Western Balkans and Turkey.

Policy template

The reform of child protection in Romania has been hailed as a model that could be replicated to other countries facing similar problems.[19] The concrete stages underpinning the Romanian reform process, along with how the EU reacted to the changing circumstances on the ground via its instruments, can be applied to other countries undergoing similar shortcomings. For instance, it has been claimed that, in relation to the countries in the region such as Ukraine or Moldova that have a big inter-country adoption market and might apply for EU membership, the example of the Romanian case should be followed, namely 'these countries should be provided with EU financial assistance to develop proper child protection services and complement that in time with modern legislation on children's rights' (Post, 2007: 230). Although the costs of the reform process in Romania were substantial, they were not as significant as they would have been in the long-run had Romania not reformed its child protection. The Romanian case provided the EU with critical lessons about how to set in train the overhaul of a child protection system in line with the CRC principles.

There are more concrete guiding principles that transpired from the Romanian case regarding the revamp of child protection system. First, Romania reformed its system within a very short timeframe, which means that the reform process did not follow an incremental pattern; for instance, the new legislation on child rights was adopted after the reform process had been ongoing for some time. At the same time, second, the reform process in Romania occurred under the strict monitoring of the Commission, while significant pressure was exerted at various political and institutional levels with respect to the issue of ICA. It has been claimed that Romania has the only childcare system, among the former communist countries, that is largely compatible with the systems in the old EU Member States in terms of how children's rights are reflected by legislative and institutional frameworks.[20] For instance, former communist countries that joined the EU in 2004, such as Poland and the Czech Republic, complained that a similar support by the EU had not been provided for their child protection systems, and, as EU members, they were now stuck with unreformed and old child protection systems (Post, 2007: 233). Ultimately, the Romanian case constitutes the 'living proof' of how substantial external financial and technical assistance can provide the lynchpin for the domestic leaders to undertake radical and costly reforms.

Child protection in Bulgaria faced similar shortcomings as the one in Romania before its accession to the EU in 2007. However, children's rights were not a salient condition on Bulgaria's accession agenda in the same way as they were on Romania's. For instance, there was a large number of institutionalized children in Bulgaria and ICA from this country thrived, without being under the radar of the EU. Unlike in Romania, in 2007 there were only 135 children in foster care in Bulgaria, while 500 Bulgarian children were approved for international adoption in 2007 (European Parliament, 2009: 25). Child protection in Bulgaria had not been reformed as part of EU accession process before 2007, when both Romania and Bulgaria become EU Member States. PHARE funding was channelled towards addressing individual aspects regarding child rights in Bulgaria: for instance, a PHARE project entitled Child Welfare Reform, with €3.5 million from PHARE and the Bulgarian government co-financing €0.5 million, was implemented through twinning (between 2002 and 2004)[21] and was aimed at assisting the authorities to improve policies towards socially marginalized children (including a significant number of Roma children and children with disabilities). Other projects provided indirect support to the child protection sector in Bulgaria, such as the project Roma Population Integration (PHARE budget: €1.65 million), which sought to improve school attendance by Roma children by removing economic and cultural barriers at pre-school and primary level.[22] Despite these disjointed attempts to support the child protection sector in Bulgaria, there was no targeted action and strategic effort on the part of the Commission to thoroughly reform the child rights provision in Bulgaria. Therefore, the Bulgarian children's case, despite being assessed by the Commission, did not benefit from the same level of EU leverage and support and, above all, the extent and depth of the EU's intervention in child protection in Bulgaria was insignificant compared with the Romanian case.

The question of Bulgarian children had an impact at the EU level after 2007, when the BBC documentary about the Mogilino case triggered the Commission's reaction and debates at the EU level. The BBC documentary[23] aired in 2007 revealed the poor situation of a children's care institution in the Bulgarian village of Mogilino. The conditions in care institutions in Mogilino were appalling, and most of the children had disabilities and suffered from severe malnutrition and neglect. The Bulgarian case bore a striking resemblance to the situation of institutionalized children in Romania unearthed by Western media in the early 1990s. However, given that Bulgaria was already a Member State, the Commission could not intervene in Bulgaria's system for the protection of children with disabilities due to the lack of legal competence in this area in relation to the Member States. Yet, in reaction to the Bulgarian case, a study was commissioned, *Deinstitutionalization and Community Living – Outcomes and Costs*,[24] on the situation of institutional care for people with disabilities across Europe. According to the findings of this study, institutional care in the EU is often of unacceptable poor quality and community-based services, when properly established and managed, can deliver better outcomes in terms of quality of life and enable people with disabilities to live as full citizens.

Child protection in Bulgaria had not undergone the same radical reform as the Romanian one had before 2007. Indeed, the vast majority of Bulgarian children in institutions had disabilities (Mihova *et al.*, 2008) and were particularly exposed to widespread discrimination and risk of social exclusion after leaving institutional care (Bogdanov and Zahariev, 2007). Furthermore, foster care and community-based social services were scarce and underdeveloped and, by 2007, Bulgaria had one of the highest number of institutionalized children in Europe (Mihova *et al.*, 2008), unlike its Northern neighbour, Romania, where the number of institutionalized children had started dropping significantly since the early 2000s. The 'root-and-branch' reform of child protection in Bulgaria had only started in late 2007, and to this end, the de-institutionalization of children constitutes the key policy objective of the Bulgaria National Strategy for the Child, 2008–2018, which also includes the development of community-based care by local authorities (Ministry of Labour and Social Policy, 2008). The principles and reform template employed in the Romanian case have been applied to child protection in Bulgaria after 2007, but within the context of EU internal policy dimension. The Bulgarian government's commitment to reform child protection after 2007 benefited from EU financial support via EU Structural Funds and consequently, through careful prioritization, the country was successful in advancing children's rights and in reforming its system. For instance, the number of children in residential care institutions dropped by over 40 per cent in terms of the rate of one hundred thousand child population between 2001 and 2010, while from 2007 to 2012 the number of foster families increased tenfold (UNICEF, 2012: 3). Additionally, in 2010 for the first time after Bulgaria had become an EU member, more children at risk were placed in alternative family care than in residential care, due to the availability of preventive child protection services (UNICEF, 2012). In the Bulgarian case, therefore, the reform process followed the same pattern as in Romania before 2007, yet with less EU leverage to intervene in the overhaul of the child protection system. Hence, the Bulgarian case brought to the fore the unevenness of EU intervention to reform the child protection of the former communist states: while the Romanian children's case received unparalleled attention and support from the EU, the child protection in Bulgaria did not benefit from the EU's accession leverage and, hence, the reform of this policy sector lagged behind. Bulgaria and Romanian faced similar problems in their child protection systems, yet EU accession conditionality in relation to this policy sector led to distinctive outcomes in practice: an overhauled child protection system in Romania before EU accession; whilst in Bulgaria, childcare system still bore the communist blueprint even in 2008.

The de-institutionalization of children is one of the policy objectives pursed by the Commission in relation to the current candidates and potential candidates. The closure of large institutions and the development of alternative care services, including community-based, constitute the guidelines for the reform of child protection, which had initially been established in relation to the Romanian case. For instance, in Turkey the Commission is supporting initiatives aimed at the creation of a community-based care approach (European Commission, 2011a), while in Montenegro and Serbia foster- and community-based care are insufficiently developed (European Commission, 2011c, 2011d). The Commission employed the same 'child protection reform' template as in the Romanian case and, therefore, demanded the de-institutionalization of children, the creation of alternative care services and the provision of EU financial support, specifically geared towards assisting the reform process. Additionally, the Commission has been supporting financially staff training and awareness campaigns of child rights and CRC, which again mirrors the reform pattern applied initially in the Romanian case. In brief, the policy template created as a result of the Romanian case covers particularly the situation of 'children in crisis', such as the plight of children in care homes, encompassing the key stages and principles underpinning the reform process in this sector.

The Romanian reform model has been replicated via children's NGOs and charities. For instance, the 'Children's High Level Group' – a charity co-founded and co-chaired by Emma Nicholson and children's author J. K. Rowling in 2005 – promotes child welfare and children's rights all over Europe. The Children's High Level Group promotes the Romanian child protection model to neighbouring countries, such as Bulgaria, Moldova, Ukraine or Russia, which face the same problems in their child protection systems as the ones faced by Romania in the 1990s.[25] For instance, according to J. K. Rowling, 'Romania is a model for other countries hoping to reform ... Romania was the state that acknowledged there was a problem and set out to do something about it' (Rowling, quoted in National Authority for the Protection of Child's Rights, 2006: 24). Apart from promoting the Romanian child welfare model externally, Children's High Level Group Romania

– established in 2006 – works with the Romanian government, and particularly with the National Authority for the Protection of Child's Rights, on the development of projects and activities aimed at promoting child welfare.[26] Thus, Emma Nicholson continues the work she had started – initially as the EP's rapporteur for Romania – regarding the protection of children's rights on a different level, via her charity, and in relation to other countries. The Children's High Level Group assisted the Romanian government to develop a strategy to prevent the abandonment of babies in hospitals and provided the Romanian authorities with an assessment of institutions for children with disabilities, which was the first assessment of its kind in Romania (Children's High Level Group, 2007). For instance, the *Report on Disabled Children in Romania* (2007) highlights the lack of specialist therapists, training and staffing, while it stresses the progress achieved in this area, namely the transformations of institutions into small, modern, family-type units, which have access to qualified medical staff (Children's High Level Group, 2007: 36). Additionally, according to the report's findings, the majority of disabled children in Romania live with their families and it is only a small minority who live in residential institutions (Children's High Level Group, 2007). Thus, the Children's High Level Group assisted the Romanian government to assess institutions for children with disability and handicaps and to develop strategies to improve care provisions (Children's High Level Group, n.d.). To cut a long story short, the Romanian children's case provided a policy template of how to reform child protection, and this reform template is currently being employed by both the EU and non-governmental actors. The key features of this policy template are the ones that initially guided the reform process in Romania, namely the de-institutionalization of children simultaneously with the creation of alternative care services focusing on child abandonment, the employment of a bottom-up approach via the inclusion of local community and authorities in the provision of childcare services and, above all, the employment of the CRC provisions to guide changes on the ground.

Children's rights as part of EU accession acquis

The weight attached to human rights in the current accession negotiations process transpires from the re-structuring of the negotiating chapters under the *acquis* section. For instance, a new *acquis* Chapter was created in 2005 – Chapter 23 on 'Judiciary and Fundamental Rights'- and human rights are now monitored and assessed both under this chapter and under the political criteria. It is widely contended that at Frattini's initiative, given his portfolio covering justice and fundamental rights matters, child rights were included in the *acquis* criteria starting with 2007, which formalized this policy sector as an accession condition.[27] The rationale behind the inclusion of children's rights into the *acquis* section was based on the experience of the Romanian children's case: with the new candidates the Commission had to ensure that it had more legal tools and leverage to address child-related matters before candidates would join the Union. Indeed, according to a Commission official, 'one of the lessons learnt was that we need to do more on fundamental rights issues, we have to raise them earlier in order to ensure that the pre-accession process and the pre-accession phase are really used to improve the situation and that we also need more instruments in order to go into details'.[28] The inclusion of human rights issues in the *acquis* section of the Progress Reports illustrates the importance attached to human rights within the current enlargement process.

According to Commission officials, one of the most striking evidence of feedback effect generated by the Romanian children's case on EU enlargement policy is the formalization of the child rights issues monitored as part of the *acquis* criteria. Chapter 23 scrutinizes some human rights areas, including children's rights, which are also still examined in the political section of the Progress Reports. Thus, according to DG Enlargement officials, child protection and children's rights are now monitored both within the Chapter 23 context – as part of fundamental rights in the *acquis* section – and under the political criteria. The decision to apply stricter conditionality to children's rights as part of an *acquis* chapter was the outcome of the Romanian case, where, at times, the pace of the reform in child protection jeopardized the accession negotiations with the EU. The monitoring of children's rights within the *acquis* context involves two aspects. First, the Commission has greater leverage to put pressure on current candidate states, because the Commission can issue benchmarks for opening and closing chapters, which is an important instrument for the Commission during accession negotiations. Second, the evaluation of progress is more straightforward and has become more institutionalized and structured, given that the Commission has now the necessary expertise and practical knowledge acquired due to the Romanian children's case.

The approach of DG Enlargement to children's rights in EU enlargement policy was strongly developed through the accession process of Romania, although the policy is widely adjusted to the local circumstances of candidate states. How to promote effectively CRC principles via EU accession tools constitutes one of many guiding lessons learnt due to the Romanian case. The lessons learnt and experience accumulated at the Commission level due to children's rights case in Romania are now employed in the accession negotiations with the current candidate countries, although it is deemed that the protection of children's rights in these countries is not as deplorable as it was in Romania. More concretely, in terms of institutional structures now there are task managers on children's rights in the European Commission Delegations – a position created for the first time in relation to child rights in Romania – assessing the children's rights provision in the current candidate countries.

The role and function of a children's rights task manager has been defined and determined by the know-how and experience accumulated due to the Commission's intervention in the Romanian case. EU financial instruments, such as the Instrument for Pre-Accession Assistance (IPA), are specifically channelled to assist local authorities with the reform of the child protection system. Furthermore, the employment of benchmarks in relation to children's rights and the inclusion of this human rights area in the *acquis* section amount to the formalization and further enhancement of the Commission's role regarding the promotion of the rights of the child in the EU's external dimension. These EU enlargement effects underscore the path-dependent aspect of child rights in EU accession process and also signal the further institutional development elements (Pierson, 2004: 15); for instance, the establishment of specific institutional structures to target children's rights. Of course, these developments increase the visibility of the Commission's involvement with children's rights matters in non-EU countries. There has been an incremental acceptance and normalization of the normative role played by the Commission in the protection of children's rights in the EU enlargement process. Taking all these into account, therefore, it can be argued that there has been institutional development at the Commission level in relation to this policy area: the Commission's clout and role in this area have significantly augmented due to the feedback effects of the Romanian case.

Children's rights in the current enlargement process

Children's rights are now monitored and assessed in all candidate and potential candidate countries. The principles guiding EU intervention in child rights as part of enlargement policy had been developed in relation to the Romanian case, yet they have to be adapted to the situation on the ground in the current candidates. By employing the main instruments at its disposal, namely the ECHR, the CRC and the EU Charter of Fundamental Rights,[29] the Commission's child rights enlargement policy has become wider in scope and more complex. In other words, the Commission, via the accession conditionality, attempts to ensure the candidates' compliance with the CRC and, therefore, aims to redress the Convention's legal anomaly (Stalford and Drywood, 2011: 204), namely its weak legal enforceability. Yet, it should be noted that the range of shortcomings encountered in the child protection systems of current candidates varies significantly and, therefore, the Commission adjusts its policy instruments and demands to the situation on the ground. While the specific children's rights issues that arise in each country may differ, in all candidates children's rights feature most prominently in the sections of the Progress Reports relating to the political criteria. Given the broad scope of the accession negotiations, the children's rights deficits identified in the candidates usually bear no correspondence to areas in which the EU has specific competence to enact legal or policy measures (Stalford, 2012). In brief, the protection of children's rights constitutes now a *sine qua non* accession condition in the current enlargement process.

The current enlargement process has seen a thematic assessment of the child rights provision in the candidate states. The extent to which rights are protected in certain fundamental sectors, along with the key institutional and legislative structures in place, are widely examined in the Commission's Progress Reports. The main recurrent thematic sectors are related to education (access and treatment within), institutionalized care, juvenile justice, poverty, health and Roma children. For instance, the de-institutionalization of children is mentioned in the majority of Progress Reports (European Commission, 2011a–e), while the template of child protection reform – a clear reminder of the Romanian case – highlights the need to prevent child abandonment via the development of alternative community-based services. The discrimination faced by children, based on gender, disability, nationality and ethnicity in compulsory education, is prevalent in the monitoring of all candidate countries. The discrimination of Roma children, an issue also addressed in the Romanian case, is particularly singled out in Turkey, Former Yugoslav Republic of Macedonia (FYROM) and Croatia. In Turkey, for instance, child poverty and child labour constitute huge and complex problems, which are also interlinked to cases of discrimination (European Commission, 2011a). Turkey's Progress Reports make more substantial references to children's rights than any other candidate. The overarching emphasis in Turkey's Reports is on juvenile justice, particularly regarding the outlawing of criminal responsibility of children implicated in terrorist crime (European Commission, 2011a: 34). The Commission has funded under IPA projects targeting child labour in Turkey. For instance, the EU-funded *Project for Eradicating the Worst Forms of Child Labour* [30] provides approximately three thousand children and their families with education, rehabilitation and support services. Other new themed areas under which child rights are scrutinized are violence and exploitation, including tackling domestic violence against children (Turkey, Montenegro and Serbia); child labour and begging, particularly in a migration and trafficking context (Turkey, FYROM, Montenegro and Serbia), sexual abuse and paedophilia (FYROM) and enhanced identification of child victims (Montenegro). Child rights matters are assessed as part of most of the *acquis* chapters: for instance, child labour and child poverty (Chapter 19 – Social Policy and Employment); children as asylum-seekers or unaccompanied minors (Chapter 24 – Justice, Freedom and Security); juvenile justice (Chapter 23 – Judiciary and Fundamental Rights); inclusive education, Roma children (Chapter 26 – Education and Culture); or children with disabilities or mental illness (Chapter 28 – Consumer and Health Protection).

The current enlargement process has seen a significant focus on the legislative and institutional deficiencies regarding children's rights provision in the current candidates. The Commission's monitoring process has become extremely detailed with regards to the institutional and legislative changes enacted by candidates in areas relevant to children. A new emphasis has emerged regarding the candidates' constitutional provisions on human rights and child rights: for instance, the Commission evaluates positively whether children's rights are enshrined in national constitutions (European Commission, 2011a–e). Along the same lines, an explicit focus is placed on the institutional mechanisms, including children's Ombudsmen and governmental child rights agencies, along with national legislation and strategies in line with the CRC principles. The Commission's evaluation of child rights provision has become more sophisticated and complex as now aspects related to constitutional provisions, primary law and institutional settings are thoroughly assessed by Commission officials. Therefore, the Commission now knows where to look and what to look for and, often, its assessment of the situation at local level reflects the CRC Committee's own evaluation. Unlike the CRC Committee, however, the Commission, by deploying the accession conditionality, has more extensive leverage to enact changes that go beyond paper provisions. In other words, the Commission is an indirect 'agent' promoting the legal enforcement and compliance with the CRC by ensuring that the necessary 'structures' – laws, institutions and policies – are in place to achieve this.

Conclusion

The EU's intervention in child protection in Romania has had unforeseen consequences on the EU's internal and external engagement with children's rights. Inside the Union, the Romanian case acted as a catalyst in pushing children's rights onto the Commission policy agenda, while in EU enlargement policy, child rights have become an entrenched accession condition. As the evidence provided in this chapter demonstrates, the emergence of feedback effects in areas where the EU has limited mandate requires a set of propitious conditions to render possible processes of policy innovation and development. Feedback effects can take various forms, but in this case they generated the emergence of new policy mechanisms and institutional structures or, in the case of enlargement policy, they amounted to the entrenchment and stability of the already existing policy and institutional structures. As has been shown here, policy entrepreneurs can have a galvanizing function in forging policy change at the EU level.

Notes

1   See Case 65/81 *Reina and Reina* [1982] ECR 33; Case 94/84 *Deak* [1985] ECR 1773; Case 7/94 *Lubor Gaal* [1996] ECR 1031; Case 85/98 *Sala* [1998] ECR 2691.
2   Some of the sections here have been published in Iusmen, I. (2013a) 'Policy Entrepreneurship and Eastern Enlargement: the Case of EU Children's Rights Policy', *Comparative European Politics*, 11(4), 511–529.
3   Author's interview with a Commission official in DG EMPL, September 2011, Brussels.
4   One of the objectives of the Hague Programme was to enhance 'the common capability of the Union and its Member States to guarantee fundamental rights' (European Council, 2004: 4).
5   Author's interview with Commission officials in DG EMPL and DG Justice, July 2011, Brussels.
6   Author's interview with Commission officials in DG EMPL and DG Justice, September 2011, Brussels.
7   Marc Dutroux kidnapped, tortured and sexually abused six girls (ranging in age from 8 to 19) from 1995 to 1996, four of whom he murdered.
8   Author's interview with Commission officials in DG Enlargement and DG JLS, May 2008, Brussels.
9   Author's interview with Commission officials in DG Enlargement, Brussels, May 2009.
10 Author's interviews with Commission officials involved in the Romanian children's case, DG ELARG, and Commission officials in DG JLS, May and September 2008, Brussels.
11 Author's interview with a Commission official in DG Enlargement, May 2008, Brussels.
12 Author's interview with Baroness Emma Nicholson, EP rapporteur for Romania, May 2008, Brussels.
13 Author's interview with a Commission official in DG EMPL, July 2011, Brussels.
14 Author's interview with a Commission official in DG EMPL, Brussels, September 2008.
15 As a Commission official put it, 'the preoccupations of the EU in the internal policy are different from the preoccupations of the EU in the external policy. By basing ourselves on the principles of the CRC, both the internal and external dimensions can reflect their consensus and the policies they develop. You say "protect children", but internally it means providing parents with the adequate means to be able to raise their children, providing access to education etc. For the external dimension "protecting children" means protecting them in armed conflicts, even providing them with the right to be registered when they are born. So we can cover under the same title many different aspects.' Author's interview with a Commission official in DG EMPL, Brussels, September 2008.
16 'Children shall have the right to such protection and care as is necessary for their well-being. They may express their views freely. Such views shall be taken into consideration on matters which concern them in accordance with their age and maturity.

In all actions relating to children, whether taken by public authorities or private institutions, the child's best interests must be a primary consideration.

Every child shall have the right to maintain on a regular basis a personal relationship and direct contact with both his/her parents, unless that is contrary to his or her interests'(Article 24).

17 'It [the EU] shall combat social exclusion and discrimination, and shall promote social justice and protection, equality between women and men, solidarity between generations and *protection of the rights of the child* ... In its relations with the wider world, the Union shall uphold and promote its values and interests and contribute to the protection of its citizens. It shall contribute to peace, security, the sustainable development of the Earth, solidarity and mutual respect among peoples, free and fair trade, eradication of poverty and the protection of human rights, in particular the *rights of the child*, as well as to the strict observance and the development of international law, including respect for the principles of the United Nations Charter' (emphases added, Article 3 TEU).

18 Some of the sections here have been published in Iusmen, I. (2012b) 'Romania's Accession to the EU and EU Children's Rights Agenda: Policy Entrepreneurship and Feedback Effects', *Perspectives on European Politics and Society*, 13 (2), 210–225.

19 Author's interview with a Commission official in the Romania team, DG Enlargement, Brussels, May 2008.

20 Author's interview with the secretary of state for the Romanian Office for Adoptions, Bucharest, July 2008.

21 *Official Journal of the European Union*, C 88 E/434, 8.4.2004.

22 *Official Journal of the European Union*, C 88 E/434, 8.4.2004.

23 The BBC documentary was titled 'Bulgaria's Abandoned Children'. The Mogilino children's institution finally closed on the 11th of October 2009 following further pressure from the BBC and EU.

24 Mansell J., Knapp M., Beadle-Brown J. and Beecham J. (2007) *Deinstitutionalization and Community Living – Outcomes and Costs: Report of a European Study* (Canterbury: Tizard Centre, University of Kent).

25 Author's interview with Emma Nicholson, the EP's rapporteur for Romania, Brussels, May 2008.

26 Author's interview the project manager for Children's Rights High Level Group–Romania, Bucharest, July 2008.

27 Author's interview with a Commission official, DG Enlargement, Brussels, July 2011.

28 Author's interview with a Commission official, DG Enlargement, Brussels, May 2008.

29 The ECHR, the CRC and the Charter of Fundamental Rights also constitute the main sources of children's rights at the EU level (Stalford, 2012: 31).

30 The project (worth €5.3 million) was implemented between November 2005 and November 2007 by ILO, while the beneficiary was the Turkish Ministry of Labour and Social Security.

5

Drivers of change, policy entrepreneurship and the institutionalization of children's rights

The joining of the three separate streams (problems, policies, politics) ... depends heavily on the appearance of the right entrepreneur at the right time.

(Kingdon, 1984: 213)

Introduction

The European Union's (EU) application of human rights conditionality in relation to child protection in Romania had feedback effects on the EU's own children's rights provision. Yet, the empirical evidence supporting this claim raises crucial analytical questions about the mechanisms of feedback effects, the push-and-pull factors and the role of entrepreneurial actions undertaken by EU actors, in essence: what are the drivers of change? This chapter provides an analytical overview of the explanatory factors accounting for the feedback effects triggered by the Romanian children's case. Two sets of factors are presented: *structural* and *agency* related. In terms of the contextual or structural conditions, the salience attached to human rights in the Eastern enlargement process sowed the seeds for broader propitious – political and institutional – conditions for addressing human rights matters more robustly inside the Union. Apart from these favourable circumstances, the availability of EU entrepreneurs, i.e. agency-related factors, to take advantage of these propitious opportunities made a substantial difference to the emergence of feedback effects. Kingdon's (1984) model of multiple streams coupling is employed to explain the emergence of children's rights as an issue on EU internal policy agenda. Both the EU's propitious context and the entrepreneurship of EU actors provide insights into broader EU processes by demonstrating how the enlargement of the EU is intimately linked with the trajectory and scope of European integration by affecting irreversibly the normative principles and values of the EU, what the EU is and does. The feedback effects are analysed by employing a historical institutionalist lens (in EU external policy dimension) and processes of policy entrepreneurship and 'EU-topianization' (in EU internal policy dimension). The last section of this chapter demonstrates that children's rights have become institutionalized at the EU level after 2006.

Drivers of change: context, conditions, entrepreneurs

The sections below provide the analytical narrative underpinning the feedback effects in relation to the EU internal policy sphere described in Chapter 4. With respect to these feedback effects, the main drivers of change involve contextual factors and the pro-active role played by policy entrepreneurs at the EU level. It is argued, therefore, that entrepreneurs always operate in a certain setting, one that can either facilitate or constrain their entrepreneurial initiatives. Eastern enlargement has created favourable conditions for the emergence of a more robust human rights agenda at the EU level. At the same time, specific factors pertaining to children's rights and in line with Kingdon's model of multiple streams coupling facilitated the emergence of entrepreneurial actions by EU actors which led to the establishment of children's rights as an overarching EU policy issue.

EU context: favourable factors

There are broad contextual factors, along with specific conditions (discussed in the section on 'Policy entrepreneurship' below), that contributed to the emergence of feedback effects inside the Union. These broad conditions involve the salience attached to human rights within the Eastern enlargement process, the emergence of a human rights script at the level of EU institutions and the perception that the violation of human rights is also a matter recurrent in the Member States. Therefore, these processes generated a favourable institutional and political context for the emergence of new human rights matters and initiatives on the EU's policy agenda. Put simply, the advancement of human rights matters in the Eastern candidates has left its mark on the EU institutions' scope and remit in relation to human rights.

Eastern enlargement has been conceived and advanced as a normative project of re-joining the two 'Europes' – Western and Eastern – divided by an ideological Iron Curtain for more than 50 years. The EU's normative endeavour, likened by some to a '*mission civilisatrice*' (Zielonka, 2011), involved the promotion of those principles and values, such as liberal and democratic norms, that have formed the fabric of the European project since its inception in the early 1950s. Indeed, given the rule-based community organization characteristics of the EU, membership decisions are based on collective identity, common values and social norms (Schimmelfennig, 2003: 89). Schimmelfennig convincingly illustrated how and why the 'rhetorical action' – the strategic use of norm-based arguments by EU institutions

– resulted in the 'rhetorical entrapment' of those Member States that opposed EU enlargement, as they felt obliged to behave in a certain way to preserve their credibility as community members (Schimmelfennig, 2001). Along the same lines, it is argued here, the EU's interventionist policy in the human rights provision of the Central and Eastern European Countries (CEECs) generated what could be described as 'normative entrapment', namely the establishment of an EU role in the promotion of certain human rights norms externally, which implicitly has had unintended consequences for the EU's internal involvement with those human rights norms. Therefore, the Commission's intrusive human rights conditionality, as part of the enlarge- ment process, yielded a propitious context for the emergence of human rights initiatives at the EU level. The contention that joining the EU is congruous with respect for a broad spectrum of human rights entailed that the EU had to live up internally to the expectations it advanced externally, namely to Eastern candidates. Meanwhile, the European publics and even the Member States became aware not only of the scale of human rights violations in the former communist states, but also of the human rights deficiencies inside the Union, which underscored the urgency of EU action to support Member States' efforts in addressing them. Despite the EU's 'lack of competence' mantra, the institutional and political contexts were propitious for the EU's, partic- ularly the Commission's, adoption of bold actions to promote human rights, even if the key instruments were soft law and, therefore, non-binding legisla- tive measures.

The EU's normative entrapment in relation to human rights is even more persuasive if the breadth and depth of the EU's intervention in the CEECs' national human rights provision is assessed. For instance, Storey (1995) has distinguished the European approach towards the prospective members along two human rights axes: minimalist–maximalist and conditionalist– non-conditionalist. The first axis refers to the type of human rights catalogue – in terms of its inclusiveness and specification – employed by the EU; while the second axis highlights whether the level of human rights observance in a given country should be a condition for political decisions or economic assis- tance. Therefore, while the 'minimalist' position stands for the recognition of 'fundamental principles that can be met with the consensus of all people across all boundaries of culture, politics, religion and levels of economic and social development', the 'maximalist' position illustrates 'a universal system of norms that should progressively expand and reshape itself to take account of every new social and technological innovations' (Storey, 1995: 133–134). The 'maximalists', therefore, argue for a detailed human rights catalogue, which cuts across cultural and political differences of states, and which amounts to an intrusive policy of conditionality in relation to a wide set of human rights sectors. As the human rights conditionality applied to CEECs demonstrates, the EU applied both a maximalist and conditionalist policy regarding the human rights demands that Eastern candidates had to meet before accession. Therefore, this human rights interventionist policy indicated that the protection of human rights constitutes one of the building blocks of the EU and, subsequently, that EU institutions had to embrace their role of upholding rights also inside the Union.

The EU's constitutional reforms and the enlargement process in the early 2000s seem to have unfolded separately, although human rights norms and principles underpinned both processes. However, there is evidence that Eastern enlargement influenced the process of European constitutionalisation (Weiss, 2005) as the two processes developed mutual inter-linkages. Indeed, accession states were allowed to participate in the Convention on the Future of Europe meetings (2001–2003), and, therefore, could influence the content of the Draft Constitution, although their leverage was less significant than that of the Member States (Walker, 2003: 381). Given the variety of human rights systems across Europe, particularly in Eastern Europe after 50 years of communist rule, the CEECs' inputs into the debates preceding the adoption of the Constitutional Treaty were widely welcomed. Therefore, accession states made contributions to the Charter of Fundamental Rights and the Draft Constitution, a fact proven by the attempts of Poland to change some parts of the Draft Constitution (Weiss, 2005: 3). Hence, there are clear inter-linkages between the EU's ongoing attempts to boost human rights protection inside the Union and the Eastern enlargement process.

The late 1990s and early 2000s saw an emergent appeal to human rights norms and values as part of the EU's constitutional 'soul searching', which led to the adoption of the EU Charter of Fundamental Rights and the doomed Constitutional Treaty. For instance, the process preceding the adoption of the Constitutional Treaty, namely the Convention on the Future of Europe (2001–2003) framework, also saw the extensive participation of civil society actors, human rights organizations and various human rights stakeholders in the consultations regarding the future constitutional framework of the Union. A greater institutional openness to input from various actors was the outcome of the Commission's *White Paper on European Governance* (2001), which explicitly prioritized the participation of civil society actors as key conditions for the Union's legitimacy. Yet, civil society organizations pushed for the EU's more robust role in human rights, signalling that the EU's constitutional reshuffle has to accommodate better economic objectives with human rights commitments (Lombardo, 2003). Indeed, the unprecedented openness of the Convention which included the participation of and contributions from a wide range of human rights non-governmental organizations (NGOs), meant that civil society actors could have a significant level of input into the drafting stages of the Charter (De Schutter, 2002). Therefore, at the time of the Eastern enlargement process, the EU was undergoing a substantial constitutional makeover, which brought to the fore the EU's attachment to values such as human rights, civil society participation or minority protection, to name just a few. Human rights matters emerged on the EU agenda as part of both EU internal constitutional debates and pre-accession negotiations with the CEECs. In sum, it is argued here that, due to the processes described above, a propitious context at the EU level took shape for the initiation of new measures and developments aimed at upholding human rights inside the Union.

Policy entrepreneurs[1]

Policy entrepreneurs are the main drivers of policy change and therefore the key shapers of EU agenda. Several definitions and roles have been ascribed in the literature to institutional entrepreneurship (e.g. Di Maggio, 1988; Fligstein, 2001), political entrepreneurship (Lopez, 2002), public entrepreneurship (e.g. Dahl, 1991; Ostrom, 2005; Schnellenbach, 2007) and policy entrepreneurship (e.g. Kingdon, 1984; Schneider *et al.*, 1995; Roberts and King, 1991). Here the focus is on the role of policy entrepreneurs in setting the EU agenda from above (Princen, 2007, 2009). Due to its ability to shape the EU policy agenda, usually the Commission, as an institution, has been described as a 'policy entrepreneur' (Sandholtz and Zysman, 1989: 96) or as a 'purposeful opportunist' (Cram, 1994: 201). Indeed, the concept of policy entrepreneurship is often applied to the European Commission (EC) (Pollack, 1997; Cram, 1997), whereby the Commission is described as a policy entrepreneur capable of exploiting the resources at its own disposal in order to generate new policies that are acceptable to various coalitions of Member States. Entrepreneurs usually play a key role in the creation and promotion of international norms (Checkel, 2001), whereby norms generally entail shared expectations about appropriate behaviour held by a collectivity of actors (Checkel, 1999; Weissert, 1991). The advancement of norms by entrepreneurs has been envisaged according to a 'life cycle' metaphor (Finnemore and Sikkink, 1998) consisting of three stages: the production of norms ('norm emergence'), the evolution of norms ('norm cascades') and their implementation ('norm internalization'). This norm evolution model can explain the application of human rights conditions, especially children's rights, to candidate countries by the Commission. Therefore, the EU's role as a norm entrepreneur involves the development and promotion of international norms in the global arena, norms which will then cascade down to the domestic level and consolidate. Of course, norm advancement does not occur randomly and it requires the emergence of the right entrepreneur to undertake policy innovation actions.

Policy entrepreneurs – either individuals or organizations – refer to 'advocates for proposals or for prominence of ideas' (Kingdon, 1984: 122). Entrepreneurs, here understood as individuals acting in specific institutional settings, possess the capacity to mobilize resources and develop proactive strategies to expand influence in certain policy spheres (McCowan, 2005). Entrepreneurship in children's rights necessitates persistent endeavour to develop and actively promote measures and principles inspired by the UN Convention on the Rights of the Child (CRC), the main normative yardstick in this area. As shown in Chapter 3, adoption lobbies got the plight of institutionalized children onto Romania's accession agenda; however, the Commission and, particularly, the EP's rapporteur for Romania (Emma Nicholson) re-framed (Rein and Schön, 1994) the plight of institutionalized children as a children's rights matter. Within the enlargement context, policy entrepreneurs, such as Emma Nicholson and the Commissioner for Enlargement (Günter Verheugen), seized the window of opportunity provided by the inclusion of institutionalized children onto Romania's accession agenda to attach an anti-intercountry adoption (anti-ICA) solution to it and thus to extend the Commission's scope and remit in the regulation of ICA from Romania via the promotion of a rights-based approach. Child rights entrepreneurship within the enlargement context, however, was not constrained by EU competence limitations. The entrepreneurship of Commissioner Verheugen and Baroness Nicholson allowed the extension of EU mandate to address child rights matters as part of EU enlargement policy, which later on had far-reaching repercussions for the EU's internal approach to child rights.

Kingdon's (1984) model of multiple streams coupling, which is employed here, pays heed to both structure and agency-related factors to explain policy innovation via entrepreneurship. Policy entrepreneurs take advantage of the available windows of opportunity to initiate policy change and, therefore, policy entrepreneurship in relation to human rights at the EU level entails favourable conditions facilitating entrepreneurial actions, given the EU's limited mandate in human rights, including child rights, in relation to the Member States. Feedback effects in EU internal policy, as outcomes of actions taken be policy entrepreneurs, are illustrated persuasively by Kingdon's (1984) model of multiple streams coupling, which provides the explanatory framework for the process of policy feedback – as policy development – described in Chapter 4. Kingdon's (1984: 191) model analyses policy process as a function of three streams providing contextual factors, namely *problems*, *policies* and *politics*, which are joined together by agents or policy entrepreneurs to forge policy change. As described in Chapter 1, the three streams flow independently of each other, yet the pro-active role played by the policy entrepreneur can seize a window of opportunity to couple the three streams together via policy innovation. Therefore, the policy window provides 'an opportunity for advocates of proposals to push their pet solutions or to push attention to their special problems' (Kingdon, 1984: 173). At the same time, a policy window highlights the available opportunities for action in certain policy areas, although it tends to stay open for only a short period (Kingdon, 1984: 174). Windows can also open in the problems or politics streams, however, they do not stay open long (Kingdon, 1984: 213) and hence, the convergence of the three streams to advance a new policy issue is largely dependent on 'the appearance of the right entrepreneur at the right time' (Kingdon, 1984: 214).

Kingdon's model, which explains agenda-setting as the outcome of policy entrepreneurship, employed evidence from American politics and, therefore, it needs adjusting to the EU's specific institutional context and policy-making process. Institutionally, the Commission is strategically positioned to set the EU agenda – given the Commission's Treaty role as the EU's agenda-setter – while with respect to the policy process, the EU's lack of competence in human rights shapes the type of action that EU institutions can take regarding human rights matters. Kingdon's model, as adapted to EU institutional structure and 'bifurcated' human rights policy (Williams, 2000, 2004), provides the explanatory framework for Frattini's entrepreneurship regarding children's rights inside the Union, which was discussed in Chapter 4. In this case, the *problems* stream entails a shared perception across Europe that child rights are violated also within the Union and, therefore, that EU action is needed to provide a supranational effort to tackle the problems faced by children (Ruxton, 2005). Stakeholder reports and studies, along with the media coverage of Marc Dutroux's case and the case of missing children, Nathalie Mahy and Stacy Lemmens, generated public outcry at the failure of national authorities in dealing with cases of child abduction and abuse. At the same time, the Romanian children's case had generated unprecedented public outrage due to images showing the conditions in Romanian orphanages, yet it was widely perceived across Europe that child abuse and violation of child rights were hurdles primarily faced by countries from the former communist bloc. The child abuse cases mentioned above and stakeholders' advocacy for EU action in relation to children's plight inside the Union underscored the fact that child rights cannot amount only to an export product, primarily promoted to candidate countries.

There had also been solutions attempted by the Commission in the *policies* stream before the Romanian children's case became a hot topic on the EU's agenda. As shown in Chapter 4, the Commission endeavoured to develop a child rights policy in the EU internal dimension under the leadership of DG Employment, Social Affairs and Inclusion (EMPL) in the mid 1990s. For instance, under the Demography programme, child-related matters were addressed as part of gender equality and employment policies. However, the context was not favourable for the development of an overarching EU child rights policy and, subsequently, at Member States' behest, DG EMPL had to curtail its initiatives in the area of children's rights due to a lack of legal mandate in the Treaties. At the same time, children's rights had been included in some of the key policy documents guiding EU relations with third countries, such as *The European Union's Role in Promoting Human rights and Democratisation in Third Countries* (2001) and *EU Guidelines on Children and Armed Conflict* (2003). In the context of EU external policy, DG RELEX had been advancing children's rights as part of its development and human right promotion policies with non-EU countries since the early 2000s. Inside the EU, however, child rights policy was lagging behind and, therefore, different Commission services, such as DG Education and Culture (EAC) and DG EMPL, were competing to embrace the ownership of the Commission's children's rights policy.[2] In other words, there was an increasing gap between the EU's external and internal actions related to child rights. Therefore, the competing policy solutions 'floating around' (Kingdon, 1984) in the policies stream amounted to how the new policy area should be framed by Commission services, and, subsequently, which Commission DG should endorse the ownership for its development. As shown in Chapter 4, the then Commissioner for Freedom, Security and Justice Franco Frattini was strategically positioned to advance child rights as an internal policy sector mainly steered from within the Area of Freedom, Security and Justice (AFSJ) framework by DG JLS, now DG Justice.

The *politics* stream, or the favourable political conditions that can facilitate policy innovation (Kingdon, 1984), include the broader contextual factors described in the first section of this chapter. Yet, as highlighted in Chapter 4, there were specific EU internal political factors that contributed to policy development processes. Having been adopted by the Member States under the Dutch Presidency, the Hague Programme (2004–2009) made no reference to children's rights, apart from the broad commitment to enhance the protection of fundamental rights inside the Union. Despite this, the first mention of children's rights as an area of EU internal policy was in the Action Plan (2005) regarding the implementation of the Hague Programme (Council of the European Union, 2005), whereby the Commission proposed to address child rights within the EU context, which was widely welcomed by the Member States. At the same time, the ongoing controversies surrounding the legislative solution adopted in relation to the Romanian case generated a favourable political context for the adoption of a bold and clear EU position and action plan regarding children's rights inside the Union. Romania's anticipated accession to the EU in 2007 and the controversy generated by its moratorium on ICA further augmented the salience acquired by children's rights at the EU level. Therefore, the Romanian case opened a window of opportunity in the politics stream, particularly due to the conflicting approaches adopted by the key EU institutions in relation to it. For instance, the entry into force of the new Romanian legislation in 2005, which maintained the ban on ICA, generated disagreement both at the Commission and Parliament's levels. It was Commissioner Frattini, however, who was well placed to seize these opportunities provided by the Romanian case and facilitated by the broader EU political and institutional context. Commissioner Frattini was fully committed to making child rights the flagship objective of the AFSJ.[3] Indeed, the normative impact of Frattini's public statements and speeches regarding children emphasizes his institutional commitment to taking firm action on child rights, on the one hand, but also his desire to have his name associated with this policy area, on the other. To this end, Frattini developed a role for the Commission as a child rights actor advancing 'the full promotion of children's rights and zero tolerance of violation of these rights' (Frattini, 2008). Indeed, the controversies stirred by the Romanian case opened windows that presented 'opportunities for the complete linkage of problems, proposals and politics, and hence opportunities to move packages of the three joined elements up on a decision agenda' (Kingdon, 1984: 213). More concretely, Frattini's coupling of the three streams engendered the emergence of child rights as an issue on the EU's internal policy agenda (Iusmen, 2013a), as evidenced by the adoption of the Communication *Towards an EU Strategy on the Rights of the Child* in 2006. In short, Frattinin was the right entrepreneur at the right time that could take full advantage of the propitious context at the EU level and, therefore, could 'strike while the iron was hot'.

The incremental development of a child rights agenda and policy initiatives at the Commission level confirm the relevance of Finnemore and Sikkink's (1998) 'life cycle' metaphor to explain norm evolution. As shown in Chapter 4, now the Commission has a fully fledged child rights agenda as part of the Stockholm Programme (2009–2014), covering objectives regarding the protection of vulnerable children. At the same time, child rights are constitutionally enshrined at the Treaty level. This norm development, therefore, substantiates the evolution of child rights norms ('norm cascades') and the current norm implementation or internalization processes. In other words, the entrepreneurial actions taken to introduce child rights as an EU issue have gradually led to the normalization of the EU's role and scope in children's rights.

Emergence of feedback processes

The Romanian children's question acted as a catalyst in shifting the focus from an EU accession policy issue to an EU internal policy sector. The EU's intervention in the Romanian children's case had feedback effects at the EU level and expanded the Commission's involvement with this human rights area as part of the AFSJ and in EU enlargement policy. Yet different feedback mechanisms account for the emergence of feedback effects in EU internal and external policy dimensions. The question arises about how to explain the significance of the observed feedback effects on EU policy processes?

The child protection case in Romania had clear feedback effects on EU children's rights policy, namely the Commission's 2006 Communication and the institutional and policy structures created by it. The Communication in turn generated further effects at the EU level, which amounted to the institutionalization and normalization of the EU institutions' role in this policy area within the EU's internal human rights dimension. Externally, child rights constitute now an entrenched EU accession condition. These clear feedback effects of the EU's engagement with the child protection case in Romania are consistent with a historical institutionalist approach (in EU external policy dimension), while inside the Union they can be conceptualized as the EU-topianization of the EU in relation to children's rights, according to which the EU has begun to import the policies which it developed initially for export to accession countries.

Import of 'EU-topia' in the field of children's rights

The feedback effects of the Romanian case on EU internal policy dimension have to be conceptualized within the context of Europeanization processes. Indeed, the developments triggered in the EU internal policy sphere constitute the consequences of the broader enlargement-led Europeanization process which occurred in the CEECs. The Romanian children's case constitutes a clear example of *policy feedback* (cf. Pierson, 1993), according to which policies – which are generally analysed as the effect of politics – in turn become causes and thus affect politics. Politics played a significant role in making child protection an accession condition for Romania. For instance, the political pressure applied by Emma Nicholson and the Commission on Romanian authorities to reform the child protection system and ban international adoptions was highly significant, amounting to the involvement of a vast number of EU actors in the creation and development of an EU policy line on the question of children in Romania. The EU's external policy line on children's rights fed back into the EU's internal human rights dimension and had a substantial impact on the EU's approach to children's rights internally due to policy entrepreneurship, as discussed in this chapter. Pierson (1993) describes two mechanisms of policy feedback: *resource–incentive effects* and *interpretive–cognitive effects*. The resource–incentive effects refer to the expertise and know-how acquired at the Commission level due to the Commission's monitoring of and intervention in the Romania case and the subsequent institutional structures established by the 2006 Communication; while the interpretive–cognitive effects describe the subsequent 'norm internalization' (Finnemore and Sikkink's, 1998) of the rights of the child at the EU level.

The Europeanization of the CEECs' human rights provision entailed the export of an EU-topia in the field of human rights, due to the disjuncture between the EU's internal and external human rights remits. It can be argued, therefore, that the feedback effects on EU internal policy dimension describe a process whereby the EU has begun to import its own EU-topia in the field of children's rights, which had initially been intended for export only. The EU-topianization of the EU, therefore, amounts to processes or actions whereby the EU, particularly the Commission, starts engaging internally with policy matters that are usually promoted or addressed within the EU's external relations framework, such as enlargement policy. As shown in Chapter 1, the human rights EU-topia contention rests on the widely accepted fact that there is a stark asymmetry – or 'policy of bifurcation' (Williams, 2000, 2004) – between the EU's external and internal human rights dimensions and, hence, it is contended that the EU promotes externally an ideal model of human rights protection, which is not applied, to the same extent, in the EU internal human rights dimension. Therefore, it is argued that the child rights EU-topia intended for export has begun to be promoted internally within the EU. The emergent EU-topianization of EU children's rights policy involves the introduction of child rights on the EU's agenda as an internal policy issue, in line with the CRC principles, via the establishment of new institutional structures, adoption of policy instruments and soft law measures targeted at this policy area. One of the key effects of the EU's import of its own EU-topia in relation to children's matters is that, for the first time at the EU level, children's rights have become a standalone area, clearly differentiated from the broader human rights sector. Moreover, these new institutional and policy structures augmented the visibility of EU institutions', particularly the Commission's, involvement with children's rights and determined Member States to cooperate and coordinate their actions and policies in this area. Put differently, the EU-topianization of the EU – conceived here as the outcome of EU intervention in child rights in Romania – can be envisaged as an unintended consequence of the enlargement-led Europeanization, which entailed the EU's application of human rights conditions for which it lacked a similar mandate and clout in relation to the Member States.

The EU-topianization of the EU in relation to children's rights is particularly illustrated by the significance of the soft law measures and actions taken by the Commission in this area within the EU, alongside the prioritization and visibility attached to this area within the EU's internal policy. Soft law instruments and measures are 'rules of conduct which, in principle, have no legally binding force but which nevertheless may have practical effects' (Snyder, 1994: 198). Although soft law measures and instruments do not prescribe obligations, they have implications and bring changes on the 'political, economic, and social life outside the law' (Snyder, 1995: 51). The feedback effects of the Romanian children's question and the EU-topianization of the EU regarding the rights of the child have become evident in a number of ways. First, the awareness raised and the visibility of children's rights has shifted the focus from an area perceived only as an external policy to a widely accepted and endorsed issue of internal policy. Second, the main actions taken by the Commission regarding children's rights revolve around fostering cooperation among Member States in this area and policy coordination at national level. At the same time, the Commission adopted instruments targeting the protection of children's rights *per se*, such as the Safer Internet Programme and Daphne Programme, to name just a few. Third, the EU's child rights policy entails the development and promotion of a child rights perspective in line with the CRC. By attaching an EU interpretation of child rights, EU institutions endeavour to both devise initiatives specifically targeting children's rights and, at the same time, ensure that all EU actions do not infringe the rights enshrined in the CRC. In other words, there is now a more clear sense of the EU institutions' accountability (Stalford, 2012) to child rights, whereby rights are upheld not simply as a result of being articulated in policy, but also due to coherent mechanisms for enforcement and evaluation. Ultimately, the EU's added value in this area is more significant if compared with, for instance, the Council of Europe's role in the protection of children's rights, due to the Commission's leverage in other policy sectors that have an indirect bearing on children's rights.

The import of an interest in children's rights into EU internal policy dimension points to the Commission's 'mission creep' (Cram, 1994; Majone, 2005) into new policy sectors as it can be claimed that the gap between the EU's internal and external promotion of children's rights has begun to bridge. There is still no hard law on and general EU competence in children's rights. However, child rights constitute a cross-sectoral area, which means that, in those areas where the EU has legal competence to act, EU institutions can adopt hard law measures that would implicitly affect the protection of children's rights across Europe. The EU adopted both legislative and non-legislative measures impinging directly on the protection of children's rights. For instance, a new Directive[4] on *Combating the Sexual Abuse and Sexual Exploitation of Children and Child Pornography*, replacing Council Framework Decision 2004/68, was adopted in 2011. This Directive requires Member States to enact legislation criminalizing all serious forms of sexual abuse and exploitation using online technologies. It also includes provision for harmonizing definitions of 'child sexual abuse', 'sexual exploitation', 'child pornography' and 'solicitation of children for sexual purposes' (Art 2); while it also includes enhanced protection for child victims of such offences. (Arts 16–19). Along the same lines, the anti-discrimination legislation will widen in scope and, therefore, will have a greater impact on the protection of children's rights. For instance, the Commission's *Proposal for a Council Directive on Implementing the Principle of Equal Treatment between Persons Irrespective of Religion or Belief, Disability, Age or Sexual Orientation*[5] is a far-reaching instrument, which, if adopted, would prohibit discrimination based on religion or belief, disability, age or sexual orientation in both the public and private sectors. Non-legislative measures, such as Europe 2020 Strategy for Smart, Sustainable and Inclusive Growth (2010), make an explicit link between enhancing labour market participation and combating child poverty.[6] These measures, both legislative and non-legislative, signal the rapid expansion of EU interest and actions focusing – either directly or indirectly – on children's rights, which indeed, render the rights of the child 'one of the most important cross-cutting issues in the EU today, similar to questions of gender or the environment' (Manners, 2008b: 228). The imported EU-topia in the field of children's rights suggests that children's rights are now an overarching EU issue, although, due to the cross-sectoral dimension of human rights in general, the competence of the EU in relation to children's matters varies across EU policy sectors.

Historical institutionalist elements

Historical institutionalist elements provide the explanatory framework for the feedback effects observed in EU external policy dimension. The Romanian children's case yielded what are known as *positive feedback effects*, thus establishing the Commission's status in relation to this issue as a self-reinforcing institution. As described in Chapter 1, institutions are reinforcing if the effects generated by them incline actors to stick with the existing institutional arrangements and this institutional reinforcement takes place through positive feedback effects, namely those effects which generate incentives for actors to stick with or expand the existing institutions. These historical institutionalist elements clearly describe the feedback effects generated by the EU's intervention in child rights in Romania in relation to the current enlargement process (Iusmen, 2012b). The entrenchment of children's rights in the current enlargement policy further strengthens the Commission's role as a self-reinforcing institution in relation to children's rights.

The Romanian children's question had clear feedback effects on the EU's external promotion of children's rights, particularly in relation to the enlargement policy as applied to the current candidate countries. A pattern of path-dependence and lock-in effects regarding the EU's external child rights policy was identified. The lock-in effects of the Commission's application of a high-profile child protection condition to Romania are evident in relation to the current and potential candidate countries. As shown in Chapter 4, children's rights are now monitored and assessed in the current and potential candidate countries both under the political and *acquis* criteria. Although child protection was a pre-accession condition for all the CEECs, the development of a child protection policy by DG Enlargement was heavily influenced by the Romanian case. Thus, the Commission's assessment of child rights provision of the future EU members has become path dependent in terms of enlargement policy and a *sine qua non* EU accession condition. The Commission's application of child rights accession conditionality has widened in scope and impact, which is particularly facilitated by the Commission's substantial leverage to forge changes within the enlargement context.

The feedback effects on the EU's children policy as part of EU accession conditionality demonstrate a clear case of *institutional development* and *policy evolution* (Pierson, 2004) at the Commission level. As detailed in Chapter 1, Pierson discusses the role of policy feedback and institutional reinforcement in explaining the processes of institutional development unfolding over significant periods of time (Pierson, 2004: 15). Thus, two key elements underpinning institutional development are *individual* and *organizational adaptations* to existing arrangements and *asset investment* (Pierson, 1993). Both these elements are applicable to the institutional development regarding children's rights at the Commission level; for instance, the Commission invested in certain assets such as expertise, institutional structures and knowledge in relation to the child protection in Romania. Thus, there is an emerging normative know-how and an institutional entrenchment with regard to the rights of the child at the Commission level (Iusmen, 2012b). Second, it is contended that there has been an organizational adaptation to the existing arrangements, namely the increasing visible involvement with children's rights by the Commission services at the Commission level. There has been an incremental acceptance and normalization of the normative role played by the Commission in the protection of children's rights in the EU's external dimension, particularly as evidenced by the assessment of child rights as part of EU *acquis* in the Progress Reports. What had initially begun as a highly politicized accession condition in relation to Romania's accession agenda now became a fully fledged policy in the enlargement process and a key feature of EU external policy dimension (Iusmen, 2012b). There has been an incremental evolution of the Commission's institutional role in and its policy on children's rights both inside and outside the Union, as shown in Chapter 4. The accession conditionality in relation to child rights provision demonstrates that that the EU employs the accession conditionality to enforce compliance with CRC principles at the national level.

Processes of institutional development and policy evolution are underpinned by what is known as *institutional learning* (Steinmo, 2008; Hay and Wincott, 1998). Prior to the Commission's intervention in child protection in Romania, there was no expertise on or experience regarding the employment of child rights as an EU accession condition. Furthermore, there was little know-how on how to address the problems faced in the Romanian children's case and, particularly, what EU instruments would be most effective in this regard. However, as shown in Chapter 4, lessons have been learnt from the EU's intervention in the Romanian case: institutional learning, particularly at the Commission level, has emerged due to 'learning by doing' in children's rights policy area. The lessons learnt due to the Romanian case are now employed in the current enlargement process, particularly in relation to the de-institutionalization of children and the promotion of the CRC principles.

The children's rights feedback effects on the Commission's human rights policy provide a useful example of policy feedback and *unintended consequences* (Thelen, 1999) in practice. The high profile role of child protection in the EU accession negotiations with Romania was not expected or intended by the Member States. Given the vagueness of the Copenhagen political accession criteria, it was the Commission's role to elaborate on what these conditions would mean in practice. At the same time, the Commission had the Member States' consent to pursue a broad and interventionist policy regarding candidates' human rights performance. However, the tacit contention was that the Commission's external engagement with human rights issues would not have repercussions on the EU's internal dimension. Yet, children's rights had an unpredicted boomerang effect on the EU's internal and external roles in this area, a fact which had not been foreseen by the Member States in relation to the accession conditionality towards Central and Eastern European countries. The boomerang effect illustrates how the original intentions of certain actions can backfire and have unforeseen consequences as Merton's ([1949], 1968) analysis of propaganda and persuasion demonstrated. Yet, the boomerang effect is particularly applicable to the feedback effects in the EU's internal sphere, where the policy innovation caused by policy entrepreneurship had not been anticipated at the time when child protection became an accession condition in relation to Romania's agenda.

Institutionalization of children's rights at the EU level

The feedback effects and the developments prompted by them illustrate that the EU's role and scope in child rights has been normalized. Due to their cross-sectoral aspect, children's rights are now advanced as part of four main frameworks (Stalford, 2012: 58): a rights-based framework for protecting children's rights, along with frameworks covering social inclusion, non-discrimination, and citizenship and fundamental rights. Of course, the EU's legal competence in relation to children's matters varies considerably across these frameworks. It is not surprising, therefore, that child rights have recently been institutionalized at the EU level. In this context institutionalization refers to the fact that child rights matters are now addressed by all the key EU institutions, in line with their respective legal mandate.

One of the clearest examples of the institutionalization of children's rights within the emerging EU human rights regime is that of the newly created human rights body at the EU level, the Fundamental Rights Agency (FRA). The EU Agency for Fundamental Rights (FRA)- which is the successor to the European Monitoring Centre on Racism and Xenophobia – became operational on 1 March 2007. Its main objective is to provide the EU institutions and the Member States with assistance and expertise regarding fundamental rights in order to support them – when they take measures or formulate courses of action within their respective spheres of competence – to fully respect fundamental rights (European Commission, 2007: 2). The main tasks entrusted to the FRA relate to the collection and analysis of information and data, the provision of advice through reports and cooperation with civil society and awareness raising (European Commission, 2007: 2). The FRA has funded and disseminated a significant body of research on issues covering child rights and child welfare aspects, such as separated, asylum-seeking children,[7] child trafficking,[8] discrimination, social marginalization and violence.[9] There are two main developments at the level of this agency which clearly illustrate that the rights of the child – initially endorsed and made visible at the EU level by the Commission's Communication (2006) – had a snowballing effect on the FRA's role in this area.

First, the Agency's Multiannual Framework from 2007 to 2012 includes, among other areas, the protection of the rights of the child (European Commission, 2007: 9). The inclusion of the rights of the child in the FRA's Multiannual Framework is directly related to the role played by the Commission in the proposal of the thematic areas. One of the reasons for this is that the FRA's remit is decided and overseen by the Commission's DG Justice. Therefore, the Commission proposed to the Council these thematic areas,[10] including children's rights, which were fully endorsed by the Council and thus included in the Agency's Multiannual Framework (European Commission, 2007). According to the Multiannual Framework, protection of the rights of the child covers aspects related to free movement, social inclusion and youth policies, the media and other relevant Community policies (European Commission, 2007: 7).

The second development regarding the FRA's role in relation to children's rights concerns the development of indicators for the protection, respect and promotion of the rights of the child in the EU, which were made public in 2009. In July 2007, the Commission asked the FRA to develop indicators measuring the protection of the rights of the child (European Union Agency for Fundamental Rights, 2009: 6). The Commission's request was in line with one of the priorities set out in the Communication, namely to collect comparable data on children's rights from 2007 onwards (European Commission, 2006a: 8). Indeed, the paucity of clear, detailed and comparable information is generally regarded as a key shortcoming at the EU level (Stalford, 2012: 190). The indicators collected by the FRA – included in the report *Developing indicators for the protection, respect and promotion of the rights of the child in the European Union* of March 2009 – cover four areas reflecting existing EU activity: family environment and alternative care; protection from exploitation and violence; education, citizenship and cultural activities; and adequate standards of living (European Union Agency for Fundamental Rights, 2009: 7). The indicators were the outcome of a 15-month period of intensive research involving detailed review of the normative and conceptual framework for children's rights, as well as extensive consultation with a set of EU, international and national stakeholders, policy-makers and children's rights experts (European Union Agency for Fundamental Rights, 2009: 6). According to the FRA, these indicators would be used for data collection and research on the impact of EU activities on children, which constitutes a significant step towards fulfilling the objectives set out in the Commission's Communication (European Union Agency for Fundamental Rights, 2009: 6). The indicators compiled by the FRA constitute a useful toolkit to support the Commission's periodic assessment of the effectiveness of its actions in relation to both internal and external measures affecting children. These indicators were developed in areas where the EU is competent to enact provision and where there is an existing body of law and policy (European Union Agency for Fundamental Rights, 2009: 9). It is hoped that the employment of these indicators by the EU Member States will lead to the development of a more coordinated approach to data collection and data comparability (European Union Agency for Fundamental Rights, 2009: 7), which is fundamental in order to assess the observance of children's rights at the EU and national levels. Indeed, it is widely acknowledged by all child rights stakeholders that the EU's capacity-building in relation to child rights relies significantly on the development of a coherent body of comparable data that would guide the policy-making process.

The potential and limitations of the FRA as an EU human rights body, including child rights, have been widely debated. In terms of its positive impact, the FRA could fill 'an important lacuna', providing EU institutions with crucial info on fundamental rights inside the Union (De Schutter, 2009: 116), which could ensure that, in the exercise of its competences, the EU does not violate human rights. However, there are significant limitations regarding what and how the FRA acts: for instance, it can only act within the scope of the application of Community (now EU) law (Council Regulation 168/2007); whilst the FRA's mandate precludes examination of individual complaints and monitoring of fundamental rights in individual Member States. Despite its limited jurisdiction as a human rights body, the FRA's positive impact on the EU's child rights policy depends on how effectively EU institutions, such as the Commission and the Parliament, employ the research outputs produced by the FRA. Indeed, in relation to child rights, the FRA can collect and provide important comparable data that can be employed by EU institutions to devise more effective instruments and policies, despite lacking jurisdiction to rule on the EU's or Member States' legality in relation to child rights.

The only democratically elected institution, the European Parliament (EP), has placed child rights on its agenda by adopting legislative and non-legislative measures targeting children. In the post-Lisbon legal framework, the Parliament played a fundamental role in passing legislation, along with the Council, aimed at targeting the violation of children's rights. Due to the new legal provisions included in the Lisbon Treaty, the Parliament, jointly with the Council, adopted *Directive 2011/92/EU on Combating the Sexual Abuse and Exploitation of Children and Child Pornography*,[11] referring explicitly to the child rights principles in to Article 24 of the Charter. The illegal trafficking of children was addressed via the adoption of the *Directive 2011/36/ EU on Preventing and Combating Trafficking in Human Beings and Protecting its Victims.*[12] Another key piece of legislation adopted by the Parliament, together with the Council, is the Audiovisual Media Services Directive 2010/13/EU, which requires all media services to take full account of the interests of EU citizens, including the most vulnerable users, and includes rules seeking to protect minors from inappropriate media audiovisual services. Violence against children is one of the priority areas on the Parliament's agenda, as illustrated by the initiatives the Daphne Programmes (I–III) aimed at promoting actions to combat violence against children, young people and women. For instance, the current Daphne III (2007–2013) focuses on actions targeting the rights of victims of violence, violence linked to harmful practices or children as victims and perpetrators of violence. The Safer Internet Programme also targets the protection of children. This instrument aims to enhance child online safety by financing projects and initiatives that facilitate collaboration between various stakeholders, such as NGOs, law-enforcement bodies, IT industry and governmental agencies. In terms of the institutional infrastructure intended to raise the visibility of child rights at the Parliament level, the Parliament set up the Alliance for Children, an informal cross-party and cross-committee group, aimed at facilitating the mainstreaming of child rights across EU actions and programmes and therefore improving the quality of EU legislation relevant to children.

The main political institutions in charge of EU external policy – the Council and the Commission – produced a considerable number of policy documents (both general and theme-specific) on children's rights in EU external action. These documents provide insights into the way in which children's rights are approached in EU external action (Council of the European Union, 2007; European Commission, 2006a, 2008a). The EU's external child rights policy is more developed and advanced than its internal counterpart due to the EU's long history of involvement with human rights matters in the external relations. The EU set out its approach to children's rights outside the EU in the *EU Guidelines for the Promotion and Protection of the Rights of the Child* (2007); while the Commission's external agenda focusing on children's rights was included in the Communication *A Special Place for Children in EU External Action* (2008). Both policy documents paid lip service to CRC principles whilst promising that children's rights had to be taken into consideration across EU trade negotiations, development cooperation and humanitarian aid policies and political dialogue (European Commission, 2008a, 2008b). The EU Guidelines specifically mention that the Commission should consider the link between relief, rehabilitation and development in the EU's external aid policy, and children's rights should be pursued both as part of the Development Cooperation Instrument (DCI) framework and as part of the broader EU human rights policy. Furthermore, the EU attached top priority to children's rights in its external relations 'via all available tools' at the disposal of the Commission (Council of the European Union, 2007: 1). The situation of children in armed conflict and emergency situations was outlined in more detail in the *Strategy on Children in Emergency and Crisis Situations* (2008) and the *EU Guidelines on Children and Armed Conflict* (2003, updated in 2008) which drew particular attention to the rights of separated children and child soldiers and the necessity of maintaining education services for children, even in times of emergency and crisis (European Commission, 2008b). The emergent EU vision of childhood in EU external policy is that of vulnerability, hence the focus on children in armed conflict, child sex tourism and child labour (European Commission, 2011f).

A concrete response to Commission Communication *Towards an EU Strategy on the Rights of the Child* (2006) was the adoption of the action plan concerning the role of children's rights in the EU's external relations, namely the Commission Communication *A Special Place for Children in EU External Action* (2008).[13] The Communication *A Special Place for Children in EU External Action* contributes to the process of developing a long-term strategy for the EU on children's rights from the EU's external perspective. This policy document fleshes out the main approaches and instruments in the external policy areas and their relevance for the promotion of children's rights in the EU external human rights dimension (Grugel and Iusmen, 2013). For instance, children's rights are covered by the existing EU development policies, such as those associated with education, health, social inclusion or human trafficking; whereas in terms of human rights and democratization policy towards third countries the EU implements the *EU Guidelines on Children and Armed Conflict* (European Commission, 2008b: 5).

The EU child rights actions in the external policy rely on the substantial input from child rights organizations. The institutionalization of child rights as part of EU external policy constitutes the outcome of more structured and effective engagement of children's NGOs and networks in the policy process (Iusmen, 2012a). Indeed, well-established working relations and consultation mechanisms with child rights NGOs have developed in EU external policy (Iusmen, 2012a; Grugel and Iusmen, 2013). Child rights NGOs active in EU external policy established efficient working relations with DG RELEX by following the EU's *modus operandi* of engaging human rights NGOs in EU external policy (Grugel and Iusmen, 2013). For instance, child rights organizations work on a regular basis with Commission external services regarding the external policy within the Council Working Group on Human Rights (COHOM), which includes Commission and Council officials responsible for the promotion of human rights via EU external relations. Stakeholder expertise and practical knowledge are provided by NGOs via networks, such as the Human Rights and Development Network (HRDN), European Confederation for Relief and Development Network (CONCORD) and Child Rights Action Group (CRAG), which hold regular consultation meetings with DG RELEX (Grugel and Iusmen, 2013). NGOs working on child rights matters in these networks are invited by the Children's Rights Task Force – steered by DG RELEX – to provide technical input into the policy drafts or documents touching on child rights matters which are on the EU's external policy agenda. For instance, child rights organizations active in the EU's external policy worked with the Commission external services to develop the 2008 Commission Communication *A Special Place for Children in EU External Action*.[14] The consultation meetings with the Children's Rights Task Force provide a structured and institutionalized dialogue with the main child rights networks, having the key objective the development of the EU's external policy on children's rights. Indeed, it can be deemed that the Commission's external services succeeded in establishing a structured and comprehensive mode of engaging civil society actors in the EU's external policy on children's rights, which has the contours of a policy network, namely 'a cluster of actors, each of which has an interest, or 'stake' in a given ... policy sector and the capacity to help determine policy success or failure' (Peterson and Bomberg, 1999: 8).

Children's rights have been addressed in EU external policy particularly as part of thematic programmes and through mainstreaming children's rights in development- and country-based projects. The Commission promised the application of a 'holistic child rights based approach [including] the respect for the views of the child, gender mainstreaming and local ownership' (European Commission, 2008b). Children's rights are addressed in four ways in EU development cooperation: first, via bilateral programmes; second, via thematic programmes; third, via cross-cutting issues; and fourth, via mainstreaming children's rights in all projects and programmes within the development framework (Vandenhole, 2011: 478). The EU's development cooperation policy targets broadly the reduction of poverty, along with sustainable economic and social development.[15] Thematic programmes usually complement the geographical programmes or geographical instruments and are intended to achieve the general objectives of the relevant EU external policy, in this case development cooperation. For instance, the Investing in People (IiP) thematic programme in particular has been employed to address a series of issues related to children in non-EU countries, including policy monitoring and advocacy for child protection and the rights of children, the promotion of policies to support the employment and decent work for young people and programmes targeting children's access to education. It has a specific budget line for children of €90 million for 2007–2013 (European Commission, 2008b), with projects for children also drawing from the IiP education budget (€80 million) and communicable diseases (€50.6 million). IiP is supported by geographical instruments, such as the European Development Fund (for the African, Caribbean and Pacific countries), the Development Co-operation Instrument (in Latin America, Asia and South Africa), and the European Neighbourhood & Partnership Instrument (in the neighbouring regions). The focus on children's needs rather than their rights is salient in the four main priority areas targeted by IiP: child labour, child trafficking, violence against children including sexual violence, and children affected by armed conflicts (European Commission, 2008a).Children's rights are also addressed in the European Instrument for Democracy and Human Rights (EIDHR), the main self-standing financing instrument for the promotion of democracy and human rights worldwide. While the IiP addresses social and economic issues that affect children, including labour, education and health, the EIDHR focuses primarily on political and civil rights, including those of children. The EIDHR has funded projects aimed at strengthening the role of civil society in promoting human rights, including child rights, and at addressing the rights of severely deprived and marginalized children, including child soldiers, as well as projects that aim to support the implementation of CRC principles. EU external policy, therefore, is shaped by the view that the violations of rights facing children outside Europe are more extensive and dramatic in scale and therefore a bolder entrepreneurial role should ensue, as the actions taken so far demonstrate. Little wonder, then, that child rights organizations regard EU actions as part of EU external policy as being more developed and effective in addressing child rights breaches in developing countries.[15]

The EU child rights policy is dominated by a normative 'rights'-based model (Stalford, 2012: 3) whereby EU formulations and actions endeavour to advance an approach inspired by the CRC, which envisages children as independent and autonomous rights holders. However, the key policies and initiatives applied in EU external policy signal a needs-based rather that rights-based approach. Indeed, the focus on children's *needs* rather than their rights is also salient in the four main priority areas requiring action at the global level, all of which focus on protection: child labour, child trafficking, violence against children (including sexual violence), and children affected by armed conflicts (European Commission, 2008a: 2). In the same vein, the Council has emphasized the particular vulnerability of children (Council of the European Union, 2008: 5). With respect to the image of the child and the view of children's rights that is being developed and promoted by EU institutions outside the Union a picture of vulnerability and victimization emerged: children are regarded as vulnerable, as victims of exploitation, who need to be helped (European Commission, 2010c: 14–15). Therefore, there is hardly any recognition of the agency and dignity-based rights of children. This results in a primarily paternalistic preoccupation with children, who are depicted only as a vulnerable category in need of protection, while any focus on child empowerment is sidelined. The emphasis on needs and protection in external action is perhaps not surprising, given that it reflects the standard approach to children's rights adopted also in EU internal action (Stalford and Drywood, 2009: 171). In both EU internal and external policy dimensions, children are mainly addressed from the perspective of child protection, which stresses children's vulnerability and their needs, rather than their self-determination. Irrespective of the approach adopted, the promotion of child rights in EU external policies has become institutionalized and entrenched: now, children's rights and child protection constitute the foci of targeted action or, more generally, they are mainstreamed in all EU external actions.

Conclusion

This chapter examined the analytical concepts explaining the feedback effects on EU internal and enlargement policies triggered by the Romanian children's case. It was argued that policy entrepreneurship, in line with Kingdon's (1984) model of multiple streams coupling, captures the policy innovation introduced by the 2006 Communication and the ensuing developments in this area, while in EU enlargement policy, historical institutionalist elements account for the entrenchment of children's rights as an EU accession condition. Particularly with respect to the EU internal policy sphere, it was contended that the feedback effects, namely the introduction of children's rights as an overarching EU issue, amount to the EU's import of the EU-topia that had initially been designed for external consumption. Although what was coined as the EU-topianization of the EU's children's rights provision did not shift the EU's legal competence in this area, this has led to the institutionalization of children's rights across the main EU institutions and policy sectors.

EU policy entrepreneurs and propitious institutional and political factors led to the establishment of children's rights as an EU policy area, which is addressed via various legislative and non-legislative instruments. Crucially important from a public policy perspective, however, is the test as to the 'added value' of EU measures to uphold children's rights, which lies in the extent to which such measures can be enforced and produce positive effects at the domestic level (Stalford, 2012: 183). Arguably, this added value test is both contingent on the EU's mandate to act, the Member States' acceptance of the EU's role in this area and the effectiveness and coherence of EU financial and policy instruments to generate an impact on children's lives. While it is easier to assess and ascertain the EU's actions' added value in EU external policy dimension, it is far more difficult to evaluate the added value of EU actions inside the Union, as the Member States are extremely reluctant to cede control over children's matters to EU institutions.

Notes

1   Some of the sections here have been published in Iusmen, I. (2013a) 'Policy Entrepreneurship and Eastern Enlargement: the Case of EU Children's Rights Policy', *Comparative European Politics*, 11(4), 511–529.

2   Author's interview with Commission officials in DG EMPL and DG Justice, July 2011, Brussels.

3   According to Frattini 'the European Union's moral duty to comply with the UN Convention of the Rights of the Child ... the protection of children's rights is one of the highest institutional priorities to be ensured ... by the European Commission' (Frattini quoted in European Foundation for Street Children Worldwide, 2006).

4   Directive 2011/92 on combating the sexual abuse and sexual exploitation of children and child pornography (OJ L335/1).

5   COM(2008) 426 final.

6   COM(2010) 2020 final.

7   *Separated Asylum-Seeking Children: An examination of living conditions, provisions and decision making procedures in selected EU Member States through child centred participatory research* (2008), Vienna.

8   *Child Trafficking in the EU-Challenges, perspectives and good practices* (2010) Vienna.

9   *Experience of Discrimination, Social Marginalisation and Violence: A Comparative Study of Muslim and Non-Muslim youth in three EU Member States* (2010) Vienna.

10 There are ten thematic areas in the Fundamental Rights Agency's Multiannual Framework; these are: (a) racism, xenophobia and related intolerance; (b) discrimination based on sex, racial or ethnic origin, religion or belief, disability, age or sexual orientation or of persons belonging to minorities; (c) compensation of victims, prevention of crime and related aspects relevant to the security of citizens; (d) protection of children, including rights of the child; (e) immigration and integration of migrants; (f) asylum; (g) visa and border control; (h) participation in the Union's democratic functioning; (i) human rights issues relating to the information society; and (j) access to efficient and independent justice (European Commission, 2007: 9–10).

11 This Directive replaced the Council Framework Decision 2004/68/JHA combating the sexual exploitation of children and child pornography.

12 This Directive replaced the Council Framework Decision 2002/629/JHA on combating trafficking in human beings.

13   *Communication from the Commission to the Council, the European Parliament, the European Economic and Social Committee and the Committee of the Regions: A Special Place for Children in EU External Action,* COM (2008) 55 final, Brussels, 5 February 2008.

14   Author's interview with Commission external services and child rights organizations, Brussels, July 2011.

15   Regulation (EC) No. 1905/2006 Establishing a Financing Instrument for Development Cooperation.

16   Author's interview with child rights organizations, Brussels, July 2011.

6

European Union human rights regime: from Eastern enlargement to the Lisbon Treaty and beyond

The Nobel Peace Prize 2012 is awarded to [the] European Union as: 'the Union and its forerunner have, for over six decades, contributed to the advancement of peace and reconciliation, democracy and human rights in Europe'.

(Nobel Committee)

Introduction

This chapter examines the key features and scope of the emergent European Union (EU) human rights regime in the light of Eastern enlargement and the Lisbon Treaty provisions. The EU has been recently hailed as a success story in contributing to the advancement of peace, democracy and human rights in Europe, according to the Nobel Prize Committee's justification for its decision to award the Nobel Peace Prize 2012 to the EU. It is argued that a more robust institutional, legal and normative EU role regarding the promotion of human rights has taken shape at the EU level. The proliferation of EU human rights initiatives, particularly in relation to politically sensitive and even controversial areas such as mental health, would not have occurred if it had not been for the interventionist human rights conditionality applied to the Central and Eastern European Countries (CEECs), as part of Eastern enlargement. The legal and constitutional changes introduced by the Lisbon Treaty, along with the binding nature of the EU Charter of Fundamental Rights, have further enhanced the EU's internal and external human rights commitments. The *acquis* accession criteria focusing on human rights issues have become more entrenched and formalized, as the accession monitoring process of current candidate countries demonstrates. Despite this, the 'lack of competence' mantra is still employed by the EU to justify its limited reach in most human rights matters inside the Union. However, more and more violations of human rights at the national level require cross-border cooperation and policy coordination, and in this respect, the EU is particularly well-placed to promote cross-national cooperation in Europe. It is not surprising, therefore, that the Member States realised the added value of EU-driven actions and policy initiatives in addressing human rights violations.

This chapter charts the key developments in areas, such as the Roma, mental health, disability and international adoption, whose profile has been augmented due to Eastern enlargement and post-accession events. This is by no means an exhaustive list of human rights areas that have been radically transformed by the last round of enlargement and the EU's internal processes. The chapter then proceeds by mapping the role of human rights in the current enlargement process and, finally, unpacks the shape and scope of the current EU human rights regime.

Eastern enlargement effects and EU human rights provision

The EU's engagement with human rights matters was substantially enhanced due to Eastern enlargement. Human rights matters strictly monitored and extensively scrutinized during accession negotiations with Eastern candidates emerged high up on the EU's internal agenda, particularly, as the case of the Roma demonstrates, after the former communist states became EU Member States. The evaluation of human rights performance of candidates was perceived as an EU external policy matter, without any expected consequences on EU internal policies and processes. However, Eastern enlargement had a boomerang effect on the EU's internal human rights agenda, particularly in relation to those areas thoroughly examined during the pre-accession process. The feedback effects of Eastern enlargement took various forms and shapes, yet, overall, they boosted the profile attached to human rights matters at the EU level, as the cases of the Roma protection, mental health and disability prove. Indeed, the unprecedented degree of scrutiny of the human rights performance of Eastern candidates unearthed the controversial double-standards approach in relation to the EU's internal and external policies, and provided a major impetus to the development of EU internal policy (De Burca, 2003). Human rights issues thoroughly addressed as part of Eastern enlargement permeated the EU's policy agenda after 2007. As the case of international adoption demonstrates, the EU adopted a pro-inter-country adoption (ICA) position after 2007 particularly as an indirect spin-off from its anti-ICA policy applied to Romania during accession negotiations. In brief, the sections below demonstrate how Eastern enlargement has had an impact on EU human rights regime by showing 'the way in which enlargement impacts upon the shape of the EU's policy profile' as 'each of the rounds of enlargement brings about significant change to the trajectory of the EU as a whole, while impacting on individual policy regimes as well' (Bulmer, 2009: 313).

The Roma

The Roma protection, apart from children's rights, perhaps acquired the highest political salience inside the EU after 2007. The increase in Romani migration across Europe has signalled that the EU could no longer treat it as merely a problem of Eastern Europe (Sigona and Trehan, 2009: 9). More specifically, the developments regarding the Roma were triggered by post–2007 incidents in France and Italy concerning the rights and freedom of movement of this minority. The way the French and Italian authorities dealt with the situation of the Roma within their national boundaries unearthed the complexity and interlinkages of the problems faced by this community and how and the extent to which EU institutions and law are equipped with tools to protect their rights as EU citizens. The soft law measures and initiatives developed at the Commission level regarding this minority rendered Roma inclusion a politically salient issue in the EU's internal dimension, despite the EU's limited mandate with respect to minority protection. Indeed, as is demonstrated below, Eastern enlargement lifted the profile of the Roma to the status of an overarching EU issue, demonstrating that an EU external policy concern had been imported into the EU's internal sphere.

The Roma resurfaced as an issue on EU policy agenda due to several factors. First, the actual increase in the size of the Roma population[1] after the 2004 and 2007 enlargements had practical implications within the EU due to the freedom of movement of this minority, on the one hand, and the reaction of EU Member States to this EU citizenship right, on the other. Second, the incidents regarding Roma settlements in Italy (2008, 2009) and France (2010) signalled the need of European concerted action to address their plight and ensure that their rights as EU citizens are protected. It is argued that the history of EU involvement with Roma issues during the accession process with the CEECs has shaped the emergent responses from the EU institutions regarding the post-accession plight of the Roma in Europe.

The political visibility of the Roma at the EU level became evident in the late 1990s. The historical background to the EU's involvement with the Roma question began in 1997, which marked the European Year against Racism and therefore, politically, this is when the Roma issue became politically and institutionally visible at the EU level. The EU's internal awareness of the Roma question was further enhanced by the adoption of the Racial Equality Directive (2000/43/EC), which established, among other things, the legal enforcement of the anti-discrimination measures targeted at the Roma. However, the main trigger for the emergence of the Roma as an EU issue was the Eastern enlargement context when, the plight of Roma communities in the CEECs – which constituted the states that had the most sizeable Roma population in Europe[2] – was monitored as part of the Copenhagen accession criteria. The accession of the former communist countries to the

EU, therefore, was expected to generate a certain impact on the protection of minorities within the EU as the increase in the size of the Roma within the EU could have posed a challenge to the overall minority protection system in Europe. In the same vein, the candidate countries were not only bringing a greater Roma population into the EU, but they were also 'importing' into the EU the underlying problems, mainly huge socio-economic exclusion, faced by the Roma communities in these countries. For instance, it has been shown that the Poland and Hungary: Assistance for Reconstructing their Economies (PHARE) programmes in the accession states demonstrated the failure of national policies and practices in Central and Eastern Europe to protect the Roma (European Commission, Employment and Social Affairs, 2004: 15–16). It is not surprising, therefore, that in 2004 EU institutions had to contend reluctantly that tackling the plight of the Roma was a long-term process, which required substantial resources over a long period of time in order to generate a real societal impact (European Commission, Employment and Social Affairs, 2004: 15).

One of the major effects of Eastern enlargement regarding the Roma was the prioritization of Roma issues within the EU's policy agenda, particularly in the aftermath of the Roma expulsions. Indeed, the accession of Bulgaria and Romania in 2007 in particular, and the ensuing events involving the Roma from these countries in Italy and France brought to the fore the extent to which the Member States and EU structures were equipped to deal with the problems faced by the Roma, which is deemed to be the most disadvantaged minority in Europe (O'Nions, 2011). While before 2007 the plight of the Roma was perceived as being primarily an enlargement concern, which could be contained to candidate countries, this has recently transformed into a wide European issue that requires the EU's and Member States' concerted efforts. For instance, ever since 2002 the EU Network of Independent Experts on Fundamental Rights described Europe's Roma as suffering from an 'apartheid situation' and exclusion in respect of every right contained within the (now legally binding) Charter of Fundamental Rights (EU Network of Independent Experts on Fundamental Rights, 2002: 176). The same network of experts highlighted the widespread and engrained forms of discrimination experienced by the Roma in Eastern Europe due to lack of employment, educational segregation, police violence, poverty and lack of access to health care and social services (EU Network of Independent Experts on Fundamental Rights, 2002). How to tackle effectively the plight of the Roma in Europe reached a tipping point after countries such as Italy and France undertook large scale Roma expulsions from their territory after 2007. Therefore, Eastern enlargement yielded the creation of a European political space for the formation and contestation of new meanings of who the Roma are, what they need and how they should be supported (Simhandl, 2006).

The accession-monitoring process raised considerable awareness at the EU level of the entrenched shortcomings faced by the Roma. Particularly countries with a sizeable Roma population, such as Slovakia and Romania, failed to address the widespread discrimination experienced by this community before they became EU Member States. Slovakia, with an estimated population of five hundred thousand Roma, struggled to meet the political criteria due to its discriminatory treatment of the Roma, including the protection of their minority rights (Vermeersch, 2003). Moreover, the former Slovak Prime Minister Vladimir Mečiar expressed publicly his dislike of the Roma during his period in office by describing them as 'socially unadaptable' and 'backward', while, overall, the Roma constitute a social problem and 'are simply a great burden on this society' (Kohn, 1996: 179). The situation of the Roma in Romania, which has the most sizeable Roma community in Europe, has been widely examined and warning signals have been raised regarding the ethnic tensions and nationalism in Romania, with the Roma being the principle targets (Verdery, 1993: 187). The Roma's way of life, including their economic opportunism and supposed 'otherness', led to the majority cultures, over a period of many years, to attempt to exclude them from mainstream society (Liegeois and Gheorghe, 1995: 8–9). There had been a long history of Roma discrimination in Eastern Europe (Jeremić and Rädle, 2011), yet the lid on the extent and depth of the discriminatory treatment faced by this community was lifted only after 1989. The Roma problem had not been solved by the time of the 2004/2007 enlargements, which illustrated that the EU institutions were poorly equipped to address the deeply entrenched discrimination and sheer complexity of the Roma problem as an EU accession matter. Meanwhile, within the EU's internal policy sphere there was little awareness of how and whether the EU institutional and legislative frameworks had the means to accommodate the situation to the Roma inside the Union.

The post-enlargement incidents involving the Roma exposed the limited success and reach of the EU accession policy towards this minority. Although the economic and social situation experienced by the Roma was targeted by various EU instruments during the accession process, the EU approach provided limited opportunity for an integrated multicultural approach, with little bottom-up input from local Roma communities. Despite the widespread discrimination and poverty faced by the Roma, it has been argued that the signals sent by the Commission to candidates were misleading as they had implied that the minority rights criteria could be interpreted as merely aspirational (Guy, 2002: 16). Therefore, the EU's approach to the Roma problem entailed a 'deep ambivalence' on this topic, while suggesting that other political and economic factors would be given greater priority than the situation of an 'impoverished and powerless minority'(Guy, 2002: 19). In the mid 2000s it became evident that the situation of the Roma was generally poor across Central and Eastern Europe due to the sheer scale of socio-economic exclusion they faced: for instance, Roma communities experienced marked discrimination and social exclusion, or engrained obstacles in gaining access to employment, education, healthcare, housing and other public services and justice (European Commission, Employment and Social Affairs, 2004: 6).

The EU, and particularly the Commission, 'discovered' the topic of the Roma as an EU internal policy matter after the 2004/2007 enlargement. Therefore, the urgency to address effectively the plight of the Roma in Europe, as a consequence of the first round of Eastern enlargement, determined the Commission to set up the Roma Inter-service Group in Directorate General Employment, Social Affairs and Inclusion (DG EMPL) in 2004. The role of the Roma Inter-service Group is to provide a forum for institutional coordination on and mainstreaming of Roma issues across Commission services. The Inter-service Group is an intra-institutional platform for the exchange of information with regard to policy instruments and mechanisms which are relevant for Roma inclusion (European Commission, 2008d: 5). Thus, there was a heightened awareness of the need to address the Roma problem as a cross-sectoral issue via the engagement of all Commission DGs. The Commission services involved in the Inter-service Group inform each other on how they mainstream Roma inclusion into their activities and, to this end, the Inter-service Group has to 'make sure that there is a Roma element in everything that is happening in the Commission'.[3] The most active DGs in this Inter-service Group are DG Justice, DG EMPL, and DG Education and Culture, given the relevance of their policy remit for the Roma in Europe. The Roma is a cross-cutting issue which, given its complexity, requires concerted action and cooperation across all Commission services in order to adopt integrated and coordinated actions focusing on the situation of this community.

The Romanian Roma question had an impact at the EU level after Romania had joined the EU in 2007. This post-accession feedback was triggered by the Romanian Roma in Italy, namely in Rome, where cases of Italian women being raped and killed by Roma ethnics were reported in November 2007. These crimes led to a number of violent attacks against the Roma in Italy, culminating in a mob arson attack on a Roma settlement in Naples. For the first time in the post-accession period it became obvious that an EU 'external' issue had been internalized as part of the fabric of the Union (Topidi, 2010: 80). The events which occurred in Italy constituted the outcome of the freedom of movement enjoyed by the new EU citizens from Eastern Europe, particularly from Romania, given that Romania is regarded as having the highest Roma population in the EU.

The incidents involving the Romanian Roma in Italy in 2007 prompted the reaction of EU institutions, such as the Parliament and the Commission, while their positions on and measures taken in response to the events in Italy further raised the profile of the Roma issue at the EU level. For instance, the European Parliament adopted a resolution on 15 November 2007 *On Application of Directive 2004/38/EC on the Right of EU Citizens and their Family Members to Move and Reside Freely within the Territory of the Member States*, whereby it reacted to the statements made by the then Commissioner for Justice, Freedom and Security, Franco Frattini, according to which Italy's decision to deport the Roma was justified on grounds of security matters in a move to crack down on crime. The public security rhetoric was employed by the Italian government, along with Commissioner Frattini, to legitimize the deportation of Roma migrants from Italy. Yet, the Parliament's Resolution signalled that, under the provisions of the Citizenship Directive 2004/38/EC and the Charter of Fundamental Rights, mass expulsions of Union citizens are prohibited. Secondly, the Parliament rejected the principle of collective responsibility – which justified the Italian government's decision to expel all Romanian Roma from Italy – and raised concerns regarding the need 'to combat every form of racism and xenophobia and all forms of discrimination and stigmatization based on nationality and ethnic origin' (European Parliament, 2007b: 4). The Parliament urged for further EU political action by requesting the Commission to develop a European Framework Strategy on Roma Inclusion which should provide policy coherence at the EU level regarding the social inclusion of Roma (European Parliament, 2007b: 3). The Parliament, therefore, seemed to support the interpretation of the EU's legal framework in line with a human rights script.

The Parliament had rung the alarm bells about Member States' violation of EU law by deporting Roma illegally and hence violating the rights they enjoy as EU citizens. Notwithstanding the Parliament's criticisms, the Italian government continued its anti-Roma actions. For instance, in 2008 the Italian government announced a state of emergency and a planned census, which included compulsory fingerprinting of camp inhabitants, most of which were Roma (ODIHR, 2009). To facilitate the smooth running of the census, powers were given to local police to collect data, including the fingerprints, of Roma camp residents. These actions led to the expulsion of many non-Italian Roma (mainly from Romania and Bulgaria), which further continued in 2009 under the guise of the 'Nomad Decree', which allowed the destruction of temporary camps, with the result that many Roma became homeless (Amnesty International, 2010). Indeed, the actions taken by the Italian government violated EU legislation, namely the provisions in the Citizenship Directive 2004/38/EC, according to which European citizens can be expelled from Member States provided that they constitute a threat to public policy, public health and public security. For instance, according to Article 27 of the Citizenship Directive, any expulsion must be proportionate and must be based exclusively on the conduct of the individual, thereby collective expulsions are deemed illegal. It has been shown that the political rhetoric of public security was deployed to justify the collective expulsions of Roma in Italy, which also infringed the non-discrimination and proportionality principles of the Citizenship Directive (O'Nions, 2011).

EU institutions, particularly the Parliament, as shown above, reacted to the incidents in Italy to reinforce the supremacy of EU law and values. The Commission as the 'guardian of the Treaties', therefore, had to take a stand in relation to the controversial situation of the Roma. For instance, the Commission adopted the Communication *Non-discrimination and Equal Opportunities: A Renewed Commitment* on 2 July 2008 by responding to the European Council Conclusions of 14 December 2007, which specifically requested that the Commission examine EU policies and instruments regarding Roma inclusion in light of the events in Italy (European Commission, 2008d: 3). This was the first time that the European Council had addressed the issue of the Roma within the EU's internal policy dimension. The main outcome of the Communication was the Commission's commitment to draft a proposal on a new Directive on anti-discrimination, which would extend the scope and reach of the two anti-discrimination Directives, namely the Race Equality Directive 2000/43/EC (establishing the legal enforcement of the anti-discrimination measures) and the Employment Equality Directive 2000/78/EC (establishing a general framework for equal treatment in employment and occupation). The new Directive to be proposed by the Commission intends to complete the European legal framework on anti-discrimination by establishing a legislative framework extending legal protection to all forms of discrimination in all areas of life (European Commission, 2008d: 3–4). Hence, the scope of the new Directive is to complement the legal framework established by the existing Directives[4] by providing legal protection against discrimination based on race and gender in all areas of life, including social protection and access to goods and services.[5]

An EU political and institutional consensus had emerged, therefore, regarding the urgency of addressing the Roma problem most effectively with the legal and policy tools available to EU institutions. It is widely contended that the core areas of Roma inclusion, such as education, employment, public health, housing and fights against poverty, fall mainly under the responsibility of Member States; however, the EU can play an important role in ensuring that the principle of non-discrimination is respected and that it provides a platform for the policy coordination of national strategies (European Commission, 2008d: 4). EU-level and national action was needed urgently given that the widespread prejudice and racism regarding the Roma was on the rise. For instance, in 2009 one in five Roma claimed to have been the victim of racist incidents at least once during the previous 12 months (Eurobarometer, 2008), while in Hungary 50 per cent of the population believed that the Roma are genetically predisposed to have criminal tendencies (Cette-France-là, 2010).

The first EU institutional initiative to engage all Roma stakeholders at the EU level in response to the events in Italy was the organization of the first Roma Summit in Brussels in late 2008. The Summit brought together for the first time 400 representatives from the key EU institutions, national governments and Roma civil society to discuss the plight of the Roma in the EU and to find effective and shared solutions to improve it. According to Commission President Barroso, the Roma Summit represented 'a unique opportunity for getting the problems of the Roma higher on the agenda than ever before' (Villarreal and Walek, 2008: 2). The Summit acknowledged that the problems faced by Roma communities, such as extreme poverty, social exclusion, discrimination and racism, became more visible within the EU after Eastern enlargement, when the number of Roma within the Union's borders increased significantly (Villarreal and Walek, 2008). The key outcome of the Summit was the establishment of an integrated European Platform for Roma Inclusion, involving all the relevant Roma stakeholders, whose first meeting took place in April 2009. The Platform aimed to implement Roma inclusion policies as well as to align them with mainstream policies on education, employment, social inclusion, public health and infrastructure (Council of the European Union, 2009: 2). One of the concrete outcomes of the first Platform meeting was the adoption of the Common Basic Principles on Roma Inclusion. These ten Common Basic Principles on Roma Inclusion include provisions such as explicit but not exclusive targeting of the Roma; aiming for the mainstreaming, which involves inserting the Roma in the mainstream of society; awareness of the gender dimension, namely taking into account the needs and circumstances of Roma women; or the involvement of civil society when developing and implementing Roma inclusion policies (Council of the European Union, 2009: 4–5). The EU's efforts are channelled towards engaging all key stakeholders in taking concerted action targeted at the Roma at EU and national levels. On its part, the EU is committed to mainstreaming the Common Basic Principles when designing and implementing policies targeting the inclusion of the Roma, including aspects related to discrimination, poverty and social exclusion. Yet, the Member States have the upper hand in addressing the plight of the Roma, and the EU can only persuade them to commit to implementing soft law measures and initiatives, such as the Common Basic Principles.

Member States are reluctant to make legal commitments regarding the Roma, particularly when faced with substantial budget cuts to welfare spending due to economic recession (Kushen, 2009). In an age of austerity and financial crisis, national governments are not willing to commit financially and politically to solving the Roma problem, particularly as the old Member States perceive it as an East European issue that ought to be tackled by the CEECs. Despite the political rhetoric regarding the Roma situation endorsed by EU institutions and Member States alike, the Roma issue was back on the EU agenda in the summer of 2010 due to Roma expulsions from France. The French government began targeting an estimated 12,000 migrant Roma from Romania by employing collective expulsions with the offer of a small cash payment to those prepared to leave 'voluntarily' (European Parliament, 2010a). As in the Italian case, by using the public security rhetoric, the French authorities destroyed unauthorized settlements and expelled over 1000 Roma to Bulgaria and Romania, while the deported Roma were paid €300 per adult and €100 per child (Impey, 2010). The question of Roma camp clearances was placed at the centre of President Sarkozy's public security agenda (Romeurope, 2010; Sarkozy, 2010: 5). For instance, in his Grenoble speech Sarkozy presented the Roma as a threat to the integrity of the French state and, to this end, their deportation constituted a key priority for the French establishment. Between 2009–2010, for instance, a reported 20,000 + Roma had been deported (Fichtner, 2010; BBC News, 2010). Yet, it was soon revealed to European publics by a leaked French government circular that the deported Roma had been the target of collective expulsion on the grounds of their ethnicity rather than security related concerns (*Guardian*, 2010). This demonstrated that the actions taken by the French government breached the EU law on European citizenship.

The EU Justice Minister Viviane Reding was particularly quick to react to the Roma expulsions from France. Her outspoken criticism of the French authorities' attitudes towards the Roma made her compare their actions with the Vichy expulsions during the Second World War (Reding, 2010). At her initiative, the Commission issued a formal request asking the French authorities to comply with the 2004 Citizenship Directive (European Commission, 2010d). Despite the available evidence from the leaked French government circular that the Roma were targeted due to their ethnicity and not due to public safety concerns, the Commission toned its criticism down by concluding that the French expulsions of the Roma had not been deliberately directed towards an ethnic group (European Commission, 2010d). Therefore, in spite of the initial bold reaction to a clear infringement of EU law by an old Member State, as Commissioner Reding's blunt statements demonstrate, the Commission accepted the reassurances of the French government, as it had done previously in the Italian case, to the effect that, despite evidence to the contrary, the Roma had not been targeted on ethnicity grounds (European Commission, 2010d). However, the cautious position endorsed by the Commission underscores its lack of genuine commitment to the provisions of EU Citizenship Directive, which, according to the evidence, the French government, like the Italian government, had breached.

Furthermore, the Parliament's position was highly critical of both the French government's actions and the Commission's failure to employ the legal instruments at its disposal to safeguard the spirit and letter of EU Treaties.

The Resolution[6] adopted by the Parliament condemned the deportations initiated by the French government, warning that this kind of action violates EU law and particularly the EU Charter of Fundamental Rights. One of the Parliament's main concerns was the widespread 'stigmatization of Roma and general anti-Gypsyism in political discourse' (European Parliament, 2010a) that seemed to generate and legitimize the mass expulsions on security grounds. Indeed, the Parliament's position highlights the potential repercussions of the precedent set by the Italian and French cases, whereby the most disadvantaged minority in Europe, i.e. the Roma, can easily be deployed as scapegoats in times of economic recession, on the one hand, and the striking lack of legal follow-up action from the Commission, the guardian of the Treaties, on the other. Additionally, the Parliament is also concerned about how the public security rhetoric and the national governments' commitment to curb illegal migration and crime can grant 'credibility to racist statements and the actions of extreme right-wing groups' (European Parliament, 2010a). The Parliament, therefore, rang the alarm bells about how national governments can justify their anti-Roma actions on public security grounds by contradicting the spirit and letter of EU law.

Eastern enlargement had far-reaching effects on how EU institutions and Member States deal with the Roma community within both EU and national settings. However, the Roma mass expulsions from Italy and France also raised pertinent questions about the effectiveness and underlying pitfalls of EU legislative framework to accommodate the rights of the Roma in light of Member States' security concerns. Indeed, particularly the French deportations uncovered some of the deficiencies and loopholes of EU law which can be easily exploited by national authorities to legitimize their actions against the Roma. For instance, as mentioned above, according to the Citizenship Directive, European citizens can be expelled legally if they constitute a threat to public policy, public health or public security. Yet, according to the Directive, the Member States 'remain competent to define and modify the notions of public policy and public security' (European Commission, 2008d: 8). The Directive provisions, therefore, demonstrate that 'EU citizenship is not a privileged category that is somehow beyond security practices' (Parker, 2012: 484) and therefore, free movement and residence – which constitute some of the key rights of EU citizenship – can be radically restricted on public security grounds. The grey areas in the Directive were employed to the Member States' advantage in order to justify their actions in line with the three conditions for expulsion. In France, for instance, the offer of payment was employed to justify the voluntary aspect of the departures; while in Italy the absence of financial means experienced by the majority of the Roma community was interpreted as generating a threat to public policy and security (O'Nions, 2011: 371). At the same time, rather than being individual cases of deportation, the Roma were targeted for expulsion from France based on their ethnicity, indicating collective deportation, which is in breach of EU law (O'Nions, 2011).

The Commission has recently adopted *An EU Framework for National Roma Integration Strategies up to 2020* (2011) aimed to support targeted action regarding the Roma at the national level. While recognizing that the Framework does not replace Member States' primary responsibility in this area, this EU soft law initiative requests that Member States develop national Roma integration strategies by focusing on key EU Roma integration objectives, such as employment, poverty and education, which will contribute to progress towards Europe 2020 (European Commission, 2011g: 4). According to the Framework, EU Roma integration targets four crucial areas: access to education, employment, healthcare and housing, and therefore progress in these sectors is assessed via regular EU reporting back mechanisms. Therefore, there is a clear commitment on the part of the Commission to employ an integrated approach that can be applied by the Member States, while the Commission oversees the national efforts in this respect.

Arguably, there are clear drawbacks regarding the effectiveness and positive impact of EU-level initiatives to tackle the plight of the Roma in Europe. It has been argued that there is a deep ambivalence inherent in the 'European' calls for addressing the situation of the Roma (Vermeersch, 2012). This is rooted particularly in the tendency to single out Roma as a '*European* priority and a special *European* concern' (emphases added, Vermeesch, 2012: 1197), which can paradoxically offer ammunition to nationalist politicians to plead against a national responsibility vis-a-vis the Roma. In other words, the Europeanization of the Roma issue is a double-edged sword: it can transfer responsibilities for providing solutions from the national level to EU level, on the one hand; whilst it sheds light on the EU's lack of legal competence and efficient tools to address the problems faced by this community, on the other.

However, the feedback effects triggered by Eastern enlargement and the Romanian Roma at the EU level bolstered the need to take concerted action at the EU and Member States' level in order to combat discrimination and forge the inclusion of the Roma into the mainstream European society. The heightened political visibility acquired by the Roma issue due to the negative incidents in Italy and France prompted EU actions aimed at supporting Member States' efforts in this area, while, at the same time, exposed the contingent character of Member States' interpretation of EU law. In sum, there has been an incremental spillover of the Roma issue at the EU level. As shown above, previous reactions of EU institutions to the impact of enlargement and the stir caused by the Romanian Roma communities in Italy and France led to further initiatives adopted by the EU institutions, particularly by the Commission. The institutional structures, processes and actions which emerged due to enlargement and post-accession events further boosted the political visibility and broader consensus that concerted and coordinated action at both EU and national levels is paramount.

Mental health

The profile of mental health at the EU level has been raised due to Eastern enlargement. The Commission's engagement with mental health issues within the Union has acquired greater visibility at the EU level starting with 2005, when a Green Paper was issued and was aimed at consulting stakeholders regarding the adoption of an EU Mental Health Strategy. Mental health had been a sensitive accession condition for countries such as Romania during the accession monitoring process. It is not surprising, therefore, that mental health became an accession condition for the CEECs simultaneously with the DG for Health and Consumers' (SANCO) adoption of the Green Paper on mental health, which placed this policy issue on the Commission's internal policy agenda.[7] Eastern enlargement broadened the array of mental health issues within the EU and, therefore, it had an indirect impact on the Commission's role in this area.

The Green Paper (2005) promoting mental health had as a key aim the adoption of an EU strategy on mental health. However, rather than developing a strategy, the Commission initiated the *European Pact for Mental Health and Well-Being*, which was the outcome of the EU high-level conference 'Together for Mental Health and Well-Being' that was held in June 2008. Therefore, incrementally, EU non-legislative measures focusing on mental health started taking shape at the Commission level. The European Pact for Mental Health and Well-Being brings together EU and European institutions, Member States and stakeholders from relevant sectors to support and promote mental health and well-being (Slovenian Presidency, 2008: 4). Thus, a flexible and pragmatic approach to promoting mental health – the European Pact – was chosen over a formal mechanism – a Strategy – in order to avoid creating reporting obligations and new bureaucracy regarding mental health due to Member States' reluctance. The Pact focuses on five priority areas such as prevention of depression and suicide; mental health in youth and education; mental health in workplace settings; mental health of older people and combating stigma and social exclusion. Coterminous to other areas where the EU lacks legal mandate, the main objective of the Pact is to forge cooperation among the Member States, the Commission and stakeholders on various aspects related to mental health via the employment of soft law measures and instruments such as the exchange of best practice and promotion of mutual learning processes regarding the five priority areas, along with the involvement of non-governmental stakeholders in the promotion of mental health-related issues.[8] The Pact clearly acknowledges the division of competence on mental health according to which the 'primary responsibility for action in this area [mental health] rests with Member States' (Slovenian Presidency, 2008: 4).

Mental health is a sensitive policy area in the Member States and therefore, the Commission has to 'tread carefully' in terms of the kind of actions it takes in this sector. The Member States are reluctant to render mental health a highly visible issue at the Commission level and particularly to cede power on this sector to EU institutions. Yet, since 2005 the Commission has been developing a wide range of soft law measures, such as improving the cooperation and coordination between Member States in this field, public health promotion and raising awareness of mental health issues. The European Parliament adopted a Resolution[9] on mental health (2009) specifically supporting a Commission proposal for a European Strategy on Mental Health and Wellbeing, while urging Member States to adopt mental health legislation in conformity with their international obligations regarding human rights. The mandate of the Commission in this area rests on the Article 168 TFEU (ex Article 152 TEC) on public health. The new Article on Public Health in the Lisbon Treaty replaces 'human health' by 'physical and mental health', which constitutes a sea change regarding the recognition of this sector at the EU level. By the same token, the scope and role of the Commission in the area of public health have been augmented according to the new Article 168 TFEU as the Commission 'may take initiative to promote Member States' coordination, especially to establish guidelines and indicators, organise exchange of best practices, and prepare the necessary elements for periodic monitoring and evaluation'. While respecting the principle of subsidiarity in public health, the Commission has greater leverage to forge the cooperation of Member States on mental health matters, while overseeing these developments. However, even if the Commission's mandate in mental health is still limited, unlike its broad mandate as part of enlargement policy, it can be contended that the visibility and salience attached to mental health outside the Union has also started to emerge in EU internal policy sphere. Mental health received a significant boost due to Eastern enlargement, which normalized and broadened the EU's involvement with human rights issues that so far had been the domain of the external human rights policy. In sum, the considerable awareness raised of mental health issues due to enlargement, alongside the ongoing developments in this area, ascribed greater political visibility and weight to mental health concerns inside the Union.

Disability

Another human rights issue that resurfaced at the EU level due to Eastern enlargement concerns the rights of persons with disabilities, despite the history of involvement with disability issues dating back to the 1990s. For instance, the two Helios programmes – Helios I (1988–1992) and Helios

II (1993–1996) – were Community programmes for people with disabilities and their objective was to promote economic and social inclusion as well as independent living for people with disabilities. The Helios programmes provided funding for disability organizations in Europe with the key objective to raise public awareness of and promote the rights of disabled people.[10] These Community programmes focused on disability insofar as it was correlated to the functioning of the common market. Yet, Eastern enlargement and the Bulgarian post-accession case, i.e. Mogilino, raised awareness of a specific category of people with disabilities, namely vulnerable categories such as institutionalized disabled children. The Mogilino case in Bulgaria in particular brought to the spotlight how institutional care rendered disabled children as one of the most vulnerable categories, whose rights are violated by the national care system. This new 'dark' side of disability triggered actions at the EU level after 2007.

The EU had already in place its own institutional mechanisms to address disability as a horizontal issue, across EU policy sectors. For instance, in 1996 the Commission set up a Disability Inter-service Group to address issues pertaining to disability across all Commission services, which, therefore, encouraged more inter-sectoral cooperation within the Commission. The Inter-service Group also forged the mainstreaming of disability issues into all Commission initiatives and policy proposals. Thus, the Commission had been involved, to a certain extent, with disability issues in relation to the functioning of the common market by the time the situation of people with disabilities became an accession condition in relation to Eastern candidates. Yet, the question of the Bulgarian disabled children had feedback effects at the EU level after 2007 due to the media coverage of the appalling conditions of Bulgarian care homes for these children. As discussed in Chapter 4, the Mogilino case in Bulgaria prompted the Commission's reaction with respect to disability at the EU level as it raised awareness within the EU of the plight of people with disabilities in institutional care across Europe. As the Bulgarian case illustrates, the gap between the old and the new Member States' protection of people with disabilities became more evident once the former communist countries had joined the EU.

The EU's commitment to upholding the rights of persons with disabilities was reinforced by its allegiance to the international instruments in this area. For instance, the Union ratified in December 2010 the UN Convention on the Rights of Persons with Disabilities, which marked the first instance when an intergovernmental organization had signed and ratified an international human rights treaty. This convention was adopted by the UN on 13 December 2006 and its purpose is to promote, protect and ensure the equal enjoyment of all human rights by people with disabilities. The Commission signed the Convention on behalf of the Community on 30 March 2007. The implementation of this convention at the EU level and in the Member States provides a human rights approach – hence a broader coverage – to ensuring the respect of the rights of people with disabilities. The adoption of the UN Convention framework further entrenches disability as a human rights issue within the EU's normative framework, while, at the same time, it provides a shift from the medical and social models of disability to a human rights approach. Unlike the previous models, the human rights approach seeks to cast a positive spotlight on difference as, in the past, the invisibility of persons with disabilities led to a depreciation of the system of basic freedoms when applied to the difference of disability (Quinn and Degener, 2002: 26). A human rights approach, therefore, restores full civil rights to persons with disabilities and entails the protection of individual freedoms enjoyed by the rest of the society. The focus on a rights-based approach to disability endorsed by the EU underscores the broader EU commitment to the protection of human rights and fundamental freedoms by all members of society.

The EU has shared competence regarding action to combat discrimination on the grounds of disability according to Article 19 TFEU (ex Article 13 TEC). There are also other Treaty Articles which are relevant for disability issues over which the EU has shared competence, such as free movement of goods, persons, services and capital (Article 28 TFEU, Articles 45–48 TFEU and Article 55 TFEU), transport by rail, road, sea and air transport (Article 91 TFEU and Article 100 TFEU) to name just a few. Disability policies are essentially the responsibility of individual Member States, yet the EU can reinforce the disability dimension in all relevant EU policies and actions – via mainstreaming- and establish a sustainable and operational approach to disability in the EU. Disability matters loom large in the EU's internal policies. For instance, the Disability Strategy 2003–2010 was adopted in 2003. The priorities of the Disability Strategy are two-fold: ensuring accessibility and rights. The main legal basis for these priorities is the Employment Directive 2000/27/EC, which establishes a general framework for equal treatment in employment and occupation. The current EU Disability Strategy[11] (2010–2020) draws on the Charter of Fundamental Rights, the UN Convention on the Rights of Persons with Disabilities and the Lisbon Treaty, which provide a more robust rights-based dimension. The overall aim of this Strategy is to empower people with disabilities across the Union so that they can enjoy their full rights. By focusing on the elimination of all barriers currently preventing persons with disabilities from enjoying their rights, the Strategy focuses on key areas for action: accessibility, participation, equality, employment, education and training, social protection, health, and external action. It should be noted that the achievement of the Strategy objectives at the EU level is conducive to the implementation of the UN Convention on the Rights of Persons with Disabilities principles by the EU institutions inside the Union. Therefore, given that the EU is a State Party to the Convention, it is expected that EU institutions will promote and mainstream the rights of persons with disabilities in all EU actions, while fulfilling the EU's legal obligations arising from the Convention.

The disability case demonstrates that Eastern enlargement had profound implications for the profile and scope of disability at the EU level. Independent of this, the EU's accession to the UN Convention on the Rights of Persons with Disabilities, along with the provisions in the Lisbon Treaty, have further augmented the EU's institutional and policy capacity in this area inside the Union. Post-enlargement developments, along with the EU's internal on-going processes, therefore, re-defined the EU's role in and approach to the rights of persons with disabilities.

International adoption[12]

Another enlargement issue that generated effects on the EU's internal sphere is the regulation of international adoption. The practice of ICA from Romania had been one of the controversial human rights matters where the EU intervened and sought change before 2007. However, after Romania had joined the EU, adoption lobbies allied with some of the EU institutions pressured the Romanian authorities to lift the ban on ICA, which was maintained by Romania's current legislation. Therefore, as a consequence of Eastern enlargement, ICA was again on the EU's agenda after 2007, but now as part of the EU internal policy sphere.

After Romania's accession to the EU in 2007, various adoption lobbies, who disapproved of Romania's ban on ICA, sought to reverse the anti-ICA legislation in Romania by employing the EU's institutional opportunity structures. Adoption groups accessed EU venues, such as DG Justice, Freedom and Security (JLS) and the Parliament's Committee on Civil Liberties, Justice and Home Affairs (LIBE), to determine Romania to re-open ICA (Iusmen, 2013b). Given that the regulation of ICA is a national matter, the lobbies petitioned the European Parliament by framing ICA as a matter of EU internal policy and, therefore, by pleading for an open market in ICA in Europe. The success of adoption lobbies depended on their making alliances with supportive EU actors – either in the Commission or in the Parliament – and therefore capitalizing on the EU's self-interest in expanding its role in ICA inside the Union by embracing the lobbies' framing of ICA. Adoption agencies, such as SERA and Amici dei Bambini (Friends of Adoption), petitioned or contacted EU politicians in the Parliament and EU officials in the Commission's DG JLS (Iusmen, 2013b) to launch an EU campaign on the need to free the market of ICA in Europe.[13] For instance, the MEPs Claire Gibault and Jean Marie Cavada signed a Joint Declaration (2008)[14] which requested the support of the Commission in addressing the situation of international adoptions in Europe. By highlighting the detrimental effects of foster and institutional care on child development, the Declaration requested that European states prohibiting ICA, such as Romania, should review their anti-ICA legislation. One of the Commission's internal services, the DG JLS, was instrumental in taking up the issue of ICA: the Commission's interest in ICA led to the organization, together with the Council of Europe, of the conference 'Challenges in Adoption Procedures in Europe' in 2009. The Commission strategically employed the conference as an opportunity to present the findings of a study[15] on the state of play of international adoptions in the 27 Member States. The Commission's intention was to raise awareness of the discrepancies in ICA regulation across Europe and, therefore, to persuade Member States of the need to liberalize international adoption inside the EU (De Luca, 2009). This represented a radical shift from the Commission's anti-ICA position as part of Eastern enlargement. Among the Member States' national legislation on ICA, the Romanian case was highlighted as standing out due to its restricted ICA provision (Brulard and Dumont, 2009). By endorsing a negative view of in-country childcare solutions, such as foster care, the Commission study advances the proposal to harmonise adoption procedures in the Member States with the Commission playing the key role in overseeing the intra-EU adoption process (Iusmen, 2013b). To justify its pro-ICA stance, the Commission advanced a biased interpretation of the international instruments on child rights and ICA by rejecting Article 21 CRC and its principle of subsidiarity in relation to ICA due to 'uncertain interpretations', and therefore, upholding a preference for ICA if national adoption is not possible (De Luca, 2009: 2). The Commission's pro-active role in international adoption, as envisaged by DG JLS, is justified by the inclusion of children's rights among the Union's objectives in the Lisbon Treaty (Article 3 TEU) and its commitment to protecting children's rights, as enshrined in the EU Charter of Fundamental Rights (De Luca, 2009: 3). The pro-ICA line embraced by the Commission in its internal policy dimension after 2007 constitutes a far cry from its anti-ICA stance in the accession negotiations with Romania (Iusmen, 2013b).

Italian adoption agencies, such as Amici dei Bambini, lobbied the European Parliament to make ICA an issue of EU internal policy. The employment of the Parliament as a lobbying venue attaches political salience to the issue of ICA in Europe. For instance, Marco Griffini, the leader of Amici dei Bambini, petitioned the Parliament by explicitly requesting the Parliament's intervention in the situation of ICA from Romania to liberalise ICA from this country (European Parliament, 2010b). The Parliament formally rejected the petition; however, it decided to address the issue of parentless children as a matter of urgency at the EU level.[16] In response to the lobbies' pressure at the Parliament level, the EP's rapporteur for children Roberta Angelilli requested the Commission's action in relation to the plight of orphans in Romania as the situation of 'abandoned children has become an increasingly serious and burning issue following [...] the restriction of

inter-country adoptions' (Angelilli, 2010) which led to children's abandonment in orphanages (Angelilli, 2011).

The Parliament's and lobbies' pleas for the resumption of ICA, however,
do not reflect the situation in child protection in Romania after 2007 (Iusmen,
2012b, 2013b). As discussed in Chapter 3, child protection in Romania has
transformed radically due to EU accession conditionality. Despite shortcomings related to the slowness of the domestic adoption procedure, there are no
legal grounds to determine Romania to relax its anti-ICA policy. For instance,
the rate of child abandonment in hospital wards averages around 700 children
per year, with the great majority of these children being either reintegrated
into their families or placed in family-based alternative care (General Office
for Child Protection, 2011). Indeed, due to the Romanian new law, the vast
majority of children abandoned in hospitals are returned to their biological families while substantially fewer children are now abandoned each year
(Jacoby *et al.*, 2009). At the same time, as discussed in Chapter 3, the development of family-based alternative care, such as fostering or guardianship,
was the key target of the reform of child protection in Romania before 2007,
while the number of families requesting to adopt nationally exceeds by far
the number of adoptable children in the system.[17] Therefore, the Parliament's
plea for the resumption of ICA from Romania is not supported by the data
describing the post–2007 child protection system in Romania.

The European Parliament further promoted its pro-ICA position by
adopting a *Resolution on International Adoption in the European Union* in
January, 2011. The Resolution reflects the Parliament's position on ICA and
was the outcome of the alliance between Italian MEPs and Italian adoption
organizations, such as Amici dei Bambini.[18] According to the Resolution,
institutional care and not international adoption is a measure of last resort
due to the primacy of the child's right to have a family (European Parliament,
2011), which contradicts the childcare hierarchy embraced by UNICEF and
the UN Committee on the Rights of the Child (Herczog, 2009). In brief, the
Resolution, although a non-binding measure, urges all EU Member States to
reconsider international adoption as a valid childcare solution by resuming
ICA. The Parliament's pro-ICA activism after 2007 has been justified as being
part and parcel of its commitment to protecting children's rights, including
abandoned children, in Europe (European Parliament, 2011: 3). Indeed, the
EU institutions justified their support for a pro-ICA policy as being part the
EU's commitment to protect children's rights as enshrined in Article 3 TEU
(Lisbon Treaty), according to which the protection of children's rights is one
of the EU's objectives. Yet, the EU's support of a pro-ICA policy fell short of
pursuing the spirit and letter of the CRC and Hague Adoption Convention.
The European Parliament in particular attached its own interpretation to
these conventions by promoting its own hierarchy of childcare solutions,
which prioritizes ICA at the expense of foster care or any other in-country

solution, except domestic adoption (Iusmen, 2013b). The Parliament seems to endorse a relaxed ICA market inside the Union as providing a quick fix for the plight of children in care, without tackling the underlying causes of child abandonment or the poor childcare conditions.

The cases examined in this sections, namely the Roma, mental health, ICA and disability, suggest that Eastern enlargement had unforeseen effects on the EU's internal policy processes regarding human rights. The accession of new Member States with specific human rights problems had a catalytic effect on EU institutions by opening Pandora's Box of EU internal human rights dimension. Despite not providing an exhaustive list of enlargement effects, the human rights issues examined in this section show the interlinkages between Eastern enlargement and EU human rights concerns inside the Union. It is no coincidence, therefore, that human rights matters thoroughly scrutinized in the CEECs emerged on the EU's internal policy agenda as well. In the same vein, post-enlargement incidents brought to the fore the inherent deficiencies of EU law and its enforceability at the national level. Therefore, the EU's reactions to rights violations due to post-enlargement incidents meant that new issues emerged on the EU's internal agenda, which reinforced the contours of the emergent EU human rights regime.

EU Accession and human rights

How the EU accession process has impacted upon the political structures and policies of states seeking accession to the EU has been widely examined (see, among others, Grabbe, 2006; Vachudova, 2005; Pridham, 2005; Kelley, 2004; Sedelmeier, 2006; Schimmelfennig and Sedelmeier, 2005a). There has been a gradual process of widening and deepening of the scope of the human rights conditionality, as applied in the accession process, since its enunciation in 1993, as part of the Copenhagen accession criteria. The human rights conditionality applied in the current enlargement process has become more entrenched and even wider in scope due to three factors: the lessons learnt from the 2004/2007 enlargements, the specific circumstances in the Western Balkans and Turkey, and the EU's internal constitutional reform and policy developments.

The EU currently pursues a more cautious enlargement strategy, which is shaped by the specific inter-ethnic and regional problems faced by Western Balkans, along with the peculiarities of the Turkish case. Most of the current candidate and acceding countries (Croatia, Iceland, Montenegro, Serbia, Turkey and the Former Yugoslav Republic of Macedonia) and the potential candidates (Albania, Bosnia and Herzegovina, and Kosovo) have signed Stabilization and Association Agreements (SAAs), which include provisions for future EU membership of the country involved. The SAAs ascribe a crucial role to human rights as part of the relationship between the EU and associated countries: according to the SAAs, for instance, the commitment to respect human rights, including the rights of persons belonging to national minorities, constitutes the very basis of the agreement concluded by the Union and these countries. The SAAs entail a dual strategy (Renner and Trauner, 2009) pursued by the Union: on the one hand, the agreements provide a pre-accession strategy regarding future EU member-ship, on the other, they also support stability through regional integration strategies. The SAAs, therefore, can be compared to the Europe Agreements, signed by the Union with the CEECs in the early 1990s, as they provide the legal and political framework for prospective candidates to be associated with the Union. The Commission employs the Instrument for Pre-Accession Assistance (IPA),[19] which provides financial and technical support, to forge changes in the human rights provision in the current candidates. The finan-cial assistance provided under IPA helps to strengthen democratic institutions and the rule of law, reform public administration, promote respect for human as well as minority rights and gender equality and support the development of civil society and advance regional co-operation. In a nutshell, the current enlargement process follows a similar path to the Eastern one: Western Balkans and Turkey are part of a legal and political framework of accession negotiations, while instruments such as IPA provide technical and financial support towards the fulfilment of the accession criteria.

The current enlargement process with the Western Balkans and Turkey can be described as differentiated integration of prospective EU states (Economides, 2008). Differentiated integration in the current accession nego-tiations entails a 'process whereby European states ... opt for other (non-EU) states to move at different speeds' (Economides, 2008: 5) towards European integration. This multi-speed enlargement process constitutes the EU's solution for dealing with the kind of problems encountered in the Western Balkans, namely ethnic rivalries, separatism, war, and lack of democratiza-tion and human rights and minority protection. Indeed, the application of the accession political conditionality corroborated with differentiated integration approach allows the EU to address both the specific and common problems faced by these countries, whilst ensuring that EU rules and policies are grad-ually transferred to the prospective Member States. For instance, in acceding countries, such as Croatia – which will join the Union on 1 July 2013 – the Commission has focused significantly on the rights of the disadvantaged minorities, a similar problem being also outlined in Macedonia regarding the intra-ethnic tensions with respect to its Albanian minority. In Montenegro, concerns regarding fundamental rights are raised, alongside issues pertaining to rule of law and fight against corruption. At the same time, the Western Balkan candidates are confronted with a different EU enlargement context than the Eastern candidates due to the higher degree of uncertainty about future enlargements and the less central role of the EU's enlargement policy towards neighbouring candidate states (Trauner, 2011). Despite the EU's and candidates' concerted efforts towards meeting the accession criteria, uncertainty prevails with respect to whether and when these countries, apart from Croatia, will join the Union.

EU accession negotiations with Turkey have raised significant concerns regarding human rights violations, particularly in light of Turkey conflict-ridden past and rocky road to EU accession. Turkish EU aspirations date back to the 1960s, but Turkey only acquired the official candidate status in 1999 and opened accession negotiations in 2005. One of the reasons for Turkey's 'long march towards Europe' (Aras and Gokay, 2003) and, therefore, for its protracted candidacy status, is related to its human rights performance and its military regime till 1982. Indeed, Turkey's membership application was often overturned in the past due to 'human rights abuses, the excessive involvement of the military in political affairs, restrictions imposed on minority rights, and limitations on political and cultural rights under the 1982 constitution' (Kilic, 2001: 86). The human rights violations were particularly more predomi-nant in those areas that used to be controlled by the Kurdish Workers' Party (PKK), namely the south-east. To this end, the rapprochement with the EU in the early 2000s required an obvious improvement of Turkey's human rights record, particularly in the Kurdish areas (Bozarslan, 2001: 49).

One of the moot issues in EU-Turkey accession negotiations process is minority protection. Turkey's minority regime had been established by the 1923 Treaty of Lausanne, which enforced a system of protection to non-Muslim communities—the Armenians, the Greeks, and the Jews—who were granted the official status of minorities. According to Turkey's minority regime only the non-Muslim communities are recognized as minorities and are granted the right to use their own language, can enjoy political and civil rights, and the right to freedom of religion, travel, and migration (Hurewitz, 1956: 22). As part of the pre-accession process, the European Commission has scrutinized extensively the shortcomings of the legal regime underpinning the protection of minorities in Turkey, particularly with respect to the rights enjoyed by the Greeks, Armenians, and Jews. Furthermore, the European Commission has particularly challenged Turkish authorities with regard to the protection afforded to those non-Muslim minorities that fall outside the scope of the Treaty of Lausanne, such as Protestants and Catholics. In order to address the minority protection deficits highlighted in the Commission's Progress Reports, Turkish authorities started reforming their minority protection regime regarding the protection of both Muslim and non-Muslim minorities in relation to three areas, namely elimination of discrimination, improvement of cultural rights and religious freedom (Toktas and Aras, 2009: 712). Nevertheless, despite the reforms initiated due to EU accession demands, it has been argued that the Turkish government has prevented any significant change with respect to its traditional minority regime (Toktas and Aras, 2009). As the Turkish case indicates, the current enlargement policy amounts to the EU's intervention in relation to the specific human rights deficiencies prevalent in each candidate country concerned, and this entails a long-term process of political, legal and cultural transformations regarding the situation on the ground. Additionally, the length of accession negotiations and slowness of progress towards meeting the accession criteria are amplified by the uncertainty about the prospective EU membership.

EU Human Rights Regime

The effects of Eastern enlargement on the EU human rights provision, the current accession process along with the constitutional and legal changes introduced by the Lisbon Treaty indicate the emergence of a clearly defined and structured EU human rights regime. The scope and function of the EU's human rights regime is shaped and influenced by a complex set of factors, including the EU's internal processes, such as the current Eurozone crisis, as well as external processes and developments, such as the current accession negotiations and the broader EU external relations. According to international relations scholarship, international regimes are described 'as principles, norms, rules and decision-making procedures around which actor expectations converge in a given issue-area' (Krasner, 1982: 185). Therefore, international regimes governing a given policy area or an issue-area are deemed to provide elements of 'order', or structured regularity, despite the salient international anarchy in world politics (Donnelly, 1986: 601). In other words, it is widely contended that international regimes instil a sense of order and predictability in relation to how norms and values impact on national and international politics. To this end, the international human rights regime has been closely associated with international peace, security, development and a global trend towards pluralist democracy, good governance and the rule of law (Nowak, 2003). At the same time, the human rights regimes developed by various international and regional organizations can complement each other's objectives or, on the contrary, their scope and aims may overlap.

At the European level, the Council of Europe is regarded as the main human rights framework for the European states. The very reason for being of the European system established by the Council of Europe in 1949 is the protection of human rights via its well-established institutions and well-defined processes (Steiner and Alston, 1996: 563). All European states are state parties to the ECHR, which constitutes the main European instrument for human rights protection equally recognized and respected by all EU Member States. The Council of Europe, therefore, is the provider of the main human rights protection system at the European level (Buergenthal *et al.*, 2002: 133), embracing as key objectives the defence and reinforcement of human rights, pluralist democracy and the rule of law. However, lately the Council of Europe's human rights mandate has been increasingly overlapping with the mandates of other European organizations and institutions, such as the Organization for Security and Co-operation in Europe (OSCE), which was founded to maintain peace and military security within Europe, but also oversees human rights promotion, monitors elections and broader processes of democratization. At the same time, the mandate of the EU, despite being initially devised as an organization responsible for promoting trade and economic stability for its members, has been gradually developing a human rights profile, and therefore overstepping the boundaries of its own turf. No wonder, therefore, that the European human rights system consists of overlapping human rights regimes, each covering human rights protection explicitly, such as the Council of Europe, or indirectly, as part of broader economic and political agendas, such as the OSCE and the EU. Some of the key features of the EU's human rights regime are sketched below, particularly as they have transpired in light of Eastern enlargement developments and the latest legal and constitutional changes introduced by the Lisbon Treaty.

The Lisbon Treaty has strengthened the EU's *constitutional* and *legal commitments* to human rights. There are three factors supporting the reinforcement of EU institutions' allegiance to human rights: the Treaty provisions, the EU's prospective accession to the ECHR and the binding nature of the EU Charter of Fundamental Rights. Most policy areas pertaining to the protection of human rights are still under the jurisdiction of the Member States, however, now there are more robust legal and constitutional tools to ensure that the actions undertaken by EU institutions do not violate international human rights standards. In other words, there are more well-defined institutional 'brakes' on the EU's potential breach of human rights principles both inside and outside the Union. For instance, the EU Charter of Fundamental Rights is now the main, legally binding, fundamental rights proofing instrument employed in the legislative and policymaking process. Externally, Article 21 TEU inserted by the Treaty of Lisbon, provides that human rights constitute a cross-cutting principle for all EU external actions, while the consolidation and promotion of human rights is one of the EU's duties as part of its common foreign and security policy (Article 23 TEU), as well as its foreign common commercial policy, development, financial, technical, cooperation and humanitarian aid (Article 205 TFEU). It is worth noting here that the EU distinguishes between human rights, fundamental freedoms and fundamental rights. Generally, 'fundamental freedoms' are deemed to refer to the four freedoms to move goods, persons, services and capital within the common market (Article 26 TFEU), also coined as 'fundamental economic rights' (Tomuschat, 2003), while the European Court of Justice (ECJ) case law, Article 6(3) TEU and the Charter refer to 'fundamental rights', which

is another term for human rights. The reference to 'human rights and fundamental freedoms' in Article 21 TEU includes, therefore, both the four
freedoms and the human rights as recognized by the ECHR, which is explicitly mentioned in Article 6(2)TEU.

The provisions in the Lisbon Treaty entail a more robust and firmly
entrenched framework for human rights protection at the EU level. One of
the main reasons for this is the clarification of the role of the ECHR in relation
to EU law. For instance, in the Lisbon Treaty the ECHR roles are defined in
relation to different legal contexts: according to Article 6 TEU, the Convention
is a source of EU law, whilst, at the same time, the same Treaty article mentions
the Convention as an international treaty to which the EU will accede; and
finally, the ECHR, along with the Member States' constitutional traditions, is
a source of inspiration for EU human rights provision (Article 6 TEU, para-
graph 3), including the case law of the ECJ. Yet, it has been claimed that the
common constitutional traditions of the Member States have not, in fact, been
such an important source of principles for the ECJ as the ECHR, which has
been ratified by all the Member States of the EU (Douglas-Scott, 2011). The
binding nature of EU Charter of Fundamental Rights at the EU level means
that the Charter provisions, along with the ECHR's, serve as standards for
the EU human rights policy. Indeed, the incorporation of the ECHR into EU
law does not prevent the latter from providing a more extensive protection
(Weiss, 2011: 72), given that the Convention standards reflected in Charter
rights serve as a minimum guarantee in the EU, while other EU standards of
fundamental rights, such as the Charter, include a broader human rights catalogue and can provide a higher level of fundamental rights protection (Craig
and De Burca, 2008: 386). Furthermore, the EU Charter of Fundamental
Rights introduces new rights into the EU's legal order, such as economic and
political rights, therefore its scope is wider due to the provision of a broader
spectrum of rights than the ECHR (Douglas-Scott, 2006: 662). The Charter
acts as a 'road map' of EU rights, as it provides a broad human rights catalogue, including rights scattered throughout many different sources such as
the ECHR, and United Nations (UN) and International Labour Organization
(ILO) agreements. No wonder, therefore, that the Charter has been hailed
as an innovative instrument containing both economic and social rights along
with the more traditional civil and political rights. To cut a long story short, the
EU human rights framework post-Lisbon has been described as multi-layered:
fundamental rights at the EU level stem from general principles of EU law,
fundamental rights enshrined in the Charter, and those of the ECHR (Weiss,
2011: 66).

The scope and key features of the EU human rights regime have to be
contextualized at the European level, particularly in relation to the human
rights system established by the Council of Europe. It has been claimed that
the EU and the ECHR human rights regimes are converging, based on the

facts that the membership of the EU is becoming similar to that of the Council of Europe due to the human rights conditions (Burchill, 2011). Another key characteristic shared by both regimes is the existence of some form of *systemic monitoring* of the observance or non-observance of human rights commitments, via information gathering by specially created bodies or institutions (De Burca, 2003). For instance, the gradual emergence of EU human rights monitoring and benchmarking processes in a number of social and economic policy fields can go beyond what other international human rights systems have done so far due to the potential of providing genuine exercise in mutual learning, reflexive standard setting, and articulation of best practices (De Burca, 2003: 684). The monitoring mechanisms are particularly well-established in EU enlargement process, whereby a wide spectrum of human rights issue are rigorously screened and assessed by the European Commission. Even inside the EU, however, bodies such as the EU Fundamental Rights Agency regularly collect data and enable the exchange of best practice and knowledge across a wide range of rights related matters.

There is a more well-defined and entrenched EU human rights regime emerging in light of Eastern enlargement and the entry into force of the Lisbon Treaty, and this fact sheds a new light on the EU's 'policy of bifurcation' on human rights. The current developments and patterns in human rights promotion undertaken by EU institutions demonstrate the EU's capacity for reflexivity regarding EU role and function in human rights. As shown in Chapter 4 and in this chapter alike, EU external involvement with human rights can trigger feedback effects on the EU's internal policies, which will eventually shape and transform the EU's broader human rights role and provision. Despite not having the same legal leverage in EU internal policy dimension as in EU external relations, the EU has started to address inside the Union, although primarily via soft law measures, some of the human rights matters pursued via EU external policy. This entails a commitment to also uphold internally those normative values, such as human rights, which constitute the lynchpin of EU external policies. As examined in Chapter 4, there are key EU drivers of change – entrepreneurial actions, feedback mechanisms, and violations of human rights in the Member States – which can render possible the EU's reflexivity with respect to its mission in human rights.

Another key feature of the EU human rights regime is the *institutional foregrounding* of the European Commission as the EU human rights actor. The Commission's mission creep in new policy sectors (Majone, 2005, 2009) is well documented; therefore it is not surprising to observe the emergence of the Commission as the champion of human rights reforms inside and outside the Union. The actions taken by the Commission to uphold human rights are largely backed by the European Parliament, which attaches a certain political legitimacy to the Commission's entrepreneurial actions to promote human rights principles. At the same time, the Commission is strategically placed, in terms of its legal remit, as its mandate covers key external human rights areas, while inside the Union, it can push human rights issues on the EU's agenda as part of the functioning of the common market. In other words, the Commission's policy functions provide a bridge between the EU's internal and external policy dimensions: hence, how the Commission decides to deploy its external human rights actions can generate impacts upon the EU's internal human rights provision.

The gradually developing EU human rights regime also distinguishes itself from the EU's earlier human eights efforts via an explicit and consistent adherence to international human rights instruments. International standards and principles constitute the main yardstick guiding EU actions to promote human rights. For instance, all EU documents relevant to child rights employ the CRC as the main template of reference. In the same vein, the Optional Protocol to the CRC on the Involvement of Children in Armed Conflict is employed to address the situation of children affected by conflict in EU external relations. Recently, the EU has signed and ratified the UN Convention on the Rights of Persons with Disability, which ensures the EU institutions' legal commitment to translate the Convention provisions into EU law and policy. In other words, in line with the EU 'normative power' (Manners, 2002) image, the allegiance to international principles and instruments attaches a normative and even ethical dimension (Manners, 2008a; Manners and Diez, 2007; Lucarelli and Manners, 2006; Whitman, 2011) to EU human rights regime. Indeed, generally the EU's normative role in international politics indicates that the 'EU promotes a series of normative principles that are generally acknowledged, within the United Nations system, to be universally applicable' (Manners, 2008a: 66), which includes human rights norms. Nevertheless, the EU attaches its own interpretation and meanings to international instruments, by filtering their contents to match the EU's context. Therefore, each broad international principle is given a European reading (Lucarelli and Manners, 2006: 202), which sometimes opens a gap between the EU's declaratory support of international principles and its concrete actions. For instance, it has been argued that the EU lacks genuine allegiance to the international children's rights principles due to the 'fickle and unpredictable nature of the EU's relationship with the CRC' (Stalford, 2011: 214). The EU's inconsistent interpretation and application of international human rights standards ties in with the EU's original mission, i.e. an economic project, whereby human rights issues were addressed only if connected to the functioning of the common market. Irrespective of these critiques, it is noteworthy that EU institutions endeavour to ensure that EU actions reflect the main international human rights standards and principles and that the EU's external policies contribute to the global protection of human rights.

The EU's human rights regime has been described as endorsing legal exceptionalism, as envisaged by the ECJ's case law and its interpretation of international decisions and instruments. This legal exceptionalism was established by the Court's ruling in the case of Kadi,[20] which asserted the primacy and autonomy of fundamental rights in the EU legal order, although the Court's ruling conflicted with the international binding decision on this case. The Court's judgment in the Kadi case demonstrates 'the autonomy of the European legal order and the priority it gives to its internally determined values' (De Burca, 2010: 46). The effects of the Kadi case indicated once again how the EU envisages its human rights role and system relative to the international human rights regime. Furthermore, the Court's decision in the Kadi case held that the obligations of an international agreement could not prejudice the constitutional principles, which include respect for fundamental rights, of the EU Treaty (Douglas-Scott, 2011: 675). ECJ's ruling has been criticized for stressing the primacy and autonomy of EU law, by upholding respect for fundamental rights at the expense of insulating the ECJ from any international human rights standards, because of its choice for EU standards, and hence ensuing fragmentation of international law (Ziegler, 2009). Yet the EU's exceptionalism in human rights is a double-edged sword: while it establishes the autonomy of EU legal order regarding human rights, stressing the EU's contribution to the protection of human rights globally, it also has the potential danger of distancing the EU from the prevailing trends and instruments in international human rights law (Burchill, 2011: 26).

The gap between EU internal and external human rights dimensions, at least in terms of declarations and rhetorical commitment, has started to close. The normative bridge building between EU internal and external human rights policies has emerged in an attempt to address the critique of double standards. Indeed, more and more human rights matters pursued in the EU external relations have started being addressed inside the Union, mostly via soft law instruments intended to support Member States' cooperation and policy coordination. Notwithstanding this, it is still the case that the EU has greater leverage to enforce compliance with human rights principles in its external relations than inside the Union, where the protection of human rights, including minority rights, is a national matter. This is even more compelling in relation to those sensitive policy areas where Member States are reluctant to acknowledge allegations of rights violations, particularly if these allegations are made by EU institutions. The Commission, for example, refrains from taking legal action against the Member States by confining its role only to declaratory statements. For instance, human rights organizations condemned the Commission's failure to pursue vigorously its duty to enforce fundamental rights, dropping proceedings against Hungary over its media law and France over Roma expulsions (Human Rights Watch, 2012b). In the same vein, the Commission's first report on the observance of the Charter inside the Union shied away from criticizing the Members States, with Fundamental Rights Commissioner Viviane Reding emphasizing that the EU Charter of Fundamental Rights was a 'compass' rather than a 'stick'(Human Rights Watch, 2012b: 1). Despite these critiques, it is noteworthy that EU institutions, particularly the Commission, endeavour to place rights matters on EU agenda where EU action can have an added value at the national level.

Another recurrent aspect of the EU's human rights regime is the establishment of an *institutional infrastructure* to address human rights matters *per se*. For instance, one of the most recent bodies, the Fundamental Rights Agency, plays a pivotal role in supplying EU institutions with empirical data consisting of comparative analyses, indicators and concrete facts on how EU measures affect human rights provision across Europe. In the same vein, there is a Fundamental Rights Commissioner (European Commissioner for Justice, Fundamental Rights and Citizenship; current position held by Viviane Reding), while various Commission services have incorporated human rights matters into their institutional mandate (for instance, there is a 'Fundamental Rights and Citizenship' directorate with a 'Fundamental Rights and Rights of the Child' unit in DG Justice). Therefore, at least institutionally, there are specific portfolios covering rights matters, which enhances the political visibility and salience attached to human rights by EU institutions. The European Commission in particular addresses various human rights issues either via targeted actions or via processes of mainstreaming. Given the cross-sectoral aspect of most human rights matters, more and more EU policy sectors include measures indirectly impinging on the domestic human rights provision.

The EU's human rights regime has become more robust and more firmly entrenched in terms of its constitutional, legal and institutional provisions. The features of the regime described above have emerged due to Eastern enlargement effects, the EU's own ongoing processes, as well as the EU's constitutional reform, as indicated by the entry into force of the Lisbon Treaty and the binding nature of the Charter. From the outset, the EU's main concern has been with market building and regulation and therefore, human rights concerns rarely made it onto the EU's policy agenda. Yet the human rights sectors scrutinized in this chapter, along with the case of children's rights, indicate a qualitative shift regarding the EU's engagement with rights protection in general: now fundamental rights are no longer viewed from a market-focused perspective, but they also constitute goods in themselves, to which EU institutions are eagerly associating their policy remit. This qualitative change entails a more mature conception of fundamental rights, whose protection and promotion are intertwined with the objectives and scope of economic integration.

Conclusion

This chapter illustrated that Eastern enlargement, post-accession events and EU ongoing processes have led to the emergence of new human rights issues at the EU level. At the same time, the human rights conditionality as applied in the current accession process has become more structured and tailored to the specific needs of the current candidate countries. The momentum provided by Eastern enlargement for the EU human rights provision was further reinforced by the entry into force of the Lisbon Treaty and binding nature of the Charter. These developments have shaped and contributed to the emergence of a more robust – from legal, constitutional and institutional perspectives – EU engagement with human rights and minority protection, coined here as an EU human rights regime. Although the remit of this regime partly overlaps with that of the Council of Europe's, at least in Europe, it is also fairly distinctive from it due to the specificity of the EU's institutional and legal architecture. Indeed, human rights matters have more 'teeth' at the EU level now, which has profound implications for what the EU *is* and *does*.

Notes

1   The size of the Roma is estimated to be around 10 to 12 million in Europe (approximately 6 million of whom live in the EU), which makes the Roma community the biggest ethnic minority in Europe.

2   According to independent estimates there are around 5 million Roma living in Central and Eastern Europe (Druker, 1997; Clark, 1998). Roma are estimated to make up 8% to 10% of the total populations of Bulgaria, Macedonia, Romania, and Slovakia. They comprise about 5% to 6% of the total populations in Hungary and Yugoslavia, but only 2% to 3% of the total population in the Czech Republic (Open Society Institute, 2001).

3   Author's interview with a Commission official in DG Employment, Social Affairs and Equal Opportunities, Brussels, September 2008.

4   These directives are: Directive 2000/43/EC implementing the principle of equal treatment between persons irrespective of racial or ethnic origin, Directive 2000/78/EC establishing a general framework for equal treatment in employment and occupation and Directive 2004/113/EC implementing the principle of equal treatment between men and women in the access to and supply of goods and services.

5   According to the Communication 'the Directive will ensure that in all 27 Member States all forms of discrimination, including harassment, on the grounds of age, sexual orientation, disability and religion or belief are prohibited and victims have effective redress. Once adopted, the Directive will complete the process of giving effect to Article 13 TEC on all grounds and will bring to an end any perception of a hierarchy of protection' (European Commission, 2008d: 4).

6   *European Parliament resolution of 9 September 2010 on the situation of Roma and on freedom of movement in the European Union*, P7_TA(2010)0312.

7   According to a Commission official 'also in 2005 the Commission started drafting a Green Paper on mental health because it was clear that they also wanted to start having this topic on the Commission agenda and I know that DG SANCO colleagues were of course in close contact with World Health Organization'. Author's interview with a Commission official in DG Enlargement, Brussels, May 2008.

8   Author's interview with a Commission official in DG SANCO, Brussels, September 2008.

9   *European Parliament resolution of 19 February 2009 on Mental Health*, P6_TA(2009)0063

10 Official Journal EC, 9.4.1999.

11 *European Disability Strategy, 2010–2020:A Renewed Commitment to a Barrier-Free Europe*, Brussels, COM(2010) 636 final, 15.11.2010.

12 Some of the sections here have been published in Iusmen, I. (2013b) 'The EU and International Adoptions from Romania', *International Journal of Law, Policy and the Family*, 27(1), 1–27.

13 Author's interview with Commission officials in DG Enlargement, Brussels, May 2008, July 2011.

14 Available at www.coe.int/t/dc/files/themes/childrens_rights/Declarationcommune _EN.asp.

15 *Comparative study relating to procedures for adoption among the Member States of the European Union, practical difficulties encountered in this field by European citizens within the context of the European pillar of justice and civil matters and means of solving these problems and of protecting children's rights*, JLS/2007/ C4/017-30-CE-0157325/00-64.

16 Author's interview with a Commission officials in DG Justice, Brussels, July 2011.

17 For instance, each year 1,100 children are declared adoptable while there are 2,500 families requesting to adopt nationally. Author's interview with the secretary of state in the Romanian Office for Adoptions, Bucharest, July 2008.

18 Author's interview with Commission official in DG Justice, Brussels, July 2011.

19 IPA replaces the five previous EU instruments for pre-accession – PHARE, ISPA, SAPARD, the Turkey programme, and CARDS. The total IPA financing for 2007–2013 is €11.5 billion.

20 Joined Cases C-402/05P and C-415/05P Kadi and Al Barakaat v Council [2008] ECR I-6351. In this case the acts of the EU were to be seen as a direct implementation of UN Security Council Resolution 1267 (1999). Mr Kadi was one of a number of persons who had been blacklisted as terrorists and had their assets frozen because of the UN Security Council Resolution in October 2001. The EU took measures to implement the resolution. Yet, Kadi argued that he was the victim of a miscarriage of justice and that the EU measure – of freezing his assets – violated his fundamental rights to property, the right to a fair hearing and judicial redress. So Kadi approached the Court of First Instance (CFI) and the ECJ. The ECJ ruled in 2008 that Kadi's rights had been violated and, therefore, proclaimed the constitutional autonomy of the EU legal order, holding that the EU is a community based on the rule of law and that respect for fundamental rights is an integral part of the EU legal order.

Conclusion

Child protection and children's rights in Romania have come a long way since the early 1990s. The European Union (EU) has exerted unprecedented leverage over the direction and pace of reforms in human rights in Romania, particularly in relation to child protection, via the deployment of the instrument of accession conditionality. Both 'negative conditionality', connected with the threat of exclusion from the negotiations process or even halting them, and 'positive conditionality', associated with the EU membership reward, have engendered changes and developments triggered by the EU's intervention in the Romanian children's case. The EU's influence, as with respect to the broader political and economic reforms in Romania, has always been mediated by domestic politics, which, despite the costly reforms that the Romanian government had to implement, was galvanised by the quest to claim the 'EU membership prize' (Papadimitriou and Phinnemore, 2008:144). As the empirical findings in this book demonstrate, the changes introduced by the EU in child rights provision in Romania were legally, politically and institutionally far-reaching, and within the context of Eastern enlargement, extremely unique.

Parallel to EU accession negotiations, the EU's own constitutional reform was gathering momentum in the early 2000s. The adoption of the EU Charter of Fundamental Rights in 2000 brought the protection of human rights, at least symbolically, into the spotlight of the EU's constitutional reform process. However, as was shown in this book, the Eastern enlargement process, including the post-accession events, have had unforeseen consequences on the EU's internal human rights policy. The accession of Central and Eastern European Countries (CEECs) to the EU, therefore, has amounted to an import of a new set of human rights issues and violations, which the EU institutions were not adequately equipped to address. As the case of the Roma minority demonstrates, the enlarged Union had to grapple with new forms of human rights breaches, the solutions to which blurred the legal and political responsibilities between national and EU levels. In light of the themes and findings discussed throughout this book, a number of conclusions can be drawn: specific conclusions related to the Romanian case and the ensuing feedback effects, and some broader, more general conclusions about the EU human rights provision(s) and the factors that shape it. These conclusions are spelled out below.

The EU and child rights agenda: from 'rags to riches'?

The EU's leverage over the structural reform in child protection in Romania occurred mainly due to a set of contextual 'push factors'. The pro-active role of EU entrepreneurs (the European Parliament's rapporteur for Romania Baroness Emma Nicholson and Commissioner for Enlargement Günter Verheugen), the international media coverage of the plight of children living in institutions, along with the political sensitivity attached to children's matters in general facilitated the application of an EU interventionist policy in this area via the use of EU accession conditionality. EU application of accession criteria to Romanian child protection had to have 'teeth' as it was perceived that no country could join the EU while its child care system was extremely precarious, and its government paid no attention to children's rights. Meanwhile, the commitment of EU actors to transform this policy sector in Romania, as part of the accession negotiations process, meant that Romanian authorities had to react to EU pressure for change. Yet, the long road to post-communist transition – in terms of institutional, legal and cultural transformations – proved to be marred with setbacks and often uncertain, particularly when radical and costly reforms had to be implemented within short timeframes. Of course, all former communist states had to catch up with the West and therefore, had to adopt and implement extensive and unpopular economic and political reforms. As the Romanian case demonstrates, however, some changes had to be implemented quicker than others, under extreme political pressure and, therefore, the EU leverage and political clout was crucial in rendering these transformations possible.

Another conclusion that can be drawn from the findings of this book is that EU-induced changes are not equally approved and supported by all EU institutions alike. Given the variety of political and institutional interests at stake, EU institutions and actors can adopt conflicting approaches or frames (Rein and Schön, 1991, 1994) in relation to the same issue-matter, which, consequently, can generate divergent effects in practice. As the EU's contradictory approach to the issue of ICA before and after 2007 demonstrates, EU institutions are subject to various internal and external influences, which can shape the EU's agenda on human rights matters. Indeed, the EU's incoherent approach to certain human rights matters unveils the variety of vested interests and ideas that shape EU institutional preferences. Both the child rights policy applied to Romania and the EU's approach to human rights breaches inside the Union highlight the lack of consensus amongst EU institutions over the direction and scope of EU involvement in human rights. As shown in the book, the actions of various non-governmental organizations (NGOs), advocacy groups and lobbies can shape EU policy agenda and subsequently, the adoption of divergent policy frames by EU institutions constitutes also the outcome of this external influence.

The connection between institutional interests and approach(es) to human rights is further shaped by how international law and standards are interpreted and applied in practice. The EU, despite not being a signatory state of the vast majority of international human rights conventions, strives to ensure that its actions comply with international human rights standards. However, in doing so, the EU often attaches its own interpretation and weight to the role played by international norms and standards at the EU level. The EU's contradictory interpretation of the UN Convention on the Rights of the Child (CRC) provisions regarding ICA before and after 2007 supports this claim. Therefore, the implementation of international law and conventions by EU institutions constitutes a moot issue, particularly as the EU aspires to be regarded as an international human rights actor in world politics. How the EU engages with human rights issues, therefore, illustrates its interpretation or misinterpretation of international human rights law and instruments.

When and why do policies and institutions change? The feedback effects and processes discussed in this book indicate the contingent nature of policy innovation and agenda-setting dynamics at the EU level. One of the key themes of the book centred on the role played by policy entrepreneurs in shaping EU policy agenda by taking advantage of the available windows of opportunity, institutional context or extension of EU external remit via enlargement policy. However, the emergence of the 'right entrepreneur at the right time' is largely a contingent fact, as incidental as the availability of propitious factors and opportunities to enact policy change. In other words, it is merely a matter of randomness when institutional and political contexts will be 'ripe' in order to allow entrepreneurial actions to take shape. It could be contended, therefore, that Romania was 'lucky' to benefit from the availability of entrepreneurs such as Commissioner Verheugen and Baroness Nicholson, while the EU human rights provision benefited from Commissioner Frattini's entrepreneurial actions to introduce children's rights as an overarching EU issue. Indeed, policy entrepreneurship is a contingent and irregular occurrence either at national or supranational institutional settings. As discussed throughout the book, the emergence of the right entrepreneur and the availability of propitious conditions to enact policy innovation constitute correlated, yet random processes. Therefore, the findings of this research can be generalised to other policy sectors, provided that the similar 'ingredients' for policy change are at work.

A key conclusion drawn from the findings of this book is that both the child protection in Romania and the EU's child rights policy have undergone a significant evolutionary transformation, which can be coined as a trend from 'rags to riches'. Arguably, the Romanian child rights provision has seen a dramatic transformation over the last twenty years, which was mainly due to the EU accession process. But also the EU's engagement with child rights experienced a substantial transformation, although not as profound as the Romanian case. Indeed, since mid-2000s the EU's involvement with various child rights aspects, both inside and outside the Union, has become more robust and well-defined, with the EU endeavouring to act like a child rights actor. Paradoxically, despite this incremental evolution observed in Romanian child protection and EU child rights role, they both face significant challenges and obstacles due to the current economic and political turmoil experienced by EU Member States.

What next for EU human rights role? New challenges and avenues on the horizon

Broader conclusions about European integration and EU human rights role transpire from the topics discussed in this book. Despite the common critique of a 'double standards' approach to human rights, there seems to be a strong link between the EU's external and internal actions to uphold human rights. Human rights issues extensively pursued as part of EU external relations do have the potential to reverberate in EU internal policy dimension. On an optimistic note, therefore, this indicates that more and more human rights issues could be addressed more rigorously inside the Union as well. Violations of human rights are more visible inside the Union, particularly as the functioning of the common market and the EU's broader remit post-Lisbon impacts indirectly upon national human rights provision. As shown in this book, therefore, EU institutions endeavour to respond to these challenges by undertaking more consistent and coherent measures in relation to human rights.

The link between EU internal and external human rights dimensions, secondly, ties in with the broader European integration process, particularly its breadth and depth. The emergence of new issues on the EU agenda entails an impetus to advance European integration in those respective policy areas. The scope and direction of the European integration process is often unpredictable, particularly in times of economic downturn or acceptance of new Member States. However, the EU's complex external role along with its internal political and policy processes eventually leave their mark on the EU agenda and, obviously, on the process and direction of European integration. Eastern enlargement and post-accession incidents opened Pandora's Box regarding human rights and minority protection violations in Europe. EU institutions reacted to these human rights breaches by taking action in relation to them, which amounted to the EU's embrace of new roles and functions in areas, such as children's rights, so far never associated with the EU.

European publics are highly sensitive to rights violations, particularly when vulnerable categories, such as children or mentally ill people, are concerned. The heightened public awareness of human rights abuses is crucial in providing the seal of approval to EU actions in human rights. Indeed, EU institutions often justified their initiatives to uphold human rights standards, as in the case of children's rights, by appealing to European publics' consent for EU-led action at the nation level. This is paramount given that, generally, the Member States are extremely suspicious of EU intervention in politically sensitive areas and, therefore, are reluctant to cede power over the national human rights provision to a regional economic organization, like the EU. Yet, in order to be effective as a human rights actor, the EU should lead by example and its actions should have concrete impact on people's lives. Nevertheless, as often the case, EU actions can fail to generate their intended effects, and subsequently, EU intentions become sheer rhetoric and idealistic declarations. New challenges and policy priorities have now to be addressed more coherently and holistically by the EU. For instance, climate change, child poverty, socio-economic exclusion have to incorporate clear and explicit connections with the protection of human rights, as advanced by EU institutions. To meet these challenges successfully, EU institutions need to be innovative to create new, more effective instruments, while cooperating better with national authorities, international organizations and civil society actors. Notwithstanding this, the EU human rights policy has come a long way since the early 1990s, and the flurry of activity in areas such as children's rights demonstrates that the 'nature of the beast' (Risse-Kappen, 1996) entails a more serious human rights function that will continue to grow and diversify in the future.

References

Aggestam, L. (2008) 'Introduction: Ethical Power Europe?', *International Affairs*, 84(1), 1–11.

Alston, P. and Weiler, J.H.H. (1999) 'An "Ever Closer Union" In Need of a Human Rights Policy: The European Union and Human Rights', in P. Alston (ed.) *The EU and Human Rights*, Oxford: Oxford University Press, pp. 3–66.

Amnesty International (2005) *Bulgaria and Romania Amnesty International's Human Rights Concerns in the EU Accession Countries*, EUR 02/001/2005, London, October.

Amnesty International (2010) *Italian Authorities Urged to Stop Forced Evictions of Roma*, 11th March, available at: www.amnesty.org/en/news-and-updates/report/italian-authorities-urged-stop-forcedevictions- roma-2010-03-11.

Amnesty International (2013) 'Ireland's EU Presidency Must Strengthen Human Rights Within Europe', Press Release, available from www.amnesty.eu/en/press-releases/all/0610-0610/.

Angelilli, R. (2010) *Parliamentary Questions. 17 August 2010. Subject: Alarming Situation of Orphans in Romania*, E-6272/2010, available at www.europarl.europa.eu/sides/. .

Angelilli, R. (2011) *Parliamentary Questions. 1 April 2011. Subject: Romania: Alleged Violation of International Adoption Standards in the EU*, available at www.europarl.europa.eu/sides/.

Aras, B. and Gokay, B. (2003) 'Turkey after Copenhagen: Walking a Tightrope', *Journal of Southern Europe and the Balkans* 5(2), 147–168.

Archard, D. (2004) *Children: Rights and Childhood*, London: Routledge.

Armstrong, K. and Bulmer, S. (1998) *The Governance of the Single European Market*, Manchester and New York: Manchester University Press.

Bainham, A. (2003) 'International Adoption from Romania – Why the Moratorium Should Not Be Ended', *Child and Family Law Quarterly* 15(3), 1–18.

Bartels, L. (2005) *Human Rights Conditionality in EU's International Agreements*, Oxford: Oxford University Press.

Barzelay, M. and Gallego, R. (2006) 'From New Institutionalism to Institutional Processualism: Advancing Knowledge about Public Management Policy Change', *Governance*, 19(4), 531–57.

Barzelay, M. and Gallego, R. (2010) 'The Comparative Historical Analysis of Public Management Policy Cycles in France, Italy and Spain: Symposium Introduction', *Governance*, 23(2), 209–223.

Baumgartner, F.R. and Jones, B.D. (1993) *Agendas and Instability in American Politics*, Chicago: University of Chicago Press.

Baumgartner, F.R., Green-Pedersen, C. and Jones, B.D. (2006) 'Comparative Studies of Policy Agendas', *Journal of European Public Policy*, 13(7), 959–974.

Baun, M. (2000) *A Wider Europe: The Process and Politics of European Union Enlargement*, Lanham: Rowman and Littlefield.

BBC News (2010) Q&A: France Roma Expulsions. *BBC News Online*, 19 October. Available at www.bbc.co.uk/news/world-europe-11027288.

Besson, S. (2006) 'The European Union and Human Rights: Towards A Post-National Human Rights Institution?', *Human Rights Law Review*, 6(2), 323–360.

Bogdanov, G. and Zahariev, B. (2007) 'Tackling Child Poverty and Promoting the Social Inclusion of Children: A Study of National Policies', available at ec.europa. eu/social/.

Bozarslan, H. (2001) 'Human Rights and the Kurdish Issue in Turkey: 1984–1999', *Human Rights Review*, 3(1), 45–54.

Brulard, Y. and Dumont, L. (2009) *Comparative Study Relating to Procedures for Adoption among Member States of the European Union, Practical Difficulties Encountered in this Field by European Citizens Within the Context of the European Pillar of Justice and Civil Matters and Means of Solving these Problems and of Protecting Children's Rights*, LS/2007/C4/017-30-CE-0157325/00-64, available at http://ec.europa.eu/civiljustice/news/docs/study_adoption_legal_analysis_en.pdf.

Buergenthal, T., Shelton, D. and Stewart, D. (2002) *International Human Rights in a Nutshell*, 3rd edition, Chicago: West Publishing.

Bulmer, S. (1994) 'Institutions and Policy Change in the European Communities: the Case of Merger Control', *Public Administration*, 72(3), 425–446.

Bulmer, S. (2009) '*Politics in Time* meets the politics of time: historical institutionalism and the EU timescape', *Journal of European Public Policy*, 16(2), 307–324.

Bulmer, S. and Radaelli, C.M. (2004) 'The Europeanization of National Policy?' *Queen's Papers on Europeanization*, No. 1.

Burchill R. (2011) 'Assessing the European Union's Position on Human Rights: Is It a Desirable One?' in J. Wetzel (ed.) *The EU as a Global Player in the Field of Human Rights*, London: Routledge.

Cassese, A., Clapham, A. and Weiler, J. (1991) *European Union: The Human Rights Challenge*, Portland: Nomos.

Cette-France-là (2010) 'L'Europe au Miroir des Roms: Nom Pluriel, Destin Singulier'. Available at http://lmsi.net/L-Europe-au-miroir-des-Roms.1096.

Checkel, J.T. (1999) 'Norms, Institutions and National Identity in Contemporary Europe', *International Studies Quarterly*, 43(1), 83–114.

Checkel, J.T. (2001) 'Why Comply? Social Learning and European Identity Change,' *International Organization*, 55(3), 553–88.

Children's High Level Group (2007) 'Assessment of Institutions for Children with Disabilities. Report of the 'Children's High Level Group' Association', January.

Children's High Level Group (n. d.) 'Children's High Level Group-Romania. Activities', Children's High Level Group internal document.

Cirtautas, A.M. and Schimmelfennig, F. (2010) 'Europeanisation Before and After Accession: Conditionality, Legacies and Compliance', *Europe-Asia Studies*, 62(3), 421–441.

Ciută, F. (2005) 'A Life Less Ordinary: Romania on the Road to NATO', in D. Deletant (ed.) *In and out of Focus: Romania and Britain. Relations and Perspectives from 1930 to the Present*, Bucharest: Cavaliotti, pp. 247–278.

Clark, C. (1998) 'Counting backwards: the Roma "numbers game" in Central and Eastern Europe', *Radical Statistics*, 69: 35–46.

Cobb, R.W. and Elder, C.D. (1972) *Participation in American Politics. The Dynamics of Agenda-building*, Baltimore, MD and London: The Johns Hopkins University Press.

Commissioner for Human Rights (2010) *Positions on Children's Rights Position Paper from the Council of Europe Commissioner for Human Rights.* Strasbourg, 3 May 2010, available at https://wcd.coe.int/.

Committee on the Rights of the Child (2008) *Forty-ninth Session. Report on the Forty-ninth Session*, Geneva, 15 September to 3 October.

Consolidated Texts of the EU Treaties as Amended by the Treaty of Lisbon, (2007) available at www.official-documents.gov.uk/document/cm73/7310/7310.pdf.

Council Directive 2000/43/EC of 29 June 2000, 'Implementing the Principle of Equal Treatment between Persons Irrespective of Racial or Ethnic Origin', *Official Journal of the European Communities,* 19 July 2000.

Council Directive 2000/78/EC of 27 November 2000, 'Establishing a General Framework for Equal Treatment in Employment and Occupation', *Official Journal of the European Communities,* 2 December 2000.

Council of Europe (2008) *Proposed 42-day Pre-charge Detention in the United Kingdom,* Doc. 11725, 30 September.

Council of the European Union (2005) 'Council and Commission Action Plan Implementing the Hague Programme on Strengthening Freedom, Security and Justice in the European Union', *Official Journal* C/236 of 24 September.

Council of the European Union (2007) *EU Guidelines for the Promotion and Protection of the Rights of the Child*, available at www.consilium.europa.eu/uedocs/cmsUpload/16031.07.pdf.

Council of the European Union (2008) *Conclusions on the Promotion and Protection of the Rights of the Child in the European Union's External Action – The Development and Humanitarian Dimensions*, Brussels, 2570 the External Relations Council meeting.

Council of the European Union (2009) 'Council Conclusions on Inclusion of the Roma', accessed from www.euromanet.eu/upload/21/69/EU_Council_conclusions_on_Roma_inclusion_-_June_2009.pdf.

Craig, P. and De Burca, G. (2003) *EU Law. Text, Cases and Materials* 2nd edition, Oxford: Claredon Press.

Craig, P and De Burca, G. (2008) *EU Law. Text, Cases and Materials* 4th edition, Oxford: Claredon Press.

Cram, L. (1994) 'The European Commission as a Multi-Organisation: Social Policy and IT Policy in the EU', *Journal of European Public Policy* 1(2), 195–217.

Cram, L. (1997) *The Politics of EU Policy-Making: Conceptual Lenses and the Integration Process*, London: Routledge.

Cullen H. (2004) 'Children's Rights', in S. Peers and A. Ward (eds) *The European Charter of Fundamental Rights*, Oxford: Hart.

Dahl, R. (1991) *Who governs? Democracy and Power in an American City*, New Haven Yale University Press.

Darrow, M. and Tomas, A. (2005) 'Power, Capture and Conflict: A Call for Human Rights Accountability in Development Cooperation', *Human Rights Quarterly* 27(2), 471–538.

De Burca, G. (2003) 'Beyond the Charter: How Enlargement Has Enlarged the Human Rights Policy of the European Union', *Fordham International Law Journal*, 27(2), 679–714.

De Burca, G. (2010) 'The European Court of Justice and the International Legal Order after *Kadi*', *Harvard International Law Journal*, 51(1), 1–50.

De Burca, G. (2011) 'The Road Not Taken: The EU as a Global Human Rights Actor', *American Journal of International Law*, 105(4), 649–693.

Delegation of the European Commission in Romania (2005) *Child Protection Information Sector Report*, July.

De Luca, P. (Civil Justice Unit, DG Justice, Freedom and Security, European Commission) (2009) *European Commission Study on Adoption – Outline of Presentation*, available at www.coe.int/t/dghl/standardsetting/family/Adoption%20conference/Presentation%20DE%20LUCA.pdf.

De Schutter, O. (2002) 'Europe in Search of Its Civil Society', *European Law Journal*, 8(2), 198–217.

De Schutter, O. (2009) 'The EU Fundamental Rights Agency: Genesis and Potential' in K. Boyle (ed.) *New Institutions for Human Rights Protection*, Oxford: Oxford University Press, pp. 93–133.

De Witte, B. and Toggenburg, G.N. (2004) 'Human Rights and Membership of the European Union', in S. Peers and A. Ward (eds) *The EU Charter of Fundamental Rights. Politics, Law and Policy*, Oxford: Hart Publishing, pp. 59–82.

Dickens, J. (2002) 'The Paradox of Inter-country Adoption: Analysing Romania's Experience as a Sending Country', *International Journal of Social Welfare*, 11(1), 76–83.

Dillon, S.A. (2003) 'Making Legal Regimes for Inter-country Adoption Reflect Human Rights Principles: Transforming the United Nations Convention on the Rights of the Child with the Hague Convention on Inter-country Adoption', *Boston University International law Journal*, 21, 179–257.

DiMaggio, P. (1988) 'Interest and Agency in Institutional Theory', in L. Zucker (ed.) *Institutional Patterns and Culture*, Cambridge: Cambridge University Press, pp. 3–22.

Dimitrikapoulos, D.G. (2001) 'Unintended Consequences: Institutional Autonomy and Executive Discretion in the European Union', *Journal of Public Policy*, 21(2), 107–31.

Donnelly, J. (1986) 'International Human Rights: A Regime Analysis', *International Organization*, 40(3), 599–639.

Douglas-Scott, S. (2006) 'A Tale of Two Courts: Luxembourg, Strasbourg and the Growing European Human Rights *Acquis*', *Common Market Law Review*, 43(3), 629–665.

Douglas-Scott, S. (2011) 'The European Union and Human Rights after the Treaty of Lisbon', *Human Rights Law Review*, 11(4), 645–682.

Druker, J. (1997) 'Present but unaccounted for', *Transitions*, 4(4): 22–23.

Duchene, F. (1972) 'Europe's Role in World Peace', in R. Mayne (ed.) *Europe Tomorrow: Sixteen Europeans Look Ahead*, London: Fontana, pp. 32–47.

Dyson, T. (2008) *Politics of German Defence and Security: Policy Leadership and Military Reform in the Post-Cold War Era*, Oxford: Berghahn Books.

Economides, S. (2008) 'The Politics of Differentiated Integration: The Case of the Balkans', *Hellenic Observatory Papers on Greece and Southeast Europe*, GreeSE Paper No 18. The Hellenic Observatory, London.

Eekelaar, J. (1992) 'The Importance of Thinking that Children Have Rights', *International Journal of Law and the Family*, 6 (1), 221–235.

EU Network of Independent Experts on Fundamental Rights (2002) *Report on the Situation of Fundamental Rights in the European Union and its Member States in 2002*, available from http://ec.europa.eu/justice/fundamental-rights/files/cfr_cdf_2002_report_en.pdf.

Eurobarometer (2008) 'Discrimination in the European Union: Perceptions, Experiences and Attitudes', available from http://ec.europa.eu/social/.

European Commission (1997) *Agenda 2000 – Commission Opinion on Romania's Application for Membership of the European Union*, DOC/97/18, Brussels, 15 July.

European Commission (1998) *Regular Report from the Commission on Romania's Progress Towards Accession*, accessed from http://ec.europa.eu/enlargement/archives/pdf/key_documents/1998/romania_en.pdf.

European Commission (1999) *Regular Report from the Commission on Romania's Progress Towards Accession*, accessed from http://ec.europa.eu/enlargement/archives/pdf/key_documents/1999/romania_en.pdf.

European Commission (2000) *Regular Report on Romania's Progress Towards Accession*, accessed from http://crib.mae.ro/upload/docs/9402_2000_Regular_Report.pdf.

European Commission (2001) *Regular Report on Romania's Progress Towards Accession*, accessed from http://crib.mae.ro/upload/docs/9402_2001_Regular_Report.pdf.

European Commission (2002) *Regular Report on Romania's Progress Towards Accession*, accessed from http://crib.mae.ro/upload/docs/9402_2002_Regular_Report.pdf.

European Commission (2003) *Regular Report on Romania's Progress Towards Accession*, accessed from http://ec.europa.eu/enlargement/archives/pdf/key_documents/2003/ rr_ro_final_en.pdf.

European Commission (2005a) *Romania 2005 Comprehensive Monitoring Report*, SEC (2005) 1354, Brussels, 25 October.

European Commission (2005b) *Communication from the Commission to the Council and the European Parliament of 10 May 2005 – the Hague Programme: Ten Priorities for the Next Five Years. The Partnership for European Renewal in the Field of Freedom, Security and Justice*, COM (2005) 184 final, Brussels, 10 May.

European Commission (2005c) *Strategic Objectives 2005–2009*, COM (2005) 12 final, Brussels, 26 January.

European Commission (2006a) *Communication from the Commission: Towards an EU Strategy on the Rights of the Child*, COM (2006) 367 final, Brussels, 4 July.

European Commission (2006b) *Commission Staff Working Document accompanying the Communication from the Commission: Towards an EU Strategy on the Rights of the Child. Impact Assessment*, SEC (2006) 888, Brussels, 4 July.

European Commission (2006c) *Communication from the Commission: Monitoring Report on the State of Preparedness for EU Membership of Bulgaria and Romania*, COM (2006) 549 final, Brussels, 26 September.

European Commission (2007) *Proposal for a Council Decision Implementing Regulation (EC) No 168/2007 as regards the Adoption of a Multiannual Framework for the European Union Agency for Fundamental Rights for 2007–2012*, COM(2007) 515 final, Brussels, 12 September.

European Commission (2008a) *Communication from the Commission to the Council, the European Parliament, the European Economic and Social Committee and the*

Committee of the Regions: A Special Place for Children in EU External Action, COM (2008) 55 final, Brussels, 5 February.

European Commission (2008b) *Commission Staff Working Document. The European Union's Action Plan on Children's Rights in External Action*, SEC (2008) 136, Brussels, 5 February.

European Commission (2008c) *Commission Staff Working Document. Children in Emergency and Crisis Situations*, COM(2008) 55 final, Brussels, 5 February.

European Commission (2008d) *Commission Communication. Non-discrimination and equal opportunities: A renewed commitment*, COM (2008) 420 final, Brussels, 2 July.

European Commission (2009) *Communication from the Commission to the European Parliament and the Council: An Area of Freedom, Security and Justice Serving the Citizen*, COM (2009) 262 final, Brussels, 10 June.

European Commission (2010a) *Dial 116 000: The European Hotline for Missing Children*, COM(2010) 674 final, Brussels, 17 November.

European Commission (2010b) *Strategy for the Effective Implementation of the Charter of Fundamental Rights by the European Union*, COM (2010) 573/4, Brussels, 19 October.

European Commission (2010c) *Staff Working Document: Combating Child Labour*, SEC (2010) 37 final.

European Commission (2010d) *Press Release. European Commission Assesses Recent Developments in France, Discusses Overall Situation of the Roma and EU Law On Free Movement of EU Citizens*, IP/10/1207, 29 September.

European Commission (2011a) *Turkey-Progress Report Accompanying the Document Communication from the Commission to the European Parliament and the Council, Enlargement Strategy and Main Challenges 2011–2012. Staff Working Paper*, COM (2011) 666 final, Brussels.

European Commission (2011b) *Croatia – Progress Report Accompanying the Document Communication from the Commission to the European Parliament and the Council, Enlargement Strategy and Main Challenges 2011–2012*, COM (2011) 666 final, Brussels.

European Commission (2011c) *Montenegro -Progress Report Accompanying the Document Communication from the Commission to the European Parliament and the Council, Enlargement Strategy and Main Challenges 2011–2012*, COM (2011) 666 final, Brussels.

European Commission (2011d) *Communication from the Commission to the European Parliament and the Council, Commission Opinion on Serbia's Application for Membership of the European Union*, COM(2011) 668 final, Brussels.

European Commission (2011e) *The Former Yugoslav Republic of Macedonia 2011e Progress Report Accompanying the Document Communication from the Commission to the European Parliament and the Council, Enlargement Strategy and Main Challenges 2011–2012*, COM (2011) 666 final, Brussels.

European Commission (2011f) *An EU Agenda for the Rights of the Child*, COM (2011) 60 final, Brussels.

European Commission (2011g) *An EU Framework for National Roma Integration Strategies up to 2020*, COM(2011) 173 final, Brussels, 5 April.

European Commission (2012) *Communications Committee. Working Document. Implementation of the reserved '116' numbers – as of 25 May 2012*, COCOM12-14 final, Brussels, 25 May.

European Commission, Employment and Social Affairs (2004) *The Situation of Roma in an Enlarged European Union,* Luxembourg: Focus Consultancy Ltd.

European Council (1993) *Conclusions of the Presidency.* SN 180/93, Copenhagen.

European Council (1997) *Presidency Conclusions,* DOC/97/24, Luxembourg, 12–13 December.

European Council (2004) *The Hague Programme-Strengthening Freedom, Security and Justice in the European Union,* 14292/04, Brussels.

European Court of Human Rights (2010) *Annual Report,* Strasbourg: Registry of the European Court of Human Rights.

European Foundation for Street Children Worldwide (2006) *Report on the EFSCW European Forum – Child Inclusion as a Challenge to the Mediterranean Partnership of the EU – The Consequences of Migration On Children at Risk in Southern European Member States: Analyses, Concepts and Strategies,* Rome, 16–17 February.

European Parliament (2000) *Report on Romania's Application for Membership of the European Union and the State of Negotiations,* A5-0247/2000 final, 21 September.

European Parliament (2001) *Report on Romania's Application for Membership of the European Union and the State of Negotiations,* A5-0259/2001 final, 24 July.

European Parliament (2004) *Report on Romania's Progress Towards Accession,* A5-0103/2004 final, 24 February.

European Parliament (2005) *Report on the Extent of Romania's Readiness for Accession to the European Union,* A6-0344/2005 final, 25 December.

European Parliament (2006) *Report on the Accession of Romania to the European Union,* A6-0421/2006 final, 27 November.

European Parliament (2007a) *Report: Towards an EU Strategy on the Rights of the Child,* A6-0520/2007, 20 December.

European Parliament (2007b) *Resolution of 15 November 2007 on Application of Directive 2004/38/EC on the right of EU Citizens and their family members to move and reside freely within the territory of the Member States,* P6_TA(2007)0534.

European Parliament (2008) *European Parliament Resolution of 16 January 2008: Towards an EU Strategy on the Rights of the Child,* P6_TA (2008)0012.

European Parliament (2009) *International Adoption in the European Union. Final Report* IP/C/LIBE/2008-003, 27 March.

European Parliament (2010a) *European Parliament Resolution of 9 September 2010 on the Situation of Roma and on Freedom of Movement in the European Union,* P7_TA(2010)0312, available from www.europarl.europa.eu/sides/.

European Parliament (2010b) *Committee on Petitions. Petition 1120/2009 by Marco Griffini on Behalf of Amici dei Bambini, on Romania's Compliance with International Conventions On Children's Rights,* available at www.europarl.europa.eu/meetdocs/2009_2014/documents/peti/cm/805/805927/805927en.pdf.

European Parliament (2011) *European Parliament Resolution of 19 January 2011 on International Adoption in the European Union,* P7_TA-PROV(2011)0013, Strasbourg.

European Union Agency for Fundamental Rights (2009) *Developing Indicators for the Protection, Respect and Promotion of the Rights of the Child in the European Union. Summary Report,* March.

Fichtner, U. (2010) 'Driving Out the Unwanted: Sarkozy's War against the Roma'. *Spiegel Online International,* 15 September, available at: www.spiegel.de/international/europe/0,1518,717324,00.html.

Fierke, K. and Wiener, A. (1999) 'Constructing Institutional Interests: EU and NATO Enlargement', *Journal of European Public Policy* 6(5), 721–742.

Fierro, E. (2003) *The EU's Approach to Human Rights Conditionality in Practice*, The Hague: Martinus Nijhoff Publishers.

Finnemore, M. and Sikkink, K. (1998) 'International Norm Dynamics and Political Change', *International Organisation*, 52 (autumn), 887–917.

Fligstein, N. (2001) 'Social Skills and the Theory of Fields', *Sociological Theory*, 19(2), 105–125.

Focus on Romania (2005) 'Letter to Jonathan Scheele', Commission internal document, 12 December.

Focus on Romania (2006) 'Letter to Mr Olli Rehn', Commission internal document, 6 April.

Fortin, J. (2009) *Children's Rights and the Developing Law*, 3rd edition, Cambridge: Cambridge University Press.

Frattini, F. (2005) *The Hague Programme: a Partnership for the European Renewal in the Field of Freedom, Security and Justice*, SPEECH/05/441.

Frattini, F. (2008) *Europe as the Guardian Angel of All Children. Second European Forum on the Rights of the Child*, available at www.eu-un.europa.eu/articles/en/article_7752_en.htm.

Freeman, M. (2000) 'The Future of Children's Rights', *Children and Society*, 14(4), 277–293.

Freeman, M. (2011) 'The Value and Values of Children's Rights', in Invernizzi, A. and Williams, J. (eds.) *The Human Rights of Children. From Vision to Implementation*, Surrey: Ashgate Publishing, pp. 21–35.

Friis, L. (1998) 'The End of the Beginning' of Eastern Enlargement – Luxembourg Summit and Agenda-Setting', *European Integration online Papers*, 2(7), available from http://eiop.or.at/eiop/texte/1998-007a.htm.

Gallagher, T. (1995) *Romania After Ceausescu: The Politics of Intolerance*, Edinburgh: Edinburgh University Press.

Gallagher, T. (2005) *Theft of A Nation: Romania Since Communism*, London: C. Hurst & Co. Publishers.

General Office for Child Protection (Directia Generala Protectia Copilului) (2011) *Situation of Children Abandoned in Hospital Wards. Sem. 1–2011 (Situatie copii parasiti in unitati sanitare)*, available at www.copii.ro/Statistici/copii_parasiti_in_unitati_sanitare_iunie_2011.doc.

Ghetau, V. (1997) *Maternal Mortality and Abortion in Romania 1990–1997*, Bucharest: UNFPA, United Nations Population Fund.

Goetz, K. (2001) 'Making Sense of Post-Communist Central Administration', Modernisation, Europeanisation or Latinisation?', *Journal of European Public Policy*, 8(6), 1032–1051.

Grabbe, H. (2001) 'How Does Europeanization Affect CEE Governance? Conditionality, Diffusion and Diversity', *Journal of European Public Policy*, 8(6), 1013–1031.

Grabbe, H. (2003) 'Europeanization Goes East: Power and Uncertainty in the EU Accession Process', in K. Featherstone and C.M. Radaelli (eds.) *The Politics of Europeanization*, Oxford: Oxford University Press, pp. 303–327.

Grabbe, H. (2006) *The EU's Transformative Power. Europeanization Through Conditionality in Central and Eastern Europe*, Basingstoke: Palgrave Macmillan.

Graff, E.J. (2008) 'The Lie We Love', available online at www.foreignpolicy.com/articles/2008/10/15/the_lie_we_love.

Grimmel, A. (2011) 'Integration and the Context of Law: Why the European Court of Justice Is Not a Political Actor', *Les Cahiers Européens de Sciences Politiques*, No. 03/2011.

Groussot, X. and Pech, L. (2010) 'Fundamental Rights Protection in the European Union Post Lisbon Treaty', *Fondation Robert Schuman*, European Issue No. 173, 14 June.

Grugel, J. and Iusmen, I. (2013) 'The European Commission as Guardian Angel: The Challenges of Agenda-Setting for Children's Rights', *Journal of European Public Policy* 20(1), 77–94.

Guardian (2010) *France's Deportation of Roma Shown to Be Illegal in Leaked Memo, Say Critics*, 13 September.

Guy, W. (2002) 'The Czech Lands and Slovakia: Another False Dawn?', in W. Guy (ed.) *Between Past and Future; The Roma of Central and Eastern Europe*, Hatfield: University of Hertfordshire Press.

Hague Conference on International Law (2008) *The Implementation and Operation of Hague Intercountry Adoption Convention: Guide to Good Practice*, Guide No. 1, available at www.hcch.net/upload/adoguide_e.pdf.

Harcourt, A.J. (1998) 'EU Media Ownership Regulation: Conflict over the Definition of Alternatives', *Journal of Common Market Studies*, 36(3), 369–389.

Hay, C. and Wincott, D. (1998) 'Structure, Agency and Historical Institutionalism', *Political Studies* 46(5), 951–957.

Hayes, P. (2011) 'The Legality and Ethics of Independent Intercountry Adoption under the Hague Convention', *International Journal of Law, Policy and the Family* 25(3), 288–317.

Herczog, M. (member of the UN Committee on the Rights of the Child) (2009) *Challenges in Adoption Procedures in Europe: Ensuring the Best Interests of the Child. Presentation for Joint Council of Europe and European Commission Conference*, available at www.coe.int/t/dghl/standardsetting/family/Adoption%20conference/Presentation%20M%20%20HERCZOG%20-%20E%20rev.pdf.

Hillion, C. (2004) *EU Enlargement: A Legal Approach*, Oxford, Portland Oregon: Hart Publishing.

Holzinger, K. and Knill, C. (2002) 'Path Dependencies in European Integration: A Constructive Response to German Foreign Minister Joschka Fischer', *Public Administration* 80(1), 125–152.

Hughes, J., Sasse, G. and Gordon, C.C. (2004) *Europeanization and Regionalization in the EU's Enlargement to Central and Eastern Europe: The Myth of Conditionality*, Basingstoke: Palgrave Macmillan.

Human Rights Watch (2012a) 'EU: Rights Abuse at Home Ignored. Alarming Decline in Europe's Record', January 22, available from www.hrw.org/news/2012/01/22/eu-rights-abuse-home-ignored.

Human Rights Watch (2012b) *European Union. Country Summary*, January. Available from www.hrw.org/sites/default/files/related_material/eu_2012.pdf.

Hurewitz, J.C. (1956) *Diplomacy in the Near and Middle East: A Documentary Record 1914–1956*, Princeton, NJ, London, Toronto, New York: D. Van Mostrand.

IGIAA (Independent Group for Inter-country Adoption Analysis) (2002) *Re-organising the International Adoption and Child Protection System*, available at www.afaener.org/Rapport_FINAL_ang.doc.

IMAS (Institute for Marketing and Polls) (2004) *Child Care System Reform in Romania*, Bucharest: United Nations Children's Fund.

Impey, J. (2010) 'France Deports more Roma in Defiance of International Criticism', *Deutsche Welle*, available at www.dw.de/about-dw/who-we-are/s-3325.

Iusmen, I. (2012a) 'Civil Society Participation and EU Children's Rights Policy', *Journal of Civil Society*, 8(2), 137–154.

Iusmen, I. (2012b) 'Romania's Accession to the EU and EU Children's Rights Agenda: Policy Entrepreneurship and Feedback Effects', *Perspectives on European Politics and Society*, 13 (2), 210–225.

Iusmen, I. (2013a) 'Policy Entrepreneurship and Eastern Enlargement: the Case of EU Children's Rights Policy', *Comparative European Politics*, 11(4), 511–529.

Iusmen, I. (2013b) 'The EU and International Adoptions from Romania', *International Journal of Law, Policy and the Family*, 27(1), 1–27.

Jacoby, W., Lataianu, G. and Lataianu, C.M. (2009) Success in Slow Motion: The Europeanization of Romanian Child Protection Policy', *Review of International Organizations* 4(2), 111–133.

Jeremic, V. and Radle, R. (2011) 'Anti-ziganism and Class Racism in Europe', *Red Thread*, Issue 3.

Jerre, U. (2005) 'The State of Knowledge About Child Protection in Romania', Working Paper, Lund University, Sweden available at: www.childrights.ro/downloads/Ulrika_Report_UNICEF.pdf.

Jonsson, U.,(2003) *Human Rights Approach to Development Programming*, Nairobi: UNICEF.

Katschnig, H. (2006) 'Report on a Peer Assessment Mission to Romanian Psychiatric and Social Care Institutions for Persons with Mental Illness or Mental Disability', available at www.ms.ro/pagina.php?id=114.

Kelley, J.K. (2004) *Ethnic Politics in Europe: The Power of Norms and Incentives*, Princeton and Oxford: Princeton University Press.

Kilic, Z. (2001) 'Human Rights in Turkey – Summary Report', *Human Rights Review*, 3(1), 86–91.

Kilkelly, U. (1999) *The Child and the European Convention on Human Rights*, Aldershot: Ashgate.

Kilkelly, U. (2001) 'The Best of Both Worlds for Children's Rights? Interpreting the European Convention on Human Rights in the Light of the UN Convention on the Rights of the Child', *Human Rights Quarterly*, 23(2), 308–326.

Kilkelly, U. (2002) 'Effective Protection of Children's Rights in Family Cases: An International Approach'. *Transnational Law and Contemporary Problems*, 12(2), 336–354.

Kilkelly, U. (2009) 'Child Law and the ECHR: Issues of Family Life, Adoption and Contact' in U. Kilkelly (eds.) *ECHR and Irish Law*, 2nd edition, Bristol: Jordans.

Kingdon, J. (1984) *Agendas, Alternatives and Public Policies*, Boston: Little, Brown & Co.

Kligman, G. (1998) *The Politics of Duplicity: Controlling Reproduction in Ceausescu's Romania*, Berkeley: California.

Knill, C. and Lehmkuhl, D. (1999) 'How Europe Matters: Different Mechanisms of Europeanization', *European Integration Online Papers*, 3(7), 1–19.

Kohler Koch, B .(2007) 'The organization of interests and democracy in the European Union', in B. Kohler Koch and B. Rittberger (eds.) *Debating the Democratic*

Legitimacy of the European Union, Lanham, MD: Rowman & Littlefield, pp. 255–72.

Kohn, M. (1996) *The Race Gallery: The Return of Racial Science,* London: Vintage.

Krasner, S. (1982) 'Structural Causes and Regime Consequences: Regimes as Intervening Variables', *International Organization,* 36(2), 185–205.

Kushen, R. (2009) 'Economics, Extremism and Roma Rights: A Dangerous Linkage', *Roma Rights Journal,* 1: 1–3.

Lambru, M. and Rosu, C. (2000) 'Actiunea statului in domeniul protectiei copilului in dificultate din Romania. Profil de reforma' [State Intervention in the Domain of Children in Need in Romania] in I. Mihailescu (ed.), *Un deceniu de tranzitie. Situatia copilului in Romania* [*A Decade of Transition: The Situation of Child and Family in Romania*], Bucharest: UNICEF.

Lataianu, C. (2001) *Social Policies for the Protection of Abandoned Children: Institutionalisation and Alternatives to Institutionalisation of Children in Post-Communist Romania,* Bucharest: BCS.

Levi, M. (1997) 'A Model, a Method and a Map: Rational Choice in Comparative and Historical Analysis', in M. I. Lichbach and A. S. Zuckerman (eds.) *Comparative Politics: Rationality, Culture and Structure,* Cambridge: Cambridge University Press, pp. 19–41.

Liegeois, J.-P. and Gheorghe, N. (1995) *Roma/Gypsies:A European Minority – Minority Rights Group International Report,* 95/4, London.

Light, D. and Phinnemore, D. (eds.) (2001) *Post-Communist Romania: Coming to Terms with Transition,* Basingstoke: Palgrave Macmillan.

Lippert, B., Umbach, G. and Wessels, W. (2001) 'Europeanisation of the CEE Executives: EU Membership Negotiations as a Shaping Power', *Journal of European Public Policy,* 8(6), 980–1012.

Lombardo, E. (2003) 'EU Gender Policy: Trapped in the Wollstonecraft Dilemma?', *The European Journal of Women's Studies,* 10(2), 159–180.

Lopez, E.J. (2002) 'The Legislator as Political Entrepreneur: Investment in Political Capital', *The Review of Austrian Economics,* 15(2), 211–228.

Lucarelli, S. and Manners, I. (eds.) (2006) *Values and Principles in European Union Foreign Policy,* London: Routledge.

MacKenzie, C. (2004) 'Policy Entrepreneurship in Australia: A Conceptual Review and Application', *Australian Journal of Political Science* 39(2), 367–386.

Mahoney, C. (2004) 'The Power of Institutions: State and Interest-Group Activity in the European Union', *European Union Politics,* 5(4), 441–466.

Majone, G. (1998) 'Europe's "Democratic Deficit": The Question of Standards', *European Law Journal,* 4(1), 5–28.

Majone, G. (2005) *Dilemmas of European Integration: The Ambiguities and Pitfalls of Integration by Stealth,* Oxford: Oxford University Press.

Majone, G. (2009) *Europe as the Would-Be World Power: The EU at Fifty.* Cambridge: Cambridge University Press.

Manners, I. (2002) 'Normative Power Europe: A Contradiction in Terms?', *Journal of Common Market Studies,* 40(2), 235–258.

Manners, I. (2008a) 'The Normative Ethics of the European Union', *International Affairs,* 84(1), 65–80.

Manners, I. (2008b) 'The EU's International Promotion of the Rights of the Child', in J. Orbie and L. Tortell (eds.) *The European Union and the Social Dimension of Globalization: How the EU Influences the World*, London: Routledge, pp. 228–241.

Manners, I. and Diez, T. (2007) 'Reflecting on Normative Power Europe', in F. Berenskoetter and M. J. Williams (eds.) *Power in World Politics*, London: Routledge, pp. 173–188.

Mansell J., Knapp M., Beadle-Brown J. and Beecham J. (2007) *Deinstitutionalisation and Community Living – Outcomes and Costs: Report of a European Study*, Canterbury: Tizard Centre, University of Kent.

Mattli, W. and Plumper, T. (2005) 'The Demand-Side Politics of EU Enlargement', in F. Schimmelfennig and U. Sedelmeier (eds.) *The Politics of European Union Enlargement. Theoretical Approaches*, London, NY: Routledge, pp. 52–71.

McCowan, T.L. (2005) 'Policy Entrepreneurs and Policy Change: Strategies Beyond Agenda Setting', Paper prepared for the 2005 Annual meeting of the American Political Science Association, 1–4 September.

McGlynn, C.M.S. (2002) 'Rights for Children: The Potential Impact of the European Union Charter of Fundamental Rights', *European Public Law* 8(3), 387–400.

McGlynn, C.M.S. (2006) *Families and the European Union: Law, Politics and Pluralism*, Cambridge: Cambridge University Press.

Merlini, C. (2001) 'Book Reviews and Notes', *The International Spectator: Italian Journal of International Affairs*, 36(3), 111–114.

Merton, R.K. (1968) *Social Theory and Social Structure*, New York: The Free Press.

Mezmur, B. (2009) 'Intercountry Adoption as a Measure of Last Resort in Africa: Advancing the Rights of a Child Rather than a Right to a Child', *International Journal on Human Rights* 6(10), 83–103.

Mihova, Z., Marinova, A. and Mateeva, A. (2008) 'Bulgarian country report', in M. Barbarotto (ed.) *2008 Report Child Abandonment: An Emergency. Studies on the Child Protection Systems of Bulgaria, France, Italy, Latvia and Romania* Milan: Amici de Bambini, pp. 101–156.

Miller, V. (2004) 'The Human Rights Clause in the EU's External Agreements', *House of Commons Library Research Paper 4/33*, 16 April.

Ministry of Health (2008) 'Recent Developments in Mental Health Policy and Legislation in Romania', accessed from www.ms.ro/fisiere/pagini_virtuale/114_174_Recent_Developments.ppt.

Ministry of Labour and Social Policy (2008) *Actions Taken to Improve the Wellbeing of Children in Bulgaria, the Deinstitutionalization of Specialized Social Services Institutions and Information on the Implementation of the Home for Children and Young People with Mental Disability in the Village of Mogilino and the Plan for Closing It*, available from www.mlsp.government.bg/en/index.htm.

Ministry of Labour, Social Solidarity and Family (2005) 'Grant Scheme for Institutional Reform in the Field of the Protection of People with Disabilities', accessed from www.anph.ro/admin/doc/upload/serviciu/Prezentare-schema%20de%20granturi_29.11.05_RO.ppt.

Ministry of Public Health (2007) *Assessment of Health Condition and Access to Medical Assistance of Roma Communities. Twinning Light Project*, Bucharest: Ministry of Public Health.

Mintrom, M. (1997) 'Policy Entrepreneurs and the Diffusion of Innovation', *American Journal of Political Science*, 41(3), 738–770.

Mintrom, M. (2000) *Policy Entrepreneurs and School Choice,* Washington: Georgetown University Press.

Mintrom, M. and Vergari, S. (1996) 'Advocacy Coalitions, Policy Entrepreneurs and Policy Change', *Policy Studies Journal,* 24(3), 420–434.

Moravcsik, A. and Vachudova, M.A. (2003) 'National Interests, State Power and EU Enlargement', *East European Politics and Societies,* 17(1), 42–57.

Morrison, L. (2004) 'Ceausescu's Legacy: Family Struggles and Institutionalisation of Children in Romania', *Journal of Family History,* 29(2), 168–182.

Muller-Graff, P.-C. (1997) 'Legal Framework for Relations between the European Union and Central and Eastern Europe: General Aspects', in M. Maresceau (ed.), *Enlarging the EU Relations between the EU and Central and Eastern Europe,* London: Longman, pp. 27–40.

Mundt, A.P, Frančišković, T, Gurovich, I., Heinz, A., Ignatyev, Y., et al. (2012) 'Changes in the Provision of Institutionalized Mental Health Care in Post-Communist Countries', *PLoS ONE* 7(6), 1–6.

Mungiu-Pippidi, A. (2002) *Politics After Communism,* Bucharest: Humanitas.

Murray, R.W. (2006) 'A True Revolution', *Transitions Online,* 2 January.

National Agency for Roma (2006) *Activity Report 2006.* Bucharest: National Agency for Roma.

National Authority for Child Protection and Adoption (2004) *Children First. PHARE 1999 Programme for Development of Child Welfare Services in Romania.* Bucharest: National Authority for Child Protection and Adoption.

National Authority for the Protection of Child's Rights (2005) *Children First. PHARE Programme 2001 and PHARE Programme 2002 for the Development of Child Protection Services in Romania* Bucharest: National Authority for the Protection of Child's Rights.

National Authority for the Protection of Child's Rights (2006) *Child Welfare in Romania,* Bucharest: National Authority for the Protection of Child's Rights.

National Council for Combating Discrimination (2005) *Different, Equal, Together,* Bucharest: National Council for Combating Discrimination.

Nicholson, E. (2006a) 'Civil society and the Media in Romania', in D. Phinnemore (ed.) *The EU and Romania: Accession and Beyond,* London: Federal Trust, pp. 64–77.

Nicholson, E. (2006b) 'My Position on Inter-Country Adoptions', *Vivid,* February.

Nicolaidis, K. (2004) 'The Power of the Superpowerless', in T. Lindberg (ed.) *Beyond Paradise and Power: Europeans, Americans and the Future of a Troubled Partnership,* London: Routledge, pp. 93–120.

Nicolaidis, K. and Howse, R. (2002) 'This is my EUtopia...: Narrative as Power', *Journal of Common Market Studies,* 40(4), 767–792.

Noutcheva, G. and Bechev, D. (2008) 'The Successful Laggards: Bulgaria and Romania's Accession to the EU', *East European Politics & Societies,* 22(1), 114–144.

Nowak, M. (2003) *Introduction to the International Human Rights Regime,* Leiden: Martinus Nijhoff.

O'Nions, H. (2011) 'Roma Expulsions and Discrimination: The Elephant in Brussels', *European Journal of Migration and Law* 13(4), 361–388.

ODIHR (Office for Democratic Institutions and Human Rights) (2009) *Assessment of the Human Rights Situation of Roma and Sinti in Italy,* Warsaw: OSCE, March.

Official Journal of the European Communities, No. L 169/1 of 29 June 1987.
Official Journal of the European Communities, No. C 191/1 of 29 July 1992.
Official Journal of the European Communities, No. L 357/174 of 31 December 1994.
Official Journal of the European Communities, No. C 340 of 10 November 1997.
Oliver, T.R. and Paul-Shaheen, P. (1997) 'Translating Ideas into Actions: Entrepreneurial Leadership in State Health Care Reforms', *Journal of Health Politics, Policy and Law*, 22(3), 721–788.
Open Society Institute (2001) *Research on Selected Roma Education Programs in Central and Eastern Europe. Final Report*, available at www.opensocietyfoundations.org/sites/default/files/romaed_combined.pdf.
Ostrom, E. (2005), *Unlocking Public Entrepreneurship and Public Economies*, EGDI Discussion Paper no. 2005/01, Expert Group on Development Issues, United Nations University.
Padoa-Schioppa, T. (2001) *Europa, Forza Gentile*, Bologna: Il Mulino.
Panait, B. (Secretary of State in Romanian Office for Adoption) (2011) *Annual Number of Adoptions Is Below the Daily Situation of the Protection System* (Numărul anual de adopţii este sub realitatea de zi cu zi din sistemul de protecţie), Interview, 8 June, Bucharest, available at www.mediafax.ro/social/.
Papadimitriou, D. (2002) *Negotiating the New Europe: The European Union and Eastern Europe*, Aldershot: Ashgate.
Papadimitriou, D. and Phinnemore, D. (2004) 'Europeanization, conditionality and domestic change: The twinning exercise and administrative reform in Romania', *Journal of Common Market Studies*, 42(3), 619–639.
Papadimitriou, D. and Phinnemore, D. (2008) *Romania and the European Union – From Marginalisation to Membership*, Abingdon: Routledge.
Parker, O. (2012) 'Roma and the Politics of EU Citizenship in France: Everyday Security and Resistance', *Journal of Common Market Studies*, 50(3), 475–491.
Pentassuglia, G. (2001) 'The EU and the Protection of Minorities: The Case of Eastern Europe', *European Journal of International Law*, 12(1), 3–38.
Pernice, I. (2008) 'The Treaty of Lisbon and Fundamental Rights', in S. Griller and J. Ziller (eds.) *The Lisbon Treaty. EU Constitutionalism without a Constitutional Treaty?*, New York: Springer, pp. 235–256.
Pescatore, P. (1981) 'The Context and Significance of Fundamental Rights in the Law of the European Communities', *Human Rights Law Journal*, 4(2), 295–308.
Peters, B.G. (2001) 'Agenda-Setting in the European Union', in J. Richardson (ed.) *European Union: Power and Policymaking*, London: Routledge.
Peterson, J. and Bomberg, E. (1999) *Decision-Making in the European Union*, Basingstoke: Palgrave Macmillan.
PHARE Implementation Unit (n. d. a) 'Access to Education for Disadvantaged Groups', Informative Bulletin No. 2, Bucharest.
PHARE Implementation Unit (n. d. b) 'Access to Education for Disadvantaged Groups', Informative Bulletin No. 3, Bucharest.
Phinnemore, D. (ed.) (2006) *The EU and Romania. Accession and Beyond*, London: The Federal Trust.
Pierson, P. (1993) 'When Effect Becomes Cause. Policy Feedback and Political Change', *World Politics*, 45(4), 595–628.
Pierson, P. (2004) *Politics in Time. History, Institutions and Social Analysis*, Princeton: Princeton University Press.

Piris, J.C. (2010) *The Lisbon Treaty. A Legal and Political Analysis*, Cambridge: Cambridge University Press.

Plumper, T. and Schneider, C. (2007), Discriminatory EU Membership and the Redistribution of Enlargement Gains, *Journal of Conflict Resolution*, 51(4), 568–587.

Pollack, M.A. (1997) 'Delegation, Agency and Agenda Setting in the European Community', *International Organization*, 51(1), 99–134.

Pollack, M.A. (2003) *The Engines of European Integration: Delegation, Agency and Agenda Setting in the EU*, New York: Oxford University Press.

Pollack, M.A. (2008) 'The new institutionalisms and European integration', *ConWEB/ Webpapers on Constitutionalism and Governance Beyond the State*, accessed from www.bath.ac.uk/esml/conWEB.

Polsby, N.W. (1984) *Political Innovation in America: The Politics of Policy Initiation*, New Haven and London: Yale University Press.

Pop, V. (2009) 'EU States Criticized for human Rights Violations', *EU Observer.com*, 15 January, available from http://euobserver.com/institutional/27413.

Post, R. (2007) *Romania: For Export Only. The Untold Story of the Romanian 'Orphans'*, Amsterdam: Hoekstra.

Pralle, S. (2006) 'Timing and Sequence in Agenda Setting and Policy Change: A Comparative Study of Lawn Care Pesticide Politics in Canada and the US', *Journal of European Public Policy*, 13(7), 987–1005.

Pridham, G. (2002) 'EU Enlargement and Consolidating Democracy in Post–Communist States – Formality and Reality', *Journal of Common Market Studies*, 40(5), 953–973.

Pridham, G. (2005) *Designing Democracy: EU Enlargement and Regime Change in Post–Communist Europe*, Basingstoke: Palgrave Macmillan.

Princen, S. (2007) 'Agenda-Setting in the European Union: A Theoretical Exploration and Agenda for Research', *Journal of European Public Policy*, 14(1), 21–38.

Princen, S. (2009) *Agenda-Setting in the European Union*, Basingstoke: Palgrave Macmillan.

Princen, S. (2011) 'Agenda-Setting Strategies in EU Policy Processes', *Journal of European Public Policy*, 18(7), 927–943.

Princen, S. and Rhinard, M. (2006) 'Crashing and Creeping: Agenda-Setting Dynamics in the European Union', *Journal of European Public Policy*, 13(7), 1119–1132.

Prot-Klinger, K. (2006) 'Peer Review 2006: Evaluation Mission on Mental Health in Romania. Draft Report', accessed from www.ms.ro/pagina.php?id=114.

Public Policy and Management Institute (2011) *The Evaluation of the Impact of the EU Instruments Affecting Children's Rights with a View to Assessing the Level of Protection and Promotion of Children's Rights in the EU*, Vilnius: Public Policy and Management Institute.

Quinn, G. and Degener, T. (2002) *Human Rights and Disability. The Current Use and Future Potential of United Nations human Rights Instruments in the Context of Disability*, United Nations, New York and Geneva.

Ratesh, N. (1991) *Romania: The Entangled Revolution*. New York: Praeger Publishers.

Reding, V. (2010) Press release. *Statement on the Latest Developments on the Roma Situation*, Brussels, 14 September, Speech 10/428.

Rein, M. and Schön, D. (1991) 'Frame-Reflective Policy Discourse' in Wagner, P., Hirschon, C., Wittrock, B. and Wollman, H. (eds.), *Social Sciences and Modern States, National Experiences and Theoretical Crossroads*, Cambridge: University Press, pp. 262–289.

Rein, M. and Schön, D. (1994) *Frame Reflection. Toward the Resolution of Intractable Policy Controversies*, New York: Basic Books.

Reinstaller, A. (2005) 'Policy Entrepreneurship in the Co-Evolution of Institutions, Preferences and Technology: Comparing the Diffusion of Totally Chlorine Free Pulp Bleaching Technologies in the US and Sweden', *Research Policy*, 34, 1366–1384.

Renner, S. and Trauner, F. (2009) 'Creeping Membership in Southeast Europe: The Dynamics of EU Rule Transfer to the Western Balkans', *Journal of European Integration*, 31 (4), 449–465.

Rhinard, M. (2010) *Framing Europe: The Policy Shaping Strategies of the European Commission*, Leiden, Boston: Martinus Nijhoff Publishers.

Risse-Kappen, T. (1996) 'Exploring the Nature of the Beast: International Relations Theory and Comparative Policy Analysis Meet the European Union', *Journal of Common Market Studies*, 34(1), 53–80.

Roberts, N.C. (1991) Public Entrepreneurship and Innovation, *Policy Studies review*, 11(1), 55–74.

Roberts, N. and King, P. (1991) 'Policy Entrepreneurs: Their Activity Structure and Function in the Policy Process', *Journal of Public Administration Research and Theory*, 1(2), 147–175.

Roby, J.L. and Ife, J. (2009) 'Human Rights, Politics and Interrcountry Adoption: An Examination of Two Sending Countries', *International Social Work*, 52(5), 661–671.

Romanian Office for Adoptions (n.d.) *Adoption in Romania*. Bucharest: Romanian Office for Adoptions.

Romanian Parliament (2012) 'Law 273/2004 as Amended on 19/042012', available at www.adoptiiromania.ro/images/custom/file/Legea%20273-2004%20 Republicata%202(2).pdf.

Romeurope (2010) 'Communique de Presse du Collectif Romeurope', 22 July.

Ruxton, S. (2005) *How About Us? Children's Rights in the European Union. Next Steps*, available at www.crin.org/docs/Ruxton%20Report_WhatAboutUs.pdf.

Sandholtz, W. and Zysman, J. (1989) '1992: Recasting the European Bargain', *World Politics*, 42(1), 95–128.

Santos Pais, M. (1999) *A Human Rights Conceptual Framework for UNICEF*, Florence: UNICEF International Child Development Centre.

Sarkozy, N. (2010) Discours de M. Le Président de la République á Grenoble.

Scheuner, U. (1975) 'Fundamental Rights in European Community Law and in National Constitutional Law', *Common Market Law Review*, 12(2), 171–191.

Schiller, W. (1995) 'Senators as Policy Entrepreneurs: Using Bill Sponsorship to Shape Legislative Agendas', *American Political Science Review*, 39(1), 186–203.

Schimmelfennig, F. (2001) 'The Community Trap: Liberal Norms, Rhetorical Action and the Eastern Enlargement of the European Union', *International Organization*, 5(1), 47–80.

Schimmelfennig, F. (2003) *The EU, NATO and the Integration of Europe: Rules and Rhetoric*, Cambridge: Cambridge University Press.

Schimmelfennig, F. and Sedelmeier, U. (2004) 'Governance by Conditionality: EU Rule Transfer to the Candidate Countries of Central and Eastern Europe', *Journal of European Public Policy*, 11(4), 661–679.

Schimmelfennig, F. and Sedelmeier, U. (eds.) (2005a) *The Europeanization of Central and Eastern Europe*, Ithaca, London: Cornell University Press.

Schimmelfennig, F. and Sedelmeier, U. (eds.) (2005b) *The Politics of European Union Enlargement. Theoretical Approaches*, London, NY: Routledge.

Schimmelfennig, F. and Sedelmeier, U. (2007) 'Candidate Countries and Conditionality', in P. Graziano and M. P. Vink (eds.) *Europeanization. New Research Agendas*, Basingstoke: Palgrave Macmillan, pp. 88–101.

Schimmelfennig, F., Engert, S. and Knobel, H. (2006) *International Socialization in Europe. European Organizations, Political Conditionality and Democratic Change*, Basingstoke: Palgrave Macmillan.

Schneider, M., Teske, P. and Mintrom, M. (1995) *Public Entrepreneurs: Agents for Change in American Government*, Princeton, NJ: Princeton University Press.

Schnellenbach, J. (2007) 'Public Entrepreneurship and the Economics of Reform', *Journal of Institutional Economics* 3(2), 183–202.

Sedelmeier, U. (2003) 'EU Enlargement, Identity and the Analysis of European Foreign Policy: Identity Formation through Policy Practice', *RSC No. 2003/13 European Forum Series*.

Sedelmeier, U. (2005) *Constructing the Path to Eastern Enlargement. The Uneven Policy Impact of EU Identity*, Manchester: Manchester University Press.

Sedelmeier, U. (2006) 'The EU's Role as a Promoter of Human Rights and Democracy: Enlargement Policy Practice and Role Formation', in O. Elgström and M. Smith (eds.) *The European Union's Roles in International Politics. Concepts and Analysis*, London, New York: Routledge, pp. 118–135.

Selman, P. (2009) 'The Rise and Fall of Intercountry Adoption in the 21st Century', *International Social Work*, 52, 575–594.

Selman, P. (2010) 'Intercountry Adoption As Globalized Motherhood', in W. Chavkin and J. Maher (eds.) *The Globalization of Motherhood: Deconstructions and Reconstructions of Biology and Care*, New York: Routledge, pp. 79–104.

Sigona, N. and Trehan, N. (2009) 'Introduction: Romani Politics in Neoliberal Europe', in Sigona, N. and Trehan, N. (eds.) *Romani Politics in Contemporary Europe: Poverty, Ethnic Mobilisation and the Neoliberal Order*, Basingstoke: Palgrave Macmillan, pp. 1–20.

Simhandl, K. (2006) ''Western Gypsies and Travellers'–'Eastern Roma': The Creation of Political Objects by Institutions of the European Union', *Nations and Nationalism*, 12(1), 97–115.

Sjursen, H. (2002) 'Why Expand? The Question of Legitimacy and Justification in the EU's Enlargement Policy', *Journal of Common Market Studies*, 40(3), 491–513.

Sjursen, H. (2006a) 'The EU as a 'Normative' Power: How Can This Be?', *Journal of European Public Policy*, 13(2), 235–251.

Sjursen, H. (2006b) 'What Kind of Power?', *Journal of European Public Policy*, 13(2), 169–181.

Skalnes, L.S. (2005) 'Geopolitics and the Eastern Enlargement of the European Union', in F. Schimmelfennig and U. Sedelmeier (eds.) *The Politics of European Union Enlargement: Theoretical Approaches*, London: Routledge, pp. 213–233.

Slovenian Presidency of the EU (2008) *European Pact for Mental Health and Well-Being*, EU High Level Conference: Together for Mental Health and Well-being, available at http://ec.europa.eu/health/ph_determinants/life_style/mental/docs/pact_en.pdf.

Smith, K.E. (1998) 'The Use of Political Conditionality in the EU's Relations with Third Countries: How Effective?', *European Foreign Affairs Review*, 3(2), 253–274.

Smith, K.E. (2003) 'The Evolution and Application of EU Membership Conditionality', in M. Cremona (ed.) *The Enlargement of the European Union*, Oxford: Oxford University Press, pp. 105–139.

Smith, K.E. (2004) *The Making of EU Foreign Policy. The Case of Eastern Europe*, 2nd edition, Basingstoke: Palgrave Macmillan.

Smith, K.E. (2005) 'Enlargement and European Order', in C. Hill and M. Smith (eds) *International relations and the European Union*, Oxford: Oxford University Press, pp. 270–291.

Smith, M.A. and Timmins, G. (2000) *Building a Bigger Europe: EU and NATO Enlargement in Comparative Perspective*, Aldershot: Ashgate.

Smolin, D.M. (2010) *Abduction, Sale and Traffic in Children in the Context of Intercountry Adoption. Information Document No 1 for the Attention of the Special Commission of June 2010 on the Practical Operation of the Hague Convention of 29 May 1993 on Protection of Children and Co-operation in Respect of Intercountry Adoption*, available at www.hcch.net/upload/wop/adop2010id01e.pdf.

Snyder, F. (1994) 'Soft Law and Institutional Practice in the European Community', in S. Martin (ed.), *The Construction of Europe*, Dordrecht: Kluwer Academic Publishers.

Snyder, F. (1995) 'The Effectiveness of European Community Law: Institutions, Processes, Tools and Techniques', in T. Daintith (ed.) *Implementing EC Law in the United Kingdom: Structures for Indirect Rule*, pp. 51–87.

Sperling, J. (ed.) (1999) *Two Tiers Or Two Speeds? The European Security Order and the Enlargement of the European Union and NATO*, Manchester: Manchester University Press.

Stalford, H. (2000) 'The Citizenship Status of Children in the European Union', *International Journal of Children's Rights*, 8(2), 101–131.

Stalford, H. (2011) 'Are We There Yet? The Impact of the Lisbon Treaty on the EU's Children's Rights Agenda', *International Journal of Children's Rights*, 19(3), 7–29.

Stalford, H. (2012) *Children and the European Union: Rights, Welfare and Accountability*, Oxford: Hart.

Stalford, H. and Drywood, E. (2009) 'Coming of Age?: Children's Rights in the European Union', *Common Market Law Review*, 46(1), 143–172.

Stalford, H. and Drywood, E. (2011) 'The Use of the CRC in EU Law and Policy-Making', in Invernizzi, A. and Williams, J. (eds.) *Children's Rights: Revisiting Visions, Assessing Progress, Rethinking Implementation*, Aldershot, Ashgate, pp. 199–218.

Stalford, H. and Schuurman, M. (2011) 'Are We there Yet?: The Impact of the Lisbon Treaty on the EU Children's Rights Agenda', *International Journal of Children's Rights*, 19(3), 381–403.

Steiner, H.J. and Alston, P. (1996) *International Human Rights in Context: Law, Politics, Morals*, Oxford: Oxford University Press.

Steinmo, S. (2008) 'What is Historical Institutionalism?', in D. Della Porta and M. Keating (eds.) *Approaches in the Social Sciences*, Cambridge: Cambridge University Press.

Storey, H. (1995) 'Human Rights and the New Europe: Experience and Experiment', in D. Beetham (ed.) *Politics and Human Rights*, Oxford: Oxford University Press.

Szyszczak, E. (2006) 'Experimental Governance: The Open Method of Coordination' *European Law Journal*, 12(4), 486–502.

Thelen, K. (1999) 'Historical Institutionalism in Comparative Politics', *Annual Review of Political Science*, 2, 369–404.

Thelen, K. and Steinmo, S. (1992) 'Historical Institutionalism in Comparative Politics', in S. Steinmo, K. Thelen and F. Longstreth (eds.) *Historical Institutionalism in Comparative Politics: State, Society and Economy*, New York: Cambridge University Press.

Tobin, J. (2009) 'Judging the Judges: Are they Adopting the Rights Approach in Matters Involving Children?' *Melbourne University Law Review*, 33(2), 579–625.

Toktas, S. and Aras, B. (2009) 'The EU and Minority Rights in Turkey', *Political Science Quarterly*, 124(4), 697–720.

Tomuschat, C. (2003) *Human Rights – Between Idealism and Realism*, Oxford: Oxford University Press.

Topidi, K. (2010) *EU Law, Minorities and Enlargement*, Antwerp: Intersentia.

Transtec (2006) 'Lessons Learnt from Romania. An Assessment of the EU Role and Intervention in the Reform of the Child Protection System in Romania', *Commission Internal Document*, Brussels: Transtec.

Trauner, F. (2011) *The Europeanisation of the Western Balkans: EU Justice and Home Affairs in Croatia and Macedonia*, Manchester: Manchester University Press.

Tun, A. A., Cave, G., Trotter, D. and Bell, B. (2007) 'The Domestic Fulfilment of Children's Rights: Save the Children's Experience in the Use of Rights-Based Approaches', in A. Alen, H. Bosley and M. De Bie (eds.) *The UN Children's Rights Convention: Theory Meets Practice*, Netherlands: Intersentia.

Turcescu, L. and Stan, L. (2005) 'Religion, Politics and Sexuality in Romania', *Europe–Asia Studies*, 57(2), 291–310.

UNICEF (2004) *Assessing the Progress of Child Care System Reform in Romania*, Geneva: UNICEF.

UNICEF (2010a) *UNICEF's Position on Inter-Country Adoption*, available at www.unicef.org/media/media_41918.html.

UNICEF (2010b) *At home or in a home? Formal care and adoption of children in Eastern Europe and Central Asia*, available at www.unicef.org/ceecis/At_home_or_in_a_home_report.pdf.

UNICEF (2012) *Revised Country Programme Document. Bulgaria(2013–2017)*, 20 July, available from www.unicef.org/about/execboard/files/2012-PL4_Bulgaria_CPD-Revised-English.pdf.

Vachudova, M.A. (2005) *Europe Undivided. Democracy, Leverage and Integration after Communism*, Oxford: Oxford University Press.

Van Bueren, G. (2007) *Child Rights in Europe*, Strasbourg: Council of Europe.

Vandenhole, W. (2011) 'Children's Rights in EU External Action: Beyond Charity and Protection, Beyond Instrumentalisation and Conditionality', *International Journal of Children's Rights*, 19(3), 477–500.

Veerman, P.E. (1992) *The Rights of the Child and the Changing Image of Childhood*, Leiden: Martinus Nijhoff Publishers.

Verdery, K. (1993) 'Nationalism and National Sentiment in Post-Socialist Romania, *Slavic Review*, 52(2), 179–203.

Vermeersch, P. (2003) 'Ethnic Minority Identity and Movement Politics: The Case of the Roma in the Czech Republic and Slovakia', *Ethnic and Racial Studies*, 26(5), 879–901.

Vermeersch, P. (2012) 'Reframing the Roma: EU Initiatives and the Politics of Reinterpretation', *Journal of Ethnic and Migration Studies*, 38(8), 1195–1212.

Villarreal, F. and Walek, C. (2008) 'European Roma Summit. Conference Report', Brussels, 16 September.

Vite, S. (2008) *A Commentary on the United Nations Convention on the Rights of the Child*, Leiden: Martinus Nijhoff Publishers.

Von Bogdandy, A. (2000) 'The European Union as a Human Rights Organization? Human Rights and the Core of the European Union', *Common Market Law Review*, 37(6), 1307–1338.

Walker, N. (2003), 'Constitutionalising Enlargement, Enlarging Constitutionalism', *European Law Journal*, 9 (3), 365–385.

Weiler, J.H.H. (1991) 'The Transformation of Europe', *The Yale Law Journal*, 100, 2405–2483.

Weiler, J.H.H. (1994) 'A Quiet Revolution: The European Court of Justice and Its Interlocutors', *Comparative Political Studies*, 26(4), 510–534.

Weiler, J.H.H. (1999) *The Constitution of Europe*, Cambridge: Cambridge University Press.

Weiss, W. (2005) 'Eastern Enlargement and European Constitutionalisation', *Queen's Papers on Europeanisation*, Queen's University Belfast.

Weiss, W. (2011) 'Human Rights in the EU: Rethinking the Role of the European Convention on Human Rights after Lisbon', *European Constitutional Law Review*, 7(1), 64–95.

Weissert, C.S. (1991) 'Policy Entrepreneurs, Policy Opportunists and Legislative Effectiveness', *American Political Quarterly*, 19(2), 262–274.

Wellens, K.C. and Borchardt, G.M. (1989) 'Soft Law in European Community Law', *European Law Review*, 14(5), 267–321.

Whitman, R.G. (ed.) (2011) *Normative Power Europe: Empirical and Theoretical Perspectives*, Basingstoke: Palgrave Macmillan.

Williams, A. (2000) 'Enlargement of the Union and Human Rights Conditionality: A Policy of Distinction?', *European Law Review*, 25(6), 601–617.

Williams, A. (2004) *EU Human Rights Policies: A Study in Irony*, Oxford: Oxford University Press.

Wilsher, K. (2010) 'Orders to Police on Roma Expulsions from France Leaked', *Guardian*, 13 September.

Ziegler, K.S. (2009) 'Strengthening the Rule of Law, but Fragmenting International Law: The Kadi Decision of the ECJ from the Perspective of Human Rights', *Human Rights Law Review*, 9(2), 288–305.

Zielonka, J. (2011) 'The Ideology of Empire: The EU's Normative Power Discourse', *2001 Dahrendorf Symposium*, available at www.dahrendorf-symposium.eu/fileadmin/Content_Images/Papers/Papers_Neu/DSP_Zielonka_The_Ideology_of_Empire.pdf.

Internet sources

National Authority for the Protection of Child's Rights website, www.copii.ro/content.aspx.
Romanian Office for Adoption website, www.adoptiiromania.ro.

Index